SOCIAL WORK AND
SOCIAL DEVELOPMENT

SOCIAL WORK AND SOCIAL DEVELOPMENT

Theories and Skills for
Developmental Social Work

Edited by

James Midgley
Amy Conley

UNIVERSITY PRESS
2010

OXFORD
UNIVERSITY PRESS

Oxford University Press, Inc., publishes works that further
Oxford University's objective of excellence
in research, scholarship, and education.

Oxford   New York
Auckland   Cape Town   Dar es Salaam   Hong Kong   Karachi
Kuala Lumpur   Madrid   Melbourne   Mexico City   Nairobi
New Delhi   Shanghai   Taipei   Toronto

With offices in
Argentina   Austria   Brazil   Chile   Czech Republic   France   Greece
Guatemala   Hungary   Italy   Japan Poland   Portugal   Singapore
South Korea   Switzerland   Thailand   Turkey   Ukraine   Vietnam

Copyright © 2010 by Oxford University Press, Inc.

Published by Oxford University Press, Inc.
198 Madison Avenue, New York, New York 10016

www.oup.com

Oxford is a registered trademark of Oxford University Press.

Library of Congress Cataloging-in-Publication Data

Social work and social development : theories and skills for developmental
social work / edited by James Midgley and Amy Conley.
p. cm.
Includes bibliographical references and index.
ISBN 978-0-19-973232-6 1. Social service—Case studies.
I. Midgley, James. II. Conley, Amy.
HV40.S61767 2010
361.3—dc22
2009042640

*Dedicated to our South African colleagues—and especially
Leila Patel and Antoinette Lombard—whose pioneering
contribution to developmental social work has been an inspiration.*

CONTENTS

Part III: Conclusion

ACKNOWLEDGMENTS

Many people inspired this book, and we are grateful for their ideas and suggestions. A major source of inspiration was a group of graduate students at the School of Social Welfare at Berkeley with experience of working in the Global South. A few years ago, they created a student organization known as the Caucus for International Awareness (or CIA) to advocate for the inclusion of more international content in the curriculum. It was through their efforts that a new course on social development was established at the school. Inevitably, the need for appropriate teaching materials led to the suggestion for a book in developmental social work. After considering the challenges, we agreed. We are grateful to the members of the Consortium, particularly to Dave Androff, Joanna Doran, Joon Yong Jo, Mark Samples, and Terry Shaw, for their support.

Another source of inspiration is the ongoing efforts of social work colleagues in South Africa to translate the developmental commitments of the Mandela government's *White Paper on Social Welfare* of 1997 into tangible practice prescriptions. South African social workers frequently use the term *developmental social work*, and their efforts to conceptualize this approach have informed developments in other countries. Although the infusion of developmental ideas into professional social work is hardly new, events in South Africa and the work of several South African scholars—notably Leila Patel and Antoinette Lombard—have been particularly important. It is for this reason that the book is dedicated to them. Although former South African scholar Mel Gray now lives in Australia, she too has contributed significantly to the articulation of social development ideas with reference to the South African context. The work of other South African social work scholars, including

Sulina Green, Vishanthie Sewpaul, and Jean Trieghaardt, has also played a significant role. The prior contribution of social workers in India, the Philippines, Ghana,
and several other African countries should also be recognized. In particular, we
acknowledge the contribution of African colleagues such as Eddie Kaseke, Roddie
Mupedziswa and Kwaku Osei-Hwedie. Colleagues in Hong Kong and China, including James Lee, Raymond Ngan, Cecilia Chan, Joe Leung, C. K. Wong, Xuilan Zhang,
and Yuebin Xu, have been committed to the promotion of developmental ideas and
discussions with them and others have been very helpful. Although the publications
of social work colleagues in Latin America are not readily available elsewhere, trans-
lations of their work—particularly their efforts to reconceptualize conventional
social work—have been highly influential in shaping social development ideas.

The work of social work scholars involved in the International Consortium for
Social Development and many publications in the journal *Social Development Issues*
also inspired this book. Richard Estes, M.C., "Terry" Hokenstad, Jack Jones, Shanti
Khinduka, Fred Ahearn, and Roland Meinert made major contributions to the formulation of the social development approach. Their work built on the earlier contributions of Dan Sanders, Rama Pandey, and Frank Paiva, among others. During
their leadership of the Consortium, Jim Billups, Peter Lee, and Chuck Cogwer
actively encouraged the academic growth of the subject. As past editor of *Social
Development Issues*, Martin Tracy played a major role in promoting scholarship in
the field. Numerous congenial discussions with Doreen Elliott and Nazneen
Mayadas about the relevance of social development to social work practice crystal-
lized these ideas and helped shape this book. We also acknowledge Lynne Healy's
important work. Collaboration with Michelle Livermore, Kwong-Leung Tang, and
Michael and Margaret Sherraden also contributed significantly to the formulation
of the developmental approach. We also acknowledge the support of Lorraine
Midanik, Dean of the School of Social Welfare at Berkeley.

We are extremely grateful to the contributors to this book, most of whom are
associated with the School of Social Welfare at Berkeley, for working so diligently
on the chapters and being responsive to our suggestions as well as those of our
anonymous reviewers. These reviewers engaged us in a high-level discussion about
diverse aspects of the developmental approach, and we benefited greatly from their
questions and helpful suggestions.

From the outset, Maura Roessner at Oxford University Press expressed enthusiastic interest in the proposal and provided invaluable support and advice. Nicholas
Liu did a fine job as assistant editor. Angela Wood has been an efficient copy editor,
and we are also grateful to Susan Lee who managed the production. It will be realized from what has been said that this book has been a collaborative team effort to
which a large number of friends and colleagues have contributed—either directly or
indirectly. We are grateful to them and many others who believe that developmental
social work offers promising prospects for the future of the social work profession.

James Midgley   **Amy Conley**
University of California, Berkeley   San Francisco State University

THE EDITORS AND AUTHORS

Mary Ager Caplan is a PhD student in Social Welfare at the University of California, Berkeley. She holds a Master's of Social Welfare from Berkeley and has worked for many years in the area of mental health policy and community planning with the City of Berkeley Health and Human Services. Her research topics include economic well-being and mental health, social welfare policy, and social welfare theory.

Amy Conley is an Assistant Professor of Child and Adolescent Development at San Francisco State University. Her teaching, research, and practice experiences are in the areas of child and family policy, family support, and child maltreatment prevention. She has published several articles on child welfare innovations, including differential response and birth parent peer support. Her most recent work involves family support in community and child care settings, including San Francisco Head Start/Early Head Start.

Kristin Ferguson is an Associate Professor at the University of Southern California School of Social Work. Her research focuses on homeless and street-living youth, social and spiritual capital, outcomes evaluation and social enterprise interventions with street youth in community-based agencies. She has published numerous articles on street children, social capital, social development and social enterprise interventions for street youth in leading domestic and international social work journals. Her 2005 article entitled *Beyond Indigenization and Reconceptualization: Towards a Global, Multidirectional Model of Technology Transfer* was awarded the Frank Turner Award for Best Article in *International Social Work*.

Nancy Giunta is a John A. Hartford Geriatric Social Work Scholar, Assistant Professor at the Hunter College School of Social Work, and Faculty Fellow at the Brookdale Center for Healthy Aging and Longevity. Her areas of interest include long term care policy, home and community-based service systems, and collaborative systems change. She also serves on the technical assistance consortium of the Community Partnerships for Older Adults, a national program of the Robert Wood Johnson Foundation to help communities develop leadership, innovative solutions and options that meet the needs of older adults.

Jennifer Knapp is a clinical social worker and graduate of UC Berkeley School of Social Welfare. She currently is working in the acute psychiatric unit at the Veterans' Affairs Hospital in Palo Alto, California where she works with the chronically physically and psychiatrically disabled. She has co-founded a solution-focused committee for high frequency users of emergency rooms and hospital services, where she actively promotes a strengths-based model in addressing this population's psychosocial needs. She also works in the community by providing counseling for trauma survivors of sexual assault and running support groups for adult children of disabled parents.

James Midgley is the Harry and Riva Specht Professor of Public Social Services and Dean Emeritus of the School of Social Welfare University of California, Berkeley. He has published widely on social development and international social welfare and is an acknowledged authority in the field. He is frequently invited to present at international conferences and meetings. His most recent books include *International Perspectives on Welfare to Work Policy* Haworth Press, 2006 (editor with Richard Hoefer); *Social Security, the Economy and Development*, Palgrave, 2008 (editor with Kwong-leung Tang), *The Handbook of Social Policy*, Sage, 2009 (editor with Michelle Livermore) and *Social Policy and Poverty in East Asia: The Role of Social Security*, Routledge, 2010 (editor with Kwong-leung Tang).

Will C. Rainford is an Associate Professor and Chair of the MSW Program at Boise State University School of Social Work. He has published book chapters on Latina teen pregnancy (co-authored with Margaret Sherraden and Rosio Gonzalez) and the profession of social work (co-authored with Daniel Harkness). He has also published research on paternalistic social policy in the United States, and theoretical approaches to social development from the individual-enterprise perspective. His work as a legislative advocate (who uses a social developmental framework) has been recognized and he has received numerous awards, including being named the NASW Social Worker of the Year.

INTRODUCTION

JAMES MIDGLEY AND AMY CONLEY

This book discusses a distinctive approach to professional social work known as "developmental social work." Because developmental social work has been informed by the wider interdisciplinary field of social development, it is also known as the "social development" approach to social work. Like other social work approaches—such as psychotherapeutic clinical social work, community organization, legislative advocacy, or policy practice—developmental social work has identifiable features that include preferred practice methods, theoretical assumptions, and principles. It also has unique historical roots. Although developmental social work draws on ideas that circulated during the profession's formative years in the West, it really emerged as a coherent approach in the developing countries of the Global South. Over the years, developmental social work has gained wider attention in international social work circles, and more recently, its relevance to the Western countries has been recognized.

A key feature of developmental social work is the use of investment strategies in professional practice. Developmental social work not only emphasizes client strengths and the importance of empowerment but also requires that those served by social workers (who are known in the professional literature as "clients") are provided with tangible social investments that enhance their capabilities and facilitate their participation in community life and the productive economy. As this book shows, these investments include job training, employment placement, childcare, adult literacy, micro-enterprise, and asset savings accounts, to name but a few. These investments, which require extensive governmental resources, are used primarily to meet the material needs of social work's clients and to help them recognize their aspirations and life goals. Poverty, deprivation, and despair characterized the lives of many of the profession's clients, and addressing these challenges is a key element in developmental practice.

In addition to emphasizing social investments, developmental social work stresses the role of community-based practice interventions. Developmental practitioners believe that the vast majority of social work's clients can be served in community settings, and despite the challenges many face, they can live independently in the community. Therefore, developmental social workers avoid the use of residential facilities that segregate needy people from the community. In addition, developmental social work is participatory. Instead of the professional, expert approach that characterizes much social work practice, developmental social work emphasizes the role of client participation and self-determination. Practitioners using the developmental approach facilitate and support, rather than prescribe, solutions. International awareness is another feature of developmental social work, and accordingly, innovations in different countries are frequently but judiciously adapted to fit practice needs in other parts of the world. Finally, developmental social work is committed to a rights-based approach and to wider social goals such as democratic participation and egalitarian social justice. Developmental social workers collaborate with other progressive organizations and groups and use their lobbying and advocacy skills to contribute to the achievement of these ideals.

Developmental social work is rooted in notions of personal growth and change that can be traced back to the profession's early years, but as noted earlier, it is more closely associated with the social development approach that originated in the developing countries in the years following World War II. Although the governments of these countries adopted economic policies designed to promote rapid growth and modernize their economies, it was recognized that the problems of mass poverty and deprivation were not being solved through economic growth alone. Despite recording respectable rates of growth, poverty remained a huge problem. Criticisms of conventional economic development policies resulted in the advocacy of an alternative people-centered developmental strategy known as *social development* (or sometimes as *human development*). Social development advocates insist that economic development policies be combined with social interventions and that the goals of economic development and social well-being be given *equal* emphasis within the development process. This requires that economic development benefits the population as a whole. It also requires that social welfare interventions contribute positively to economic development. Accordingly, social development gives priority to interventions that are investment-oriented and consonant with wider developmental goals. This emphasis on social investment is also sometimes referred to as the *productivist* approach to social welfare.

Although developmental social work and social development are closely linked, social development comprises a broader set of activities than those of developmental social work. Developmental social work is, as the term suggests, a distinctive form of social work practice, but social development is a broader interdisciplinary field closely associated with economic development projects and programs in the

Global South. Few social development projects and programs are implemented by professional social workers; more often, they are the purview of economists, development policymakers, the staff of nongovernmental organizations, and grassroots community workers. Nevertheless, social development informs and inspires developmental social work. As shown in the next chapter of this book, social workers in the Global South made a major contribution to formulating social development theories and practice interventions. Although social workers in the Western countries also contributed, it is largely through the experience of working in developmental settings that the key principles and practice approaches of development social work have evolved.

Developmental social work is often viewed as best suited to the needs of the developing nations, but many social workers in the West have become interested in how it can be adapted to fit social work practice in their own countries. This interest has been sparked by a greater awareness of international innovations in social work and social welfare. A growing number of social workers now believe that developmental ideas have relevance throughout the world. Through organizations such as the International Consortium for Social Development and the journal *Social Development Issues*, as well as numerous articles, books, and research reports, they have sought to promote developmental social work in the Western nations. They have also fostered debates about its theoretical assumptions, scope, and international applicability.

Despite a greater awareness of developmental social work's potential, there is uncertainty about what it involves. Even in the Global South, where developmental ideas have been popularized, some social workers have difficulty in distinguishing between "conventional" and "developmental" social work practice. It is often believed that developmental social work is implemented through community development projects and other indirect or macro-practice activities and that it is of little relevance to social work's mainstream practice commitments. Social work services for abused and neglected children, people with mental illness, the homeless, people with disabilities, young offenders, and the elderly are not thought to be amenable to "developmental" interventions. Many social workers believe that these clients can best be helped through conventional remedial programs and that social work practice designed to meet their needs is radically different from developmental social work.

But, as this book endeavors to show, the principles and practice interventions used in developmental social work can be applied in mainstream social work practice with the clients who have traditionally been served by social workers. It will be argued that developmental social work is not only concerned with indirect or macro-practice but also can be applied to core, conventional fields of practice such as child welfare, mental health, social work with disability, gerontological social work, social assistance, and corrections. It will also be argued that the skills social workers use in conventional practice can be applied in developmental social work.

On the other hand, it should be recognized that developmental social work diverges from much conventional social work practice. Accordingly, developmental social workers do not place much emphasis on therapeutic counseling, which remains the profession's most prestigious and popular practice modality. Also, as noted earlier, they avoid using residential care. They are also critical of interventions that maintain clients in an ongoing, maintenance relationship with service providers. This does not mean that they reject the need for services and supports, but they do believe that these should be configured in ways that recognize strengths and promote self-determination and meaningful participation in community life. Also, although they recognize that counseling can be helpful, they are critical of its central role in social work today. Similarly, they recognize that some clients will require extensive supports and even residential care. However, as mentioned earlier, advocates of developmental social work transcend conventional remedial and maintenance practice approaches through adopting social investment strategies that build on peoples' capabilities to be productive citizens and lead normal and fulfilling lives.

Some social workers find this notion troubling. For example, those who have been schooled in a "helping" tradition, in which social work services are delivered on the basis of compassion, will have doubts about the emphasis in developmental social work on the promotion of economic participation through skills training, micro-enterprise, employment, asset development, and similar interventions. Others who are persuaded by a critical approach will regard the advocacy of productive participation as little more than promoting the integration of clients into the capitalist system. Yet others, who are influenced by postmodernist ideas, will regard the economistic emphasis in developmental social work as irrelevant to contemporary realities where the struggle for identity, recognition and respect are prioritized. Although these concerns are understandable, it will be explained later in this book that developmental social work's commitments are not, in fact, incompatible with social work values—particularly with a commitment to human rights and social justice. Developmental advocates make no apology for promoting community living and the integration of clients into the productive economy, but they believe that social investments require extensive state intervention and a broader egalitarian environment in which people can truly realize their potential.

The Scope of this Book

The following chapters of this book describe the key features of developmental social work and show how it can be applied in mainstream social work practice. In particular, it shows how developmental interventions can be applied in the major fields of social work practice with client groups that have historically formed the core of social work's professional activities. As mentioned earlier, these core fields of practice include child welfare, mental health, social work with disability, gerontological social work, social assistance, and corrections. It is on these traditional practice fields that most of the book's chapters are focused. It will be noted that the authors of the book's chapters sometimes use terms such as *productive aging, social enterprise*, and *rights-based* social work. Terms such as *strengths, empowerment, recovery*, and *re-entry* are also associated with developmental social work. Although potentially confusing, these different terms share common underlying principles and commitments with developmental social work.

This book is primarily designed for graduate and upper-level undergraduate students in schools of social work and related academic departments, as well as faculty and practitioner colleagues in the United States. Although there has been a growing awareness and interest in the relevance of social development ideas to professional social work in the United States over the years, many still believe that social development is primarily applicable to the developing countries in the Global South and of limited use in the West. By showing how social investment strategies can be applied in conventional fields of practice in the United States, the book hopes to demonstrate the universal relevance of the developmental approach. Of course, it is hoped that the book will also be of value in other countries. It draws extensively on the experience of international colleagues who have implemented developmental ideas and should be of interest to social workers everywhere.

The book has three parts. The first, which consists of an introductory chapter, offers an overview of developmental social work's historical evolution, principles, and practice approaches and discusses the major investment strategies that are used in the field. Part II shows how developmental social work can be adopted by social workers in their daily practice with families and children, people with mental illness, homeless youth, people with disabilities, the elderly, and those in the correctional system. These fields of practice have been chosen for inclusion in the book because they are illustrative of the application of developmental principles to social work. They are also the most popular fields of social work practice. Of course, they are not exhaustive. Because these are the primary client groups with whom social workers have been engaged for many years, approaching the topic from a fields of practice perspective will hopefully demonstrate how developmental ideas and interventions can inform everyday social work practice. Also, these chapters provide information about those interventions that are most frequently associated with developmental social work. Interventions such as child care, literacy programs, investment-oriented income transfers, micro-enterprise, and asset savings accounts are widely used by developmental social workers. Finally, in Part III, the book concludes by discussing some of the limitations of the developmental social work approach in the context of its future potential to inform social work practice and improve the lives of the people social workers serve.

The introductory chapter by **James Midgley** in Part I provides an overview of developmental social work by tracing its history, theoretical assumptions, and key practice interventions. The author discusses the contribution of social workers from both the developing and Western countries in formulating developmental ideas. He also reviews the debates that have taken place on issues of definition, principles, and practice interventions. Midgley emphasizes the importance of the concept of social investment, which is consonant with the strengths and empowerment approaches in social work. He then outlines the skills social workers use in developmental practice and discusses developmental social work's core investment interventions.

As noted earlier, Part II focuses on the application of social development's investment strategies in the major fields of social work practice. These chapters focus on social work practice with client groups that have traditionally been served by the profession.

Chapter 2 by **Amy Conley** discusses the developmental approach to child welfare. A number of scathing indictments have been leveled against the traditional Western child protection approach, suggesting that new ideas are needed to meet the needs of children and families. She argues that the American child welfare system has traditionally taken a residual approach to serving families, intervening only in the worst cases of child maltreatment. By contrast, developmental social work enhances the capacities of parents and communities to care for children and addresses the problem of poverty, which is endemic to child maltreatment. Conley compares conventional child welfare practices with the developmental approach, and while recognizing that the developmental approach is still being formulated, international innovations in childcare and family support point the way forward.

Nancy Giunta then examines the notion of productive aging and discusses its relevance to developmental social work in Chapter 3. She notes that the aging of the worldwide population has profound demographic, economic, and socio-cultural implications. Over the next several decades, the population will be increasingly comprised of older adults. Although seniors have benefited from various policies and programs, older adults and their caregivers are at risk of increased isolation and dependency and decreased economic, physical, and mental well-being. Conventional social work approaches have largely sought to address individual needs without considering the larger social, physical, or economic context of an aging society. Although the concept of productive aging addresses this concern, recent theoretical contributions have recognized that "productivity" is not only defined as the economic value of an individual's actions but may also be measured in terms of social or civic participation. Older adults have the capacity to participate fully in community life and help build a community's social and economic capital.

The following Chapter 4 by **Mary Ager Caplan** is concerned with social investment strategies—particularly the role of social enterprise in mental health. She notes that the conventional model of treatment for mental illness involves a dynamic of expert and patient. By contrast, a developmental approach to treating mental illness embraces the core tenets of the client-led wellness, recovery, and resiliency movement. This chapter compares the two approaches and explores how a social development approach can harness social and human capital to promote wellness and integrate mentally ill people into their communities. These principles are explored through a case study of the Village, a consumer-managed organization in Southern California, where clients are involved in every level of decision making, provide peer-support services, and run businesses, including catering and a credit union.

In Chapter 5, **Jennifer Knapp** and **James Midgley** describe the developmental approach to social work with people with disabilities, which is largely rights-based and focused on independent living. Drawing on social development ideas, the authors discuss the campaigns of the disability rights movement to normalize the lives of people with disabilities and to ensure their integration into economic, cultural, and political life. Three aspects of the developmental approach are discussed—namely, the emergence and institutionalization of disability rights, the mainstreaming of people with disabilities into community living, and their active engagement and participation in the productive economy. Although the outmoded expert and medical approaches still exert considerable influence in disability services, the chapter shows that much has been done to implement a rights-based, developmental approach and that social work has a major contribution to make by collaborating with people with disabilities and their organizations to promote this approach.

The role of social work in addressing the problems of poverty through social assistance and related programs is discussed in Chapter 6 by **James Midgley**. He notes that when social work first emerged as a profession in the late 19th century, social workers were actively involved in poverty alleviation and in the administration of social assistance programs. They continued to play an important role in the field for many years. During the New Deal, for example, social workers in the United States participated extensively in the administration of public assistance. However, in the latter half of the 20th century, they disengaged from programs of this kind and much more emphasis was placed on psychotherapeutic interventions. The author argues that social workers have a key role to play in formulating and implementing social assistance programs designed to reduce poverty. Several international examples are given to illustrate this point. He also shows that these programs can be configured in ways that replace minimalist, Poor Law type of cash transfers and enhance investments.

In the following chapter (Chapter 7), **Will C. Rainford** observes that social workers have been involved with issues of delinquency, crime, and corrections since the profession's inception in the late 19th century. However, as crime rates have continued to soar and as prison populations have reached unprecedented levels, new approaches are needed. Focusing on the role of social workers within correctional facilities, the author discusses innovative social investment strategies that enhance the strengths and capabilities of those in prison and prepares them for successful reentry into society. Emphasis is given to human capital programs, employment preparation and placement, asset accounts, and micro-enterprise programs that integrate offenders into the community and productive economy. The role of social workers in linking these activities to community resources, and the professional supports that facilitate re-entry into the community are discussed.

Chapter 8 by **Kristin Ferguson** discusses the social enterprise approach to social work practice with homeless youth. She notes that traditional service delivery for homeless youths consists of residential as well as outreach and shelter services. Although these services aim to mitigate their health, mental health, and other social problems, this approach fails to replace their street-survival behaviors with other legitimate, income-generating activities. In the case of homeless youths, successful strategies to move them from the informal to the formal economy require more than employment in low-paying positions, because their formal labor-market participation is often hindered by the challenges inherent in living on the streets. Ferguson describes existing intervention models for homeless youths and suggests that through social enterprises these youths can acquire vocational and business skills, mentorship, clinical treatment, and linkages to services to facilitate their economic and social self-sufficiency.

Next, Chapter 9 by **James Midgley** discusses the developmental approach to community social work practice. Although community organization and other forms of macro-practice are usually associated with developmental interventions, the author contends that conventional community practice approaches such as neighborhood building, social services planning, and social action have not effectively utilized investments that address peoples' material needs. Drawing on the experience of community development in the Global South and local economic development innovations in the United States, he argues for a greater focus on economic projects that raise standards of living and address the problem of poverty and deprivation in poor communities.

The final chapter in Part III by **James Midgley** and **Amy Conley** draws the previous material together, recognizing that there are limitations to the developmental approach in social work but also that this approach has much future promise, particularly in the context of economic challenges and resource constraints. The authors argue that social workers can use investment strategies in professional practice to promote the participation of social work's clients in normal community life and in the productive economy and, in this way, contribute positively to their long-term well-being. The developmental approach, they contend, is highly compatible with social work's historical values and commitment to achieving social justice and human rights.

SOCIAL WORK AND
SOCIAL DEVELOPMENT

PART I

The Developmental Perspective in Social Work

The Theory and Practice of Developmental Social Work

JAMES MIDGLEY

This chapter discusses the meaning and key characteristics of developmental social work. It traces its history and examines its theoretical concepts and key practice interventions. The chapter shows that developmental social work has not only been influenced by ideas associated with economic and social development but also by historic debates about social work's features, scope, functions, and mission. Ever since social work emerged as an organized profession in the early years of the 20th century, there have been sharp differences of opinion among practitioners and scholars on this issue. There have also been disagreements about the practice approaches that should be used to achieve its goals. These debates are relevant to an understanding of developmental social work.

Contemporary social work draws on divergent historical roots. One of these is the individualized casework approach, which emerged out of the poor relief activities of the urban charities in the 19th century. Another was the neighborhood organizing approach associated with the settlements. A third was the statist approach, resulting from the expansion of government social services and income maintenance programs. Although disparate, these different activities were forged into a coherent although sometimes fractious professional identity by social work practitioners and academics in Europe and North America in the early decades of the 20th century. The emergence of social work as an organized profession was aided by the creation of university-based schools of social work and the introduction of standardized curricula and educational expectations.

By the mid-decades of the 20th century, there was general agreement that social work is based on a common set of principles and values and that it has an evolving body of knowledge. It was also agreed that social work's goals would be realized through different practice methods, including casework, group work, and community organization. Although other practice modalities such as administration, research, and policy practice have also been identified, the three core methods of casework, group work, and community organization form the core modalities of social work practice. It should be noted that casework is also known as direct practice or more recently as clinical social work and that community organization is also known as community work or community practice. Of these practice modalities, individualized clinical social work is the most widely used form of social work practice.

These practice methods are generally applied in agency settings and in specialized fields such as child welfare, mental health, social assistance, medical social work, gerontological social work, and corrections. These fields of practice emerged in the early 20th century as the original poor relief functions of the charities were gradually superceded by specialized practice in hospitals, correctional facilities, public welfare agencies, mental health clinics, residential facilities, rehabilitation centers, and family and child welfare agencies. Agency-based social work practice is dominated by individualized casework. On the other hand, group work and community work are associated with distinctly different fields of endeavor, such as youth work and the planning of community social services.

Social work's functions, preferred practice methods, mission, and other issues are perennially debated. Regarding functions, social work's remedial function has long been given priority. Social work also has a maintenance function by which the profession provides long-term support and assistance to those in need. Social work's preventive function has also been discussed in the literature, but unfortunately, prevention is not always given high priority. Closely aligned to prevention is the idea of promoting social integration and fostering solidarity at the community and societal levels. Social work also has a social change function by which it promotes improvements in people's well-being and in wider social conditions. This change function is also referred to as social work's developmental function.

Many scholars believe that social work's different functions are discharged through different practice methods. Individualized social casework or clinical social work is usually associated with the remedial function, whereas residential care and the provision of social assistance is associated with the profession's maintenance function. Group work is often said to promote social work's integrative function. Community social work practice is believed to be best suited to attaining social work's change or developmental function. The developmental function is also realized through social work advocacy and lobbying as well as through engaging in policy practice. On the other hand, social work practice in child welfare, medical social work, mental health, and other the fields of practice is usually associated with remedial social work.

The literature on developmental social work frequently differentiates between remedial, or "mainstream," social work on the one hand and developmental social work on the other. Whereas the former is said to rely primarily on individualized casework in specialized fields of practice agencies, the latter is believed to take place through community organization or "macro-practice," which includes advocacy, lobbying, policy practice, and organizing. Macro-practice is believed to offer a congenial opportunity for social work to transcend its conventional remedial pre-occupation and to realize its social change goals. However, as was suggested in the introduction to this book, the bifurcation of "mainstream," remedial, and develop-mental social work has not been helpful. Although it is true that community and other forms of macro-social work are conducive to promoting the developmental approach, its tenets can also be applied in the core social work practice fields men-tioned earlier. As this book hopes to show, social work practice in these fields is amenable to developmental principles and approaches. This involves the use of investment strategies, as well as the adoption of community-based, participatory, and rights-based interventions.

This argument is articulated in the remainder of this chapter by tracing the evolution of developmental social work during the 20th century and highlighting practice innovations as well as academic efforts that have conceptualized develop-mental ideas. The chapter then examines some of the theoretical concepts that inform developmental social work. Finally, it discusses some of the key interven-tions that characterize developmental social work and distinguish it from other social work approaches.

The Evolution of Developmental Social Work

The ideas on which developmental social work are based can be traced back to the profession's early years, when the founders of the settlements and the advocates of governmental social welfare intervention offered an alternative to the casework model. The settlements provided educational, recreational, and youth activities and sought to mobilize local people to improve their neighborhoods. Statists urged the expansion of public social services based on universalism and social rights as well as the large-scale employment of social workers in government agencies. These alternatives challenged the individualized casework approach but were not success-ful in undermining its dominant position.

However, as suggested earlier, it is an oversimplification to strictly classify individualized casework as being remedial and community organization as being developmental. As scholars such as Karger (1987) have shown, community organi-zation as practiced by the settlements was not always progressive. Indeed, some settlements were very paternalistic and controlling, particularly toward immigrants whom they sought to assimilate into mainstream American society. To complicate matters, some social work scholars have argued that clinical social work can be developmental. In the 1930s, the diagnostic, medical casework model developed by Mary Richmond and the psychiatric approach of Mary Jarrett were criticized by Jessie Taft and Virginia Robinson of the Functional School, who stressed the impor-tance of growth within the therapeutic relationship. Anticipating later scholars, they argued that social workers should pay attention to client strengths rather than deficits and help them to realize their potential for personal growth. Nevertheless, notions of pathology and treatment continued to dominate social casework.

Although community social work remained a minority field, it provided an opportunity for the application of developmental ideas, particularly through the work of Jane Adams and her followers. Their contribution to settlement work and neighborhood building and to advocacy and political lobbying helped shape social work's social change function. Also relevant was the pioneering role of activists such as Florence Kelley, Lillian Wald, and Bertha Reynolds, who inspired those committed to bringing about progressive change. As the work of Saul Alinksy was absorbed into community social work practice in the 1950s, the idea that social workers could contribute effectively to social change through social action gained wider support. These events contributed significantly to the emergence of developmental social work.

Social work's commitment to social change was given a boost during the Great Depression, when social workers in the United States became involved in various New Deal programs. Important members of the Roosevelt cabinet, such as Harry Hopkins and Frances Perkins, were closely associated with the emerging social work profession and actively supported the expansion of social work education and the employment of qualified social workers within governmental bureaucracies. Hopkins appointed Jane Hoey (who was one of the first federal officials to obtain a professional social work credential) to head the government's expanding social assistance program. Social workers were also firmly in control of the Children's Bureau and shaped the emerging field of statutory child welfare practice.

The programs of the New Deal were largely developmental in character. They integrated economic and social policy and placed emphasis on securing full employment. Major economic and social reforms were introduced, and the role of the unions was strengthened. Workers' rights and minimum wages reinforced prevailing notions of economic justice. In addition, the income maintenance and social services introduced with enactment of the 1935 Social Security Act provided a comprehensive safety net and formalized the idea of the right to welfare. The New Deal also emphasized investments in education, health, and housing. The subsequent enactment of the Servicemen's Adjustment Act (or the GI Bill of Rights) in 1944 confirmed this commitment to social investment and developmental social welfare. There were similar developments in Britain after the adoption of the recommendations of the Beveridge Report by the Post-War Labour Government as well as in other European countries that implemented a variety of "welfare-state" policies.

Social Development and Developmental Social Work in the Global South

As in the West, social work in the developing countries of the Global South has also been largely remedial in character. In many countries, social work was introduced by the colonial authorities after World War II to staff the new social welfare services that had been introduced to respond to growing urban social problems, such as juvenile delinquency, child neglect, begging, and vagrancy. Professionally qualified social workers were imported from the metropolitan countries to serve in the new departments of social welfare that were created in many of the colonial territories and local staff were sent abroad to obtain professional social work credentials. Social workers were assigned responsibility for managing the institutions for young offenders and homes for the destitute elderly and people with disabilities that were established in many of these territories at the time. In addition to providing residential services, they also engaged in casework and provided limited social assistance benefits.

As many developing countries secured independence from European imperial rule, high priority was given to economic development. Their nationalist leaders were not content with securing political sovereignty but wanted to modernize their economies and raise the standards of living of their citizens. They and their economic advisors believed that by stimulating industrial development, those laboring in the subsistence, agrarian sector would be drawn into wage employment and that this would create a spiral of growth that would eventually denude the subsistence sector and significantly reduce the incidence of poverty. A major policy recommendation was that governments should reduce consumption expenditure and prioritize economic development.

It was in this context that the emerging social welfare programs of the developing countries came under sustained criticism for consuming scarce resources on allegedly "unproductive" activities that detracted from the overriding goal of achieving rapid economic growth. Although most social welfare officials reacted defensively to this criticism, some were motivated to identify interventions that did indeed contribute to economic development. In India, the developmental potential of community-based activities associated with the work of indigenous leaders such as Gandhi and Tagore laid the foundations for the country's social development programs. In West Africa, where communal grain storage and cooperative farming were commonplace, welfare administrators realized that local needs could be addressed through community projects. They proposed that the remedial emphasis of the welfare departments be augmented by community-based interventions such as literacy education, building roads, bridges, and local irrigation systems, promoting small-scale agriculture and animal husbandry, developing crafts and village industries, and constructing community health centers and schools.

These programs were enthusiastically endorsed by the Colonial Office in London, which facilitated their replication in the other British colonies. The Colonial Office also convened several meetings of social workers and welfare administrators from the colonies, and it was at these meetings that the terms *community development* and *social development* were adopted. Whereas community development referred to local activities, social development involved, as one official document put it, "nothing less than the whole process of change and their advancement of a territory considered in terms of the progressive well-being of society and the individual" (United Kingdom, 1954, p. 14).

The global spread of community development and social development owed much to the United Nations and other international organizations. The United Nations provided technical advice and funding to assist governments in implementing social development programs, and it convened numerous international meetings and conferences where social development interventions were discussed. A major event of this kind was the United Nations Conference of Ministers Responsible for Social Welfare, which took place in New York in 1969. The ministers discussed the different functions of social welfare and recognized that remedial services had a major role to play in meeting social needs and addressing social problems. They also recognized that many of those served by social workers would require "maintenance" in the form of long-term benefits and supports. However, they urged that an appropriate balance between remedial, maintenance, and developmental interventions be found and, in particular, that social welfare services should contribute to national development. Although the conference is seldom mentioned in the social development literature, it questioned the prevailing emphasis on remedial social work and contributed to the spread of developmental ideas.

Although community development and social development were initially viewed as a governmental responsibility, the statist emphasis was eventually challenged by those who believed in a grassroots, participatory approach in which ordinary people rather than government officials and their appointees controlled local affairs. Despite its promise of involving local people, government-sponsored community development was based on a "top-down" approach in which civil servants made decisions and directed development projects. It was also noted that community development often involved patronage politics and supported corrupt officials and local leaders.

In response, a more activist form of community development emerged in the 1970s. Advocates of the new radical approach criticized governmental and traditional power structures and sought to increase popular participation in development projects. This development was consonant with the rapid growth of the voluntary sector at the time, and with popular movements that were inspired by the anticolonial writings and struggles of Third World activists. The notion of empowerment and the work of Freire (1970, 1973) on *conscientization* fueled the new activism. The rise of the Women's Movement in both the West and the Global South also contributed significantly to the activist approach and infused conventional social development thinking with a new radicalism that some believe offered an alternative to the "welfare developmentalism" that characterized state-sponsored developmental social work. Antiracist and other campaigns for equality, such as the gay rights struggle, have also contributed to the popularization of the activist approach.

Conceptualizing Social Development and Developmental Social Work

These developments laid the foundation for the conceptualization of social development and developmental social work in 1970s and 1980s. Although social development had taken root by this time, it was largely a practical affair in which theoretical ideas played a minimal role. Social development's subsequent theoretical growth owed much to social work scholars who had experience of development in the Global South. Although they focused broadly on social development rather than social work, their writings had relevance for the conceptualization of developmental social work as a distinctive form of social work practice.

In the 1970s and 1980s, theoretical work in social development was facilitated by the establishment of the Inter-University Consortium for International Social Development. The Consortium, which has since been renamed the International Consortium for Social Development (or ICSD) was initially comprised largely of social work educators at midwestern universities in the United States. One of their primary goals was to introduce social development to American social workers through convening conferences and publishing a new journal, *Social Development Issues*. Also relevant was the creation of a social work program committed to teaching and scholarship in social development at the University of Minnesota, Duluth. Under the leadership of John (Jack) Jones, the program made a major contribution to the conceptualization of developmental social work. However, it encountered accreditation difficulties and the experiment was eventually terminated. Nevertheless, these events facilitated lively debates and a growing body of academic literature on the subject.

The first book on social development by social workers was an edited collection by Jones and his colleague Rama Pandey in 1981, and this was closely followed in 1982 by another edited book by Dan Sanders of the University of Hawaii. Both books contained an eclectic set of chapters dealing with different aspects of social development. At about this time, Paiva (1977) and published seminal articles on social development in leading social work journals that helped to publicize the social development approach among social workers in the United States and other countries.

However, these publications revealed that no standardized definition of social development had emerged and that the field was infused with rhetorical and hortatory claims that were in themselves inspiring but lacked clear practical prescriptions for practice. Nevertheless, it is possible to identify two strands in this formative literature. The first views social development as a process of personal growth and self-actualization that has wider social effects. For example, drawing on earlier functional casework ideas, Maas (1984, p. 3) defined social development as a process in which "people become increasingly able to interact competently and responsibly resulting in the creation of a caring and sharing society." Pavia (1977, p. 332) offered a similar interpretation, arguing that social development is "the development of the capacity of people to work continuously for their own and society's welfare."

A second approach comes from scholars such as Hollister (1977), who equated social development practice with macro-social work practice and noted that social development combines community organizing, policy analysis, planning, administration, and program and project evaluation. Spergel (1978) adopted a similar approach, suggesting that there was little difference between developmental social work and community organizing. Stein (1975) also associated social work's developmental function with social planning and the implementation of social policies. On the other hand, Sanders (1982) argued that social development is applicable to all forms of social work, but he did not provide specific examples of how developmental ideas could be implemented in mainstream professional practice. This issue was subsequently addressed by social work scholars Billups (1994) and Elliott and Mayadas (1993, 1996) who showed how social development principles could be incorporated into different social work practice modalities.

Despite this flurry of academic activity, commentators such as Lloyd (1982) concluded that the advocates of social development had failed to define developmental social work in tangible terms and that the literature on the subject had only produced a set of "values aspirations and heuristic notions" that were "hortatory rather than prescriptive" (pp. 44–45). Equally pessimistic was Khinduka's (1987) contention that despite a good deal of academic effort, social development remained "an incorrigibly elusive concept" (p. 22).

In the 1990s, attempts to offer conceptualizations of social development practice were overshadowed by the rise of market liberal ideology. This development challenged the statist interventionism that was implicit in much social development thinking. Derived from European social democratic ideas and Keynesian economics, social development scholars and practitioners generally approved of government intervention in social and economic affairs. The advocates of neoliberalism successfully challenged this assumption. In the United States and Britain, the Reagan and Thatcher administrations attacked economic planning and state welfare, whereas in Chile, General Pinochet's military régime aggressively sought to eradicate all traces of state intervention. The International Monetary Fund and the World Bank were also infused with neoliberal ideas and increasingly required the governments of indebted developing countries to reduce social expenditures as a condition for financial aid. Development economics also reflected a growing commitment to market liberalism and, coupled with frequent populist attacks on government development programs by activists in the nongovernmental sector, social development programs in many developing countries were enfeebled.

Despite the near hegemony of market liberalism, social development advocates continued to believe that state intervention was needed to deal with the increasingly serious social problems affecting many developing countries. Despite the gains recorded in the post-World War II decades, economic growth in many parts of the Global South stagnated, the incidence of poverty increased, and problems of malnutrition, ill health, and illiteracy became more evident as government social services were retrenched. Generally, the neoliberal dispensation impeded social progress and in some cases reversed earlier developmental gains. This was particularly evident in South Asia and sub-Saharan Africa as well as in the former Soviet Union, where the destruction of state socialism resulted in a precipitous rise in unemployment and social deprivation. These problems were exacerbated by the emergence of new social challenges such as the AIDS pandemic and genocidal civil wars.

Recent International Developments

In the early 1990s, staff at the United Nations Secretariat in New York persuaded the organization's leadership that a renewed commitment to social development was needed. In 1995, this resulted in a landmark conference in Copenhagen, known as the World Summit on Social Development. The Summit was attended by an unprecedented number of world leaders. It set specific long-term social development targets, which, it was hoped, would be met both through domestic and international effort. The *Copenhagen Declaration*, which enshrined these targets, again brought social development to the forefront of international attention (United Nations, 1996). Subsequently, these targets were reformulated and adopted as the Millennium Development Goals by the United Nations General Assembly at a special session in September, 2000. Among these goals is a commitment to halve the incidence of global poverty by 2015 and to bring about improvements in social conditions including nutrition, the status of women, and maternal and child health. Emphasis was also placed on the need for greater international cooperation (United Nations, 2005).

Although the World Summit and the adoption of the Millennium Development Goals undoubtedly reinvigorated social development, significant differences about the nature of social development practice and the conceptual ideas underlying different interventions persist. Although the statist approach has been undermined, its role is still recognized. On the other hand, community-based interventions have become very popular. With the rapid expansion of the nongovernmental sector in many parts of the Global South, social development is now widely associated with community-based activities managed by local people or by nongovernmental organizations. Since the 1970s, many new nongovernmental organizations have emerged to promote local community development. Many are managed by women and have a strong commitment to promoting the well-being of women and securing gender inequality. A major development has been the adoption of micro-enterprise and microfinance. Although micro-enterprise had been encouraged for many years, it was largely after the innovations of the Grameen Bank in Bangladesh became widely known that peer lending to cooperative groups of women became a popular social development strategy. Also relevant has been the rise of the Environmental Movement, which has vigorously campaigned for sustainability in development policy. The concept of sustainable development has been well-received the social development circles and has informed many social development projects, particularly at the community level.

These events facilitated new efforts to conceptualize social development. One example is Midgley's (1993, 1995) account, which contends that social development draws on diverse normative theories, including statism, populist communitarianism, and market individualism. Although they inform different approaches to social development, he suggests that they can be synthesized into a holistic model in which the role of the state, community, and market are integrated. However, this pluralistic conception requires management and oversight by the state. Using this normative framework, Midgley stresses the need to integrate economic and social policies within a broad, progressive development process. He contends that economic development should produce tangible improvements in people's welfare and, conversely, that social policies should contribute to economic development.

The ideas of Sen (1985, 1999) have provided an important conceptual basis for social development. Sen believes that development involves the freedom of people to choose different "functionings." These functionings refer to the different states of "being and doing" that people may value. To maximize their choice to achieve different functions, their capabilities need to be enhanced. The concept of capability has since been popularized in social development circles. It has also had a wider impact in both development and mainstream economics, where it is compatible with prevailing neoclassical and rational choice ideas.

The concept of capabilities is similar in many respects to that of assets—particularly to the way it is used in community development by Kretzman and McKnight (1993), who believe that communities have many unrecognized assets and that it is the task of community practitioners to map these assets and educate local people about using them effectively. This notion has been adapted to the international development context by Moser and Dani (2008) who explicitly link the notions of assets and capabilities, and by Mathie and Cunningham (2008), who believe that poor communities can be educated to recognize and utilize their assets with very limited external intervention. This usage differs from that of Sherraden (1991), who has focused on financial assets by advocating the use of matched savings accounts, or Individual Development Accounts (IDAs).

Although these ideas have relevance for developmental social work, few attempts to formulate a coherent conceptual definition of developmental social work practice have been made. One significant contribution comes from Elliott and Mayadas (1996, 2001) who contend that concepts of growth, strengths and empowerment can inform all forms of social work practice including clinical practice. They argue for the abolition of the division between clinical and macro-practice showing that social investment, economic participation, empowerment and human investment are relevant to all systems and forms of social work intervention. Another comes from South African social work scholars, who were inspired by the promotion of developmental social work and social welfare in South Africa. In the late 1990s, the Mandela government published a White Paper that proposed a comprehensive reorganization of the country's social welfare system. With the adoption of the White paper, social workers in South Africa were urged to engage in developmental, rather than conventional, remedial social work practice, which had characterized social work in the country for many years. Although the government launched several community-based projects designed to show how developmental ideas could be applied in social work practice, confusion about the differences between "mainstream" and developmental social work have not been resolved. Nevertheless, leading South African social work scholars such as Patel (2005) and Lombard (2008) have made a major contribution to the conceptualization of developmental social work.

Gray (1998), a former South African now living in Australia, has also contributed to debates about developmental social work in South Africa. Patel's experience as a senior government administrator and as author of the White Paper has informed her work and contributed to her seminal formulation of the development practice.

Theoretical Dimensions of Developmental Social Work

Although social work scholars and practitioners have grappled with the notion of developmental social work over the years, no standard definition of developmental social work has been adopted. Of course, given the diversity of interests that comprise professional social work, this is not surprising, and it is unlikely that a universally accepted definition will emerge. Nevertheless, it is possible to identify common themes that provide a basis for a systematic conceptual perspective on developmental social work. These include agreements about the importance of facilitating change, the use of strengths, empowerment and capacity enhancement, the notion of self-determination and client participation, and a commitment to equality and social justice. Also relevant are concepts that are not always recognized in the literature, such as social investment and social rights. The following examines these ideas and attempts to integrate them into a tentative exposition of developmental social work.

The notion of change is central to developmental social work. As shown in the previous section, change has been a recurring theme in debates about social work's goals and functions. In developmental social work, the notion of change is progressive and linear in that it posits a process of ongoing improvement. In direct social work practice, this involves personal growth. In macro-social work practice, change has less to do with individual development; rather, collective improvements are stressed. In addition to focusing on process, the goals of change have also been debated. Many caseworkers and group workers who emphasize the need for change have invoked Maslow's (1943) notion of self-actualization to characterize both the change process and its desired end-state. Similar ideational notions are to be found in macro-social work practice, where the goal of change is often defined as achieving social integration, effective community functioning, greater equality, or social justice. On the other hand, some scholars place more emphasis on material welfare goals, contending that the process of change should produce tangible improvements in standards of living, health and education, and a concomitant reduction in poverty, malnutrition, and illiteracy. It is this emphasis on material welfare that is given particular emphasis in the social development literature, and it has special significance for the conceptualization of developmental social work.

Theoretical debates about the nature and purpose of change in developmental social work are permeated by a cluster of related concepts that concern the factors and interventions that bring about change. These include the concepts of strengths, empowerment, conscientization, capabilities, assets, and capacity enhancement among others. Although they evoke similar images, they have different emphases and are used in different contextual settings. They have direct relevance to social work practitioners seeking to facilitate change and development.

Strengths-based social work practice has become popular in social work. As Saleebey (1992) notes, it offers a radical alternative to the profession's conventional, problem-focused preoccupations. Social workers adopting the strengths approach help clients to recognize and utilize their inner resources, skills, and capacity for growth. Although their clients may face serious challenges, social workers using the strengths perspective believe that clients are innately resilient and that their ability to identify and negotiate solutions should be supported. Accordingly, adversities should be regarded as opportunities for social workers to collaborate with clients and to facilitate the expression of strengths. This process allows for learning new skills in negotiating the challenges of everyday life and for building effective coping mechanisms.

The concept of empowerment is equally popular and perhaps even more frequently used in social work today. Although similar to the notion of strengths, it has a stronger contextual connotation, suggestive of the relationship between individuals and the negating, disempowering, and oppressive environments in which they find themselves. Not surprisingly, the concept has frequently been invoked with reference to ethnic and gender oppression, where it offers a solution to the helplessness that oppressed people often feel when faced with institutionalized racism, sexism, and other forms of discrimination (Solomon, 1976; Guiterrez & Lewis, 1999). However, it is also used in a more general way to respond to situations where despair, fatalism and apathy are widespread. Often, this situation characterizes the lives of poor and vulnerable families, who comprise the majority of the profession's clients. It is in this context that advocates of empowerment practice such as Lee (1994) invoke Freire's work and his concept of *conscientization* to urge social workers to engage in a dialogical relationship with clients, helping them to understand the power structures that impede their functioning and assisting them to a learn various techniques that will help them to challenge these structures.

The notion of community building in macro-social work practice also reflects these ideas, implying that strengths and empowerment are integral elements in bringing about change at the community level. The contention that community social workers should recognize the assets—rather than deficits—of poor communities offers an alternative to the negative way that low-income communities have been portrayed in the media and are often perceived by middle class people (Kretzman & McKnight, 1993). Community interventions that address these problems avoid the "pathology" approach and seek instead to build on local assets and resources by enhancing community capacity. This involves a process by which community workers mobilize leadership, local organizations, and resources for positive social change (Chaskin et al., 2001).

Although these concepts are primarily used in social work, they are similar to Sen's notion of capabilities, which, as noted earlier, has been widely invoked in social development circles. However, it is often used to exhort rather than to provide specific, programmatic, or policy prescriptions for bringing about change. Whereas it is assumed that by virtue of their activities development workers will enhance the capabilities of impoverished households and communities, the literature fails to show, in tangible terms, how this can be achieved. In particular, little reference is made to the role of state institutions and resources in capability enhancement.

It is in this context that a critical attitude is needed to question the assumption that significant material gains in social welfare can be achieved simply by exhorting poor families and communities to meet their needs by drawing on their strengths and capabilities. Nor is it sufficient to help these clients recognize their position in oppressive and exploitative systems or power and to resist them. Although it is indeed highly desirable that strengths and capabilities be emphasized and that oppression be resisted, concrete investments in the form of resources and services are also needed. For some social development writers (Midgley, 1999: Midgley & Sherraden, 2009; Midgley & Tang, 2001), social investments are vital to social development. These investments involve a cluster of interventions that, for example, mobilize human and social capital, facilitate employment and self-employment, promote asset accumulation, and in other ways bring about significant improvements in the material welfare of individuals, families, and communities. These investments, which are a key component of the developmental approach to social work, are discussed in more detail later in this chapter.

The concepts of social integration and normalization are also central to the theory of developmental social work. These concepts allude to the goal of facilitating the integration of social work's clients into the community and promoting normal community living. Although social work's dominant pathology perspective assigns clients to roles in which their "deficits" require perennial treatment and supports, and even segregation in specialized residential facilities, developmental social work is committed to restoring them to independent community living.

The restorative approach not only informs direct practice interventions that provide brief and intensive services to those with serious personal and familial challenges but also applies to those facing long-term adversities. These challenges may require ongoing supports, but developmental social workers believe that these supports and services should be provided in the community rather than in residential institutions. Although it is true that social workers today do not favor the use of residential care, it is still widely used in child welfare, disability, and especially gerontology, where the numbers of elderly people in nursing homes has increased steadily in recent decades. Also, although deinstitutionalization has resulted in a significant decline in the numbers of mental health consumers in residential facilities, the lack of adequate community services impedes the realization of normal community living. The notion of community integration therefore requires significant investments that facilitate normal community living such as access to housing services, transportation, education, medical care, and recreational and cultural facilities. It is also closely associated with the idea that those living in the community should be afforded opportunities to participate in the productive economy.

Developmental social work also invokes the concepts of self-determination and participation. Self-determination has been accorded canonical status in social work since the profession's early years. Despite its importance, social work has in fact relied extensively on a professional "expert" model in which social workers, together with other professionals, prescribe solutions. Because social workers acquire professional credentials (often at prestigious institutions of higher education) and base their practice interventions on an established body of knowledge, it is not surprising that they should utilize an expert perspective. The expert model is not only employed in clinical practice but is also found in other forms of social work. As Simon (1994) notes, it is often manifested in subtle ways, such as when community practitioners act as "liberators" who use their superior status and expertise to "rescue" the poor and vulnerable from oppression. Similarly, the tendency toward paternalism finds expression in the way social workers function as "benefactors" who exude compassion and relieve suffering. These tendencies should be resisted, and social workers should facilitate authentic client decision making. This involves fostering a dialogical relationship with clients so that their voices are heard and their decisions respected. Client participation also requires that professionals accept these decisions even though they may counter their own views and recommendations.

Developmental social work relies extensively on sharing international innovations. In fact, as its history reveals, the field has been largely shaped by international exchanges. However, these exchanges are today increasingly reciprocal and mutually beneficial, and challenge the previous practice of uncritically replicating Western theories and practice interventions (Gray, 2005; Midgley, 1981, 2008a). Provided social workers in different parts of the world inform themselves about developments elsewhere and judiciously evaluate the relevance of international experiences, they have much to learn from each other.

In developmental social work, the notion of social rights reflects the belief that those served by social workers not only have a right to make decisions but to benefit from services and supports. It also recognizes the inherent worth and dignity of all people. However, it is only relatively recently that this idea found expression in international human rights instruments. The Universal Declaration of Human Rights of 1948 and subsequent conventions addressing social and economic conditions enshrined this principle. These instruments urge the world's governments to adopt policies that raise the standards of living of their people, create opportunities for employment, ensure decent working conditions, and provide social security, education, health care, and other social services. Similar international instruments have sought to abolish discrimination against women, end slavery and human trafficking, and challenge racism and other forms of oppression.

The rights-based approach to social development has attracted more attention in recent years. It has infused social development discourse with the language of human rights, helped to define the goals of social development, and facilitated the implementation of social development policies and programs (Midgley, 2007). Human rights ideas have also been adopted in social welfare policy, particularly through the writings of Marshall (1950), who argued that the struggle for civil and political rights over the centuries reached fulfillment in the 20th century with the achievement of social rights as a condition of citizenship. Today, the notion of rights promotes social development through both political and judicial processes. As Lombard (2008) notes, the South African courts have issued several rulings that have benefited the recipients of social welfare provisions. Indigenous groups and community activists in other parts of the world have also made increasing use of the rights-based approach (Grugel & Piper, 2009; Molyneaux & Lazar, 2003). Although human rights have not been emphasized in social work, the publication of several books on the subject by social work scholars (Ife, 2001; Reichert, 2003) has exposed the profession to the relevance of human rights to social work practice.

Finally, theoretical debates in developmental social work have often addressed social and political concerns that transcend a narrow preoccupation with social work practice. These include peace, democratic participation, toleration, equality, and social justice. Of course, these ideals are perennially referred to in social work's literature, and although there is a danger that they achieve little more than rhetorical status, they express the profession's commitment to promote these ideals. In the past, some members of the profession have effectively engaged in advocacy and have formed coalitions with political leaders, trades unions, and other progressive organizations. These efforts are actively supported by developmental social workers who believe that political action is needed to challenge discrimination, racism, sexism, and other impediments to progress. They have recognized that improvements in material welfare are not only the result of economic progress, education, and similar interventions but of wider social and political changes that produce peaceful, democratic, egalitarian, and just societies.

Developmental Social Work Practice

The introduction to this book noted that developmental social work differs significantly from other social work approaches, such as psychotherapeutic clinical social work, residential care, community organization, legislative advocacy, or policy practice. Nevertheless, it has much in common with these forms of social work. Many theoretical concepts used in developmental social work are also used in other types of social work, and in some cases, there is a significant overlap. This is perhaps most obvious with regard to community practice. However, as shown in Chapter 9, not all forms of community social work make purposeful use of the notion of social investment or adequately emphasize the need for economic development. These are essential features of developmental social work.

Differences between developmental social work and other forms of social work are particularly marked when developmental social work and psychotherapeutic counseling are compared. Although developmental concepts such as growth, strengths, and empowerment are also used in psychotherapy, clinical social work is permeated with notions of pathology and medicalized treatment. The common use of the *Diagnostic and Statistical Manual* in social work education in the United States attests to the popularity of this approach. Although developmental social workers may serve people facing psychiatric challenges and use counseling techniques, they are not psychotherapists.

Developmental social workers also avoid the use of residential services, except on a temporary basis or when it is not possible to place people with special needs in the community. Although it is true that developmental correctional practice (as discussed in Chapter 7) occurs in a custodial setting, the emphasis on successful re-entry and the use of interventions that promote re-entry reflect a commitment to community-based practice. This is also fostered by the close links maintained between correctional social workers within custodial settings and those based in the community.

Developmental social workers facilitate the inclusion of clients in all aspects of community living. Accordingly, they are actively involved in the community and work closely with community groups to secure resources, access networks, and establish local projects. They avoid office-based practice and instead are out and about working with clients and community groups. Community-based practice is facilitated by locating practitioners in neighborhood centers that are in close geographic proximity to their clients. This may be a generalist social services center, where various social work programs are located, or specialized programs such as youth outreach or AIDS prevention agencies. This approach derives from the settlement houses and community centers that were a focal point for community social work practice in the late 19th and early 20th centuries. Today, many local community centers are either situated in the old settlement houses or otherwise utilize their community-based approach (Yan, Laurer, & Sin, 2009).

Community-based interventions are closely linked to the notion of integrating clients into the productive economy. This is revealed in the way developmental social work practice typically gives priority to local economic and social development projects. Case studies of developmental social work usually highlight the activities of community-based women's groups, micro-enterprises, health and nutritional projects, infrastructural development programs, daycare centers, adult literacy, and similar projects. These projects make extensive use of productivist social investments that enhance client participation in the economy and improve material well-being. These investments are described below, but first, reference to the skills used in developmental practice is discussed.

Practice Skills for Developmental Social Work

Social work is based on relationships established by practitioners with their clients. Although other professions also make use of interpersonal relationships, these are not always accorded primary importance. For example, in architecture, engineering, and medicine, the application of knowledge and the skillful use of technologies is given more emphasis than relationships. Of course, social workers also draw on the profession's established body of knowledge and are committed to its values and ethical principles. Skills, knowledge, and values applied through interpersonal relationships characterize all forms of social work, including direct clinical practice, group work, and community social work practice.

Interpersonal relationships also serve as a conduit through which particular agency routines and procedures are implemented. In statutory agencies, policies, procedures, and regulations based on legislative directives are particularly important, but similar routines shape social work practice in nongovernmental agencies. Standardized procedures are also integral to settings where service delivery rather than counseling is given priority. This is especially true of established fields of practice such as child welfare, corrections, medical social work, and mental health. Despite the emphasis placed on the individual worker's practice skills in much of the profession's academic literature, skills are often subordinated to the procedural rules that dominate service delivery in these practice fields.

In addition to operating within agency policies and procedures, developmental social work practice is linked to wider systems of resources. The effective utilization of these systems has long been valued in social work. The ability to help local groups and communities access resources and networks is also given high priority in developmental social work and is an important skill. This requires that practitioners be familiar with local services and wider social policies and programs. In addition to utilizing networks and resources effectively, Patel (2005) points out that generalist skills applicable to many forms of social work practice are also used in developmental settings. The following offers a brief discussion of the application of these skills in developmental social work. These range from skills usually associated with direct practice to those that are viewed as being more appropriate to community practice.

Counseling and other skills associated with direct practice are important if effective relationships are to be established with clients. Developmental social workers must be able to communicate effectively with individuals, families, and community groups and be able to use interpersonal relationships for this purpose. These skills also involve building trust and helping clients to develop self-confidence and make decisions that affect their lives and the well-being of their communities. Counseling skills are also needed when developmental practitioners encounter clients who face emotional and mental health challenges or who have been abused or traumatized. For example, developmental social workers helping local communities to operate a childcare center providing preschool education and nutritional services may discover that a child attending the center has been physically abused. On closer investigation, the child's mother may reveal that she too has been beaten by the child's father. Although counseling will be needed in situations like these, referral to more specialized agencies may be appropriate.

Because developmental social work relies on mobilizing local groups of community members, skills in working with these groups are given high priority. Again, building relationships and trust with group members is of the utmost importance, but this is accompanied by the use of facilitating and enabling skills that help group members to work together, define group goals, and engage in effective problem solving. Social work skills that mobilize local people to engage in developmental projects are also needed if local needs are to be addressed. This involves identifying local leaders who can assist in mobilizing local support. The development of leadership is another vital skill in developmental social work. Another relevant skill is brokering, by which practitioners help groups to access wider resources. For example, a womens' group seeking to establish a small enterprise will need credit and expertise that community practitioners are able to access.

Skills that facilitate decision-making in group meetings and educating group members to engage effectively in decision-making tasks are used in developmental social work. Groups establishing community projects will invariably encounter challenges that need to be addressed. The social worker's enabling skills are used to help clients solve these problems collaboratively. Although developmental social workers do not prescribe solutions, they are a resource to the group, providing knowledge and information that will help them achieve their goals. Also relevant are mediation skills, which are used when group members come into conflict and are unable to resolve difficulties.Many of the skills used by developmental social workers with groups also apply to community practice, which largely depends on mobilizing, facilitating, organizing, and planning the activities of local groups and community organizations. On the other hand, community practice also takes place at the neighborhood level, where groups may not have formed or developed sufficiently to engage purposefully in local activities. Developmental social workers are cognizant of the differences between these different levels of community practice and use their skills appropriately.

In neighborhood capacity building, skills in forming local community groups and identifying local leaders able to initiate action are widely used. Recognizing that universal participation is unlikely, practitioners nevertheless seek to enhance people's involvement and to ensure that neighborhood groups are representative of local families. Skills that enable collaborative action and empower local people are given high priority. At the wider community level, developmental social workers seek to facilitate cooperative action among a variety of neighborhood, women's, youth, and other groups and to link them to more established, community-based developmental agencies. Coordination and networking skills are obviously important to achieve this goal. Irrespective of whether developmental social workers are employed by local governmental or nonprofit bodies, or by particular projects or agencies, high priority is given to networking and ensuring that community effort is cooperative and coordinated. Mediating skills may also be needed to insure cooperation between different projects and agencies.

Advocacy skills and the ability to mobilize local people and groups for social action are also relevant. When advocacy involves facilitating a link between local groups and those who have resources, it is similar to brokering. But it also involves wider advocacy for social justice such as when community members face entrenched inequalities in resources and power or when they are exploited or discriminated against. An important aspect of social justice advocacy is educating and empowering local people to develop their own voice and act in their own interests. Freire's notion of *conscientization*, which was mentioned earlier, is a major inspiration for social justice advocacy. Social workers seeking to mobilize local people for social justice need to ensure that they do not themselves assume leadership roles and speak for local people. As the experience of indigenous activism has shown, people are able to draw on their strengths and mobilize on their own behalf (Mathie & Cunningham, 2008). However, this does not mean that practitioners have no role to play. For example, they can help by accessing the legal resources local people need to claim their rights. The realization of a right-based approach to developmental social work often requires expertise of this kind.

Investment Strategies in Professional Practice

Because of its historic association with development in the Global South, developmental social work is primarily concerned with improving the material well-being of individuals, families, and communities living in conditions of poverty and deprivation. Although it is seldom recognized that most of the profession's clients in the Western countries are also poor and face material challenges, many of their personal and familial problems are closely associated with poverty (Lowe & Reid, 1999). This is one reason that developmental social work is relevant to both the developing and Western nations.

When addressing these problems, developmental social workers make extensive use of interventions that specifically enhance standards of living. These interventions are *productivist* in that they foster economic participation and raise incomes and assets. In using these interventions, developmental social workers believe that economic participation is a major source of empowerment. However, these strategies are not employed in isolation from broader, community-based interventions but require national policies that promote a holistic development process designed to raise the standards of living of the population as a whole. This requires that economic development policies be people-centered in that they improve the material well-being of all. As Midgley and Tang (2001) note, it also requires that social development policies contribute positively to economic growth. In addition, development policies should be sustainable in that they protect the environment and ensure that natural resources are not depleted but remain available to future generations. As will be recognized, these principles are compatible with the ideal of creating egalitarian and just societies.

Numerous developmental interventions that contribute to improvements in material well-being have been identified by social development scholars. These investments have been extensively discussed in the literature on social development (Midgley, 1999; Midgley & Sherraden, 2009; Midgley & Tang, 2001) and are only summarized briefly here.

A distinguishing feature of these interventions is that they are community-based, utilize capabilities, and foster empowerment. They also facilitate the integration of clients into community living by providing access to housing, medical services, education, and recreational facilities. Also relevant are human capital investments, employment, microcredit and micro-enterprises, asset programs, and social capital interventions. These investments require resources, including funds, expertise, and a political commitment from governments. It is not always recognized that social development requires significant budgetary allocations.

Various social investments are needed if the people served by developmental social workers are to be integrated into the community and live fulfilling and productive lives. It has been a major failure of deinstitutionalization that mental health consumers are not provided with adequate supports that enable them to live normally in the community. Although the mental health experience dramatizes the problem, similar investments are needed in other fields of social work as well. The transformation of the conventional child protective services system to a community-based system will require extensive investments. Similar investments are needed to facilitate the integration of other social work clients (including seniors, people with disabilities, and former prisoners) into the community. The costs of providing housing, access to medical care, transportation, and other services that promote community integration are considerable and pose a huge challenge to those who advocate integration. On the other hand, the costs of maintaining people in custodial and residential facilities and of neglecting those who struggle to cope with the demand of community living are even higher.

Although human capital investment programs are primarily concerned with inculcating the knowledge and skills that people need to participate effectively in the productive economy, they also include investments in health and nutrition. By fostering economic participation, these programs contribute to poverty eradication. Human capital is generated through the wider educational and health-care systems; however, it is also promoted by developmental social workers. As noted earlier, adult literacy, job training, preschool childcare centers, women's educational programs, and similar projects are all associated with social development interventions in low-income communities. Of particular interest to developmental social workers is the role of preschool centers for poor children. As shown in Chapter 2, these centers play a key role in reconfiguring conventional child welfare services by creating an alternative community-based approach.

Employment and self-employment programs are also given high priority in developmental social work. Although it is widely accepted that wage employment generates income and raises standards of living, employment activation has not been emphasized in conventional social work even though many of social work's clients, including those with disabilities, street children, and unemployed youth, are eager to secure employment. Beginning with sheltered employment for people with disabilities, employment activation and placement programs have expanded over the years and now facilitate the employment of clients with special needs in the open labor market. This has been supported by antidiscriminatory legislation such as the Americans with Disabilities Act in the United States, which requires employers to make a reasonable accommodation for those with disabilities. Employment activation has also been more widely used for clients receiving long-term social assistance benefits. As shown in Chapter 6, these "welfare-to-work programs" (as they are also known) provide job referral and placement, training, and supports to encourage economic participation. However, there are wide variations in the way these programs are conceived and implemented in different countries. Fortunately, the coercive caseload reduction model introduced in United States in the mid-1990s has not been widely emulated.

Employment placement programs have been augmented by the more frequent use of micro-enterprise and microcredit programs (Jurik, 2005; Midgley, 2008b; Remenyi & Quinones, 2000). Many nonprofit organizations and governments around the world now support programs of this kind by providing technical assistance, subsidies, and preferential access to credit. The government of the Philippines has been a major promoter of micro-enterprise (Quieta et al., 2003), and the activities of the Grameen Bank in Bangladesh (Yunus, 1999) have done much to popularize this approach. Several international organizations also support micro-enterprise, and commercial banks have also become involved. Typically, loans are made to poor individuals and families who have no collateral and little access to conventional sources of credit. Originally, the Grameen Bank used a peer lending system by which cooperatives of poor women assumed collective responsibility for loans and the success of projects. However, this approach has since been replaced by an individual lending model (Dowla & Barua, 2006). As shown in several of the chapters of this book, micro-enterprises are widely employed in developmental social work to foster economic participation among poor people and those with special needs.

Investments that subsidize wages or mandate the payment of minimum or living wages also facilitate participation in the productive economy. Employment is hardly an effective mechanism for poverty eradication if wages are too low to maintain a decent standard of living or if employers unscrupulously exploit workers. Although minimum wage laws require employers to meet a prescribed minimum income level, this level has been eroded by inflation in many countries. In the United States, minimum wages are increasingly augmented by living wages. These are mandated by progressive local governments contracting for goods and services with commercial providers. In cities such as San Francisco, for example, the wages paid by contracting firms are significantly higher than the federal government's minimum wage. Also relevant are wage subsidies, such as the Earned Income Tax Credit in the United States and the Working Families Tax Credit in Britain. Both subsidize the incomes of poor families in regular employment and have contributed significantly to poverty alleviation.

Although social welfare policies and programs have been primarily concerned with maintaining incomes, the importance of asset accumulation has also been recognized, particularly through the work of Sherraden (1991), who criticized the conventional consumption approach in social welfare and argued for policies that help low-income families to accumulate financial assets. He originally proposed that children be provided with a savings account at birth, but this was subsequently modified by the introduction of matched savings accounts for all low-income savers known as IDAs. In the United States, IDAs have been established by numerous nonprofit organizations and foundations and are also supported by the state and federal governments. Although IDAs usually provide opportunities for short-term savings, they have helped poor families to accumulate assets, improve their credit-worthiness, meet educational expenses, and inculcate a stronger orientation toward the future among savers (Schreiner & Sherraden, 2007). Although Sherraden's work has been primarily concerned with savings accounts, assets are also an important element in community development (Green & Haines, 2008; Kretzman & McKnight, 1993; Moser & Dani, 2008).

The notion of social capital has been popularized in social science and policy circles over the last decade and is now widely used as a synonym for community building. However, in its original conceptualization by Putnam and colleagues (1993, 2000), social capital had an "economistic" connotation, suggesting that civic engagement is positively associated with economic development. Since then, developmental social workers have recognized the link between community organization and community building on the one hand and local economic development on the other. Today, greater efforts are being made to link community organization with economic development projects, including access to credit, job creation, micro-enterprise development, and asset building. Although social work has historically been concerned with organizing, planning, and building networks, there is now a greater interest in combining these conventional activities with economic development projects (Midgley & Livermore, 1998; Sherraden & Ninacs,1998).

The removal of barriers that inhibit economic participation and create equal opportunities are also emphasized in developmental social work. Reflecting the field's commitment to social justice and the use of advocacy, developmental social work challenges institutionalized obstacles to economic participation, including discrimination based on race and ethnicity, gender, nationality, disability, age, and other factors that impede the realization of the aspirations of social work's clients. Social investment programs will be ineffective if these obstacles are not removed. Unfortunately, racism, sexism, ageism, homophobia, and other forms of hatred continue to impede the efforts of many who seek to achieve their life goals. In addition, income and wealth inequalities that prevent people from realizing their goals need to be addressed. Although equal access to education and particularly higher education has been recognized for many years, in countries such as the United States, these opportunities have diminished as the costs of higher education have increased steadily (Sacks, 2007).

Finally, developmental social work requires the use of cost-effective interventions and evidence-based methodologies that promote effective practice. Social work has not in the past stressed the need for rigorous evaluation to determine whether its interventions are effective. It has often been assumed that professional judgment and expertise is a guarantor of effectiveness. This has opened the profession to the criticism that social welfare programs are wasteful, introduced for political reasons, and have negative unintended consequences. In recent times, the need for systematic evaluations of social work and social welfare interventions has been recognized, and the use of evidence-based interventions has also been more vigorously advocated (Gambrill, 1999; Gibbs, 2003). Although not welcomed by all social workers, there is a greater recognition today that claims about social work's effectiveness need to be substantiated. This is equally true of developmental social work, where the challenge of rigorously evaluating developmental interventions provides new and interesting opportunities for social work research. Because developmental social workers are committed to using intervention that produces positive rates of returns to clients, communities, and society as a whole, there is an urgent need to demonstrate that social investments in professional practice do, in fact, achieve this goal.

REFERENCES

Billups, J. (1994). 'The Social Development Model as an Organizing Framework for Social Work Practice', in R. G. Meinert, J. T. Pardeck and W. P. Sullivan (Eds.) *Issues in Social Work: A Critical Analysis*. Westport, CT: Auburn House. pp. 21–38.

Chaskin, R., Brown, P., Venkatesh, S., & Vidal (2001). *Building Community Capacity*. Hawthorne, NY: Aldine de Gruyter,.

Dowla, A. & Barua, D. (2006). *The Poor Always Pay Back: The Grameen II Story*. Bloomfield, CT: Kumarian Press.

Elliott, D. (1993). 'Social Work and Social Development: Towards an Integrative Model for Social Work Practice', *International Social Work*, 36 (1): 21–37.

Elliott, D. and Mayadas, N. (1996). 'Social Development and Clinical Practice in Social Work.' *Journal of Applied Social Sciences*, 21 (1): 61–68.

Elliott, D. and Mayadas, N. (2001). 'Psychosocial Approaches, Social Work and Social Development. *Social Development Issues*. 23 (1): 5–13.

Freire, P. (1970). *Pedagogy of the Oppressed*. New York: Herder and Herder.

Freire, P. (1973). *Education for Critical Consciousness*. New York: Seabury Press.

Gambrill, E. (1999). Evidence-based Practice: An Alternative to Authority based Practice. *Families in Society*. 80 (4): 341–350.

Gibbs, L. E. (2003). *Evidence-based Practice for the Helping Professions: A Practical Guide*. Pacific Grove, CA: Brooks/Cole.

Gray, M. (2005). Dilemmas of International Social Work: Paradoxical Processes in Indigenization, Universalism and Imperialism. *Journal of International Social Work*, 14 (3): 231–238.

Gray, M. (1998) *Developmental Social Work: Theory and Practice*. Cape Town: David Philip.

Green, G. P. & Haines, A. (2008) *Asset Building and Community Development*. Thousand Oaks, CA: Sage.

Grugel, J. & Piper, N. (2009). Do Rights Promote Development? *Global Social Policy*. 9 (1): 79–98.

Gutierrez, L. & Lewis, F. A. (Eds.) (1999). *Empowerment and Women of Color*. New York: Columbia University Press,

Hollister, C. D. (1977). Social Work Skills for Social Development. *Social Development Issues*, 1 (1): 9–16.

Ife, J. (2001). *Human Rights and Social Work: Towards Rights Based Practice*. New York: Cambridge University Press.

Jones, J. & Pandey, R. (Eds.) (1981). *Social Development: Conceptual, Methodological and Policy Issues*. New York: St. Martin's Press.

Jurik, N. C. (2005). *Bootstraps Dreams: US Micoenterprise Development in an Era of Welfare Reform*. Ithaca, NY: Cornell University Press.

Karger, H. (1987). *Sentinels of Order: A Study of Social Control and the Minneapolis Settlement House Movement, 1915–1950*. Lanham. MD: University Press of America.

Khinduka, S. (1987). Development and Peace: The Complex Nexus. *Social Development Issues*, 10 (3): 19–30.

Kretzman, J. & McKnight, J. (1993). *Building Communities from the Inside Out: A Path Toward Finding and Mobilizing a Community's Assets*. Evanston, IL: Institute for Policy Research, Northwest and University.

Lee, J. A. B. (1994). *The Empowerment Approach to Social Work Practice*. New York: Columbia University Press.

Lloyd, G. A. (1982). Social Development as a Political Philosophy, in D. S. Sanders (Ed.) *The Development Perspective in Social Work*. Manoa, HI: University of Hawaii Press, pp. 43–50.

Lombard, A. (2008). The Implementation of the White Paper for Social Welfare: A Ten-year Review. *The Social Work Practitioner-Researcher*, 20 (2): 137–153.

Lowe, G. R. & Reid, N. P. (Eds.) (1999). *The Professionalization of Poverty: Social Work and the Poor in the Twentieth Century*. New York: Aldyne de Gruyter.

Maas, H. (1984). *People and Contexts: Social Development from Birth to Old Age*. Englewood Cliffs, NJ: Prentice Hall.

Marshall, T. H. (1950). Citizenship and Other Essays. Cambridge: Cambridge University Press.

Maslow, A. (1943). A Theory of Human Motivation. *Psychological Review*, 50 (4): 370–396.

Mathie, A. & Cunningham, G. (Eds.) (2008). *From Clients to Citizens: Community is Changing the Course of their Earlier Development*. Rugby, Warwickshire: Intermediate Technology Publications,

Midgley, J. (1981). *Professional Imperialism: Social Work in the Third World*. London: Heineman.

Midgley, J. (1993). Ideological Roots of Social Development Strategies, *Social Development Issues*, 15 (1): 1–13.

Midgley, J. (1995) *Social Development: The Developmental Perspective in Social Welfare*. Thousand Oaks, CA: Sage Publications.

Midgley, J. (1999). Growth, Redistribution and Welfare: Towards Social Investment. *Social Service Review*, 77 (1): 3–21.

Midgley, J. (2006). Development, Social Development and Human Rights, in E. Reichert (Ed.). *Challenges in Human Rights: A Social Work Perspective*. New York: Columbia University Press, pp. 97–121.

Midgley, J. (2008a). Promoting Reciprocal International Social Work Exchanges: Professional Imperialism Revisited, in M. Gray, J. Coates, and M. Yellow Bird (Eds.) *Indigenization and Indigenous Social Work Around the World: Towards Culturally Relevant Social Work Education and Practice*. Brookfield, VT: Ashgate Publishers.

Midgley, J. (2008b). Microenterprise, Global Poverty and Social Development. *International Social Work*. 51 (4): 1–13.

Midgley, J. & Livermore, M. (1998). Social Capital and Local Economic Development: Implications for Community Social Work Practice. *Journal of Community Practice*. 5 (1/2): 29–40.

Midgley, J. & Sherraden, M. (2009) The Social Development Perspective in Social Policy', in J. Midgley & M. Livermore (Eds.). *The Handbook of Social Policy*. Thousand Oaks, CA: Sage Publications, pp. 263–278.

Midgley, J. & Tang, K.L. (2001). Social Policy, Economic Growth and Developmental Welfare. *International Journal of Social Welfare*. 10 (4): 263–278.

Molyneux, M. & Lazar, S (2003). *Doing the Rights Thing: Rights-based Development and Latin American NGOs*. London: ITDC Publishing.

Moser, C. & Dani, A. A. (Eds.). (2008). *Assets, Livelihoods, and Social Policy*. Washington, DC: The World Bank.

Omer, S. (1979). Social Development, *International Social Work*, 22 (3): 11–26.

Paiva, F. J. X. (1977). A Conception of Social Development. *Social Service Review*, 51 (2): 327–336.

Patel, L. (2005). *Social Welfare and Social Development in South Africa*. Johannesburg: Oxford University Press.

Putnam, R. D. with Leonardi, R. & Nanetti, R. Y. (1993). *Making Democracy Work: Civic Traditions in Modern Italy*. Princeton: Princeton University Press.

Putnam, R. D. (2000). *Bowling Alone: The Collapse and Revival of American Community*. New York: Simon and Schuster,

Quieta, R. et al. (2003). *Self-Employment Assistance Program: Three Decades of Enabling People to Help Themselves*. Quezon City: University of Philippines Press.

Reichert, E. (2003). *Social Work and Human Rights: A Foundation for Policy and Practice*. New York: Columbia University Press.

Remenyi, J. & Quinones, B. (Eds.). (2000). *Microfinance and Poverty Alleviation: Case Studies from Asia and the Pacific*. New York: Pinter, pp. 25–64.

Sacks, P. (2007). *Tearing Down the Gates: Confronting the Class Divide and American Education*. Berkeley, CA: University of California Press.

Saleebey, D. (1992). *The Strengths Perspective in Social Work Practice*. New York: Longman.

Sanders, D. S. (Ed). (1982). *The Development Perspective in Social Work*. Manoa, HI: University of Hawaii Press,

Sen, A. (1985). *Commodities and Capabilities*. Amsterdam: North-Holland.

Sen, A. (1999). *Development as Freedom*. New York: Knopf.

Schreiner, M. & Sherraden, M. (2007). *Can the Poor Save?: Saving and Asset Building in Individual Development Accounts*. New Brunswick, NJ: Transaction.

Sherraden, M. (1991). *Assets and the Poor: A New American Welfare Policy*. Armonk, NY: M. E. Sharpe.

Sherraden, M. S & Ninacs, W. (Eds.). (1998). *Community Economic Development and Social Work*. New York: Haworth.

Simon, B. L. (1994) *The Empowerment Tradition in American Social Work*. New York: Columbia University Press.

Solomon, B. (1976). *Black Empowerment: Social Work in Oppressed Communities*. New York: Columbia University Press.

Spergel, I. (1978). Social Development and Social Work, in S. Slavin (Ed.) *Social Administration*. New York: Haworth Press, pp. 24–35.

Stein, H. D. (1975). Social Work's Developmental and Change Functions: Their Roots in Practice. *Social Service Review*, 50 (1): 1–10.

United Kingdom, Colonial Office (1954). *Social Development in the British Colonial Territories*. London: HMSO.

United Nations (1969). *Proceedings of the International Conference of Ministers Responsible for Social Welfare*. New York.

United Nations (1996). *Report of the World Summit for Social Development: Copenhagen, 6–12 March 1995*. New York.

United Nations (2005). *Investing in Development: A Practical Plan to Achieve the Millennium Development Goals*. New York.

Yan, M. C., Lauer, S., & Sin, R. (2009). Issues in Community Rebuilding: The Task of Settlement Houses in Two Cities. *Social Development Issues*, 31 (1): 39–54.

Yunus, M. (1999). *Banker to the Poor: Micro-lending and the Battle Against World Poverty*. New York: Public Affairs Press.

PART II

Social Investment Strategies and Social Work Fields of Practice

2

Social Development, Social Investment, and Child Welfare

AMY CONLEY

In the field of child welfare, social work in Anglo-American countries such as the United States, Canada, and the United Kingdom has historically been committed to a child protection approach that places emphasis on protecting children from harm through in-home services to their families or out-of-home care when they cannot be maintained safely in their own homes. The problem of child maltreatment is perceived as a result of the incompetence, irresponsibility or "degeneracy" of parents or other caregivers. Cases are generally brought through the judicial system to investigate what is regarded as the "crime" of child maltreatment and to compel parental compliance with services. The relationship between the child welfare system and parents is often adversarial. Involvement by other social welfare systems and the broader community is tangential and often minimal.

Scathing indictments of the child protection paradigm have emphasized its crisis orientation, coercive treatment of families, removal of children from their homes and communities, use of residential care, and challenges in providing better alternatives for children in placement, among other problems. As these criticisms have multiplied, more effort in the field has gone toward reforming child welfare services. However, rather than tinkering around the edges, many child welfare experts believe that a fundamental shift is required that emphasizes prevention and builds family strengths. This chapter hopes to contribute to the ongoing debate about child welfare reform. It advocates for a developmental approach that recognizes child welfare expenditures as investments in the functioning of children and families.

A developmental approach to child welfare enhances the capacities of families and communities to care for their children. This approach has several distinctive features. First, it stresses a more coherent approach to prevention in which child welfare social workers do not assume that prevention will be undertaken by schools, youth clubs, churches, or other community resources but systematically seek to engage in prevention and coordinate preventive services. A commitment to prevention is closely associated with poverty alleviation. Most children who are brought into the formal, statutory child welfare system come from poor families and live in poor neighborhoods. A developmental approach to child welfare draws on the experience of developing countries where the promotion of child well-being is closely linked to poverty alleviation policies and programs. The developmental approach also emphasizes the importance of social investments in the form of specific interventions such as early childhood care and asset accumulation. Finally, developmental child welfare is based on a rights-based approach in which notions of human rights are explicitly invoked. By linking child protection with early child-hood care programs, community and extended family involvement and asset accu-mulation, among other practices, the developmental approach seeks to address some of the challenges facing children and families in ways that differ significantly from the conventional child protection approach. The chapter begins by discussing the child protection approach and then examines some of the key elements of the developmental approach to child welfare.

The Challenge of Child Maltreatment

Child maltreatment is not a clear and objective reality. It is rather a social construc-tion that is culturally defined and shaped by prevailing values and norms about children, child development, and parenting (Parton, Thorpe, & Wattam, 1997). Anglo-American notions of family have tended to emphasize individual rights and responsibilities, with the expectation that the primary obligation for the welfare of children lies within the family. This understanding has lead to the development of "threshold systems" in Anglo-American countries such as the United States, the United Kingdom, and Canada, which define child maltreatment as failure to provide a legal minimum of care and proscribe intervention in matters related to child safety but not under other deleterious conditions, such as extreme poverty (Cameron et al., 2007). The child protection paradigm has clear implications for how child maltreatment is defined and how its root causes are understood in these countries.

In countries with a child protection paradigm, child maltreatment is largely understood to result from parental deficiencies rather than systemic issues like lack of social safety nets and supports for families. The child protection discourse depends on a notion of an "abnormal" family, constructed in comparison to a "normal" family (D'Cruz, 2004). This approach to child welfare can be seen as reflective of historical biases against women, the poor, and people of color, which has translated into a belief that children must be saved from their parents by philanthropists and professionals (Lubeck and Garett, 1990). There are several key questions that can provide insight for understanding how governmental entities define child maltreatment: who may be implicated as a perpetrator; which types of acts may be categorized as child maltreatment; if the scope of the definition of child maltreatment is broad or narrow; and how allegations of maltreatment are substantiated.

Legal definitions of child maltreatment in countries with a child protection orientation have some broad commonalities. For example, they generally specify that only family members or caregivers can be perpetrators of child abuse and neglect. Caregivers are those who look after children in an out-of-home care setting (group homes, foster care, childcare centers). Abusive behavior by other individuals, whether known to the child or strangers, is considered assault (Trocmé et al., 2001; English, 1998; May-Chahal & Cawson, 2005). Focusing on individual caregivers and families presume that the problem of child maltreatment emerges from the micro-level, suggesting micro-level solutions such as therapy and case management, rather than the macro-level of institutions and society, a perspective that would suggest a radically different approach.

Taking the parent or caregiver and their behavior as a target, legal definitions of child maltreatment generally make distinctions between two types of acts: commission (the act of committing or perpetrating) and omission (the failure to do something) (English, 1998). At minimum, most jurisdictions define four types of maltreatment: physical abuse, sexual abuse, neglect, and emotional abuse (U.S. Department of Health and Human Services [US DHHS], 2009). Although specific legal definitions vary by jurisdictions, these categories can be broadly characterized in the following ways. Physical abuse is an act of commission in which physical harm or threatened harm is committed against a child. Sexual abuse is an act of commission in which children are sexually exploited or used to provide sexual gratification for the perpetrator. Neglect is an act of commission or omission whereby children's basic needs are unmet. Emotional abuse is a sustained pattern of omission, which may entail neglecting a child's emotional needs, or commission, involving causing emotional pain (English, 1998).

Depending on the language used and the intentions of lawmakers, definitions of child maltreatment may be narrow or broad. Researchers debate the merits of these two types of definitions. A narrow definition of child maltreatment offers greater protection for family privacy, as the bar for child welfare intervention would rise to a level of observable harm. This would also simplify the task of investigating child maltreatment because demonstrable proof, like a broken bone or bruise, would be required to substantiate an allegation of abuse or neglect. However, less tangible types of maltreatment, such as neglect or emotional abuse, are difficult to prove with physical evidence, although they may have detrimental effects. A broader definition may better capture harm posed by emotional maltreatment, threatened maltreatment, and persistent, long-term forms of maltreatment (English, 1998).

The concepts adopted in definitions of child maltreatment influence estimations of the size and scope of the child maltreatment problem. Findings also vary depending on the measures used to collect data and the populations studied (Lawrence-Karski, 1999). For example, the United States Child Abuse Prevention and Treatment Act mandates two periodic national studies that differ along these dimensions. The Administration for Children, Youth, and Families through the National Child Abuse and Neglect Data Systems issues a yearly report entitled *Child Maltreatment*, which aggregates and analyzes case-level data from states on children reported, investigated, and served by child welfare agencies. All states that accept certain federal funds for child maltreatment services must provide the federal government with specific types of data on children suspected or confirmed to be maltreated (US DHHS, 2009). Referring back to the dimensions mentioned earlier, the data used by this yearly report have no uniform definition, as they rely on state definitions of maltreatment, making comparison of incidence levels between states somewhat problematic. The measures used for data collection are the reporting, investigation, and assessment procedures used by each state, which can vary between and even within states for county-administered child welfare systems. The population included in the statistics is limited to those children who have come to the attention of child protective services.

National Incidence Studies (NIS) have been conducted approximately once a decade in the United States since the 1970s, using a nationally representative sample of counties (Sedlak, 2001). This study is designed quite differently from the previously described study, with uniform definitions of child maltreatment types, standardized data collection, and efforts to identify cases of child maltreatment beyond the pool of children known to child welfare authorities by inclusion of data from both CPS staff and "sentinels." Sentinels are professionals who work with children across a variety of settings, such as schools, social services agencies, and medical facilities. These "sentinels" are asked to complete a data form on children whom they suspect are being maltreated (Westat, n.d.). Two definition standards are used: the "harm standard," under which children are considered to be maltreated only if they have experienced harm from abuse or neglect, and the "endangerment standard," under which children who have experienced abuse or neglect that has placed them at risk of harm are considered to be maltreated.

Findings from most recent version of this study (NIS-3) conducted in the 1990s found that substantially more children were maltreated during this time period as compared to the previous study in the 1980s (NIS-2). The total number of maltreated children was two-thirds higher under the harms standard (1,553,800 children in 1993 compared to 931,000 in 1986) and nearly doubled under the endangerment standard (2,815,600 children in 1993 compared to 1,424,400 in 1996). Findings also suggest that child welfare agencies have not been able to keep pace with this increase in the incidence of child maltreatment; the number of children investigated by CPS remained fairly stable from the previous wave in the 1980s, although the number of children identified to be harmed or endangered by maltreatment shot up dramatically. Whether this results from investigation practices by child welfare agencies, confusion on the part of professionals regarding reporting procedures for potential child maltreatment cases, or some combination of both is unclear (Sedlak & Broadhurst, 1996). The fourth wave of this study is underway (from 2001–2009) (Administration for Children and Families, n.d.).

These two studies illuminate some of the challenges in measuring incidence and prevalence of child maltreatment. Not all countries have a formal surveillance and administrative data system to identify and monitor cases of child maltreatment (International Society for the Prevention of Child Abuse and Neglect [ISPCAN], 2008). There is no standard definition, as legal definitions vary from jurisdiction to jurisdiction. The judgment of professionals working with children and investigated reported cases of maltreatment also differs. What one person/agency may identify as abuse, another may not. Not all abuse is reported; indeed, the National Incidence Studies suggest that large proportions of cases are either unreported or unknown to child welfare agencies in the United States alone. Assessments of neglect and emotional abuse are particularly difficult, as there is generally no physical evidence. Child maltreatment is often described as an iceberg phenomenon, with only a small portion of cases (the "tip" of the iceberg) visible to the child welfare system (Pecora et al., 1992).

Given these challenges, it is difficult to estimate the incidence of child maltreatment—globally or even within a nation. However, there is some evidence of a trend toward increased rates of children identified as maltreated; whether this results from greater awareness of the issue or an actual increase in child maltreatment in unclear. A biennial survey conducted by the International Society for the Prevention of Child Abuse and Neglect of key informants on the topic of child maltreatment in 75 countries found that the majority (about two-thirds) reported an increase in both the reported incidence of child maltreatment and the public's perception of the problem. Looking specifically at official report rates from 1997 to 2006 for Australia, Canada, the United Kingdom, and the United States, trends related to child maltreatment reporting, investigation, and substantiation depended on the type of maltreatment: cases of child neglect and emotional abuse had experienced small to moderate increases; cases of child sexual abuse appeared to be declining in all four countries; and cases of physical abuse increased in two countries and declined in two others (ISPCAN, 2008). While noting an across the board rise in reports of child maltreatment from the mid-1980s to early 1990s, Gilbert (1997) pointed out that Anglo-American countries with a child protection approach appear to have a much higher reported incidence of child maltreatment than Scandinavian countries, which have child welfare systems that emphasize family services and support over investigation and child placement.

The Child Protection Paradigm

The origins of the child protection approach to child welfare are rooted in the child-saving movement in the 19th century. The term "child-saving" had a dual meaning: saving children from degenerate parents or life on the streets and saving society from the threat of future delinquents. In 1854, Charles Loring Brace, an ordained Methodist minister and director of the Children's Aid Society of New York, initiated a movement of "placing out" orphaned or impoverished children from New York City to rural families in the Midwest. The stated goal was to increase these children's life opportunities; a subtext was also to remove the offspring of the poor and immigrant class from the streets of New York City so they did not become a drain and a nuisance to society and to permanently sever their tie with unworthy, perhaps dangerous parents. Between 1854 and 1930, this Society and other agencies relocated 150,000 children and youth from New York City to the Midwest (Cook, 1995). With similar motivations, 80,000 British children were placed with Canadian farming families as part of Britain's Child Immigration Scheme (Barter, 2001; Bagnell, 1980). The practicing of "boarding out"—paying families to care for children—gradually replaced "placing out." As states and eventually the federal government became involved in the funding and oversight of boarding out, it evolved into the modern foster care system (Hacsi, 1995).

The last quarter of the 19th century brought a heightened public awareness of child abuse and neglect. The case of Mary Ellen Wilson, a child who was severely physically abused and neglected by her guardians, is often cited as the beginning of public awareness and legislative attention to the issue of child maltreatment in the United States. In 1874, a caseworker named Etta Wheeler heard of the child's sad plight and approached Henry Bergh, the founder of the American Society for the Prevention of Cruelty to Animals, for assistance. Together, they initiated a legal process to have Mary Ellen removed from her caregivers. That same year, Bergh and others established the first New York Society for the Prevention of Cruelty to Children. This chapter of the organization, and others that followed, were active in investigating suspected cases of child maltreatment and encouraging legislation to make child maltreatment illegal (Jalongo, 2006).

Two predominant models of child welfare practice emerged from the work of the Society for the Prevention of Cruelty to Children (SPCC). The New York chapter used a coercive social control model: rescue children, place them in an institution or with a family, and punish the "cruelist" (maltreating parent) as a deterrent to others who would cruelly treat or shamefully neglect children. The Boston chapter broke away from this model and instead adopted a family support approach, using casework and friendly visiting (in-home services) in an attempt to keep families together (Costin, 1991). These predominant approaches to child welfare practice remain in place today: a combination of the quasi-police style adopted by the New York chapter (investigative techniques, removing children from their homes) and the family preservation model (keeping children within their homes, provision of services) adopted by the Boston chapter (Costin, Karger & Stoesz, 1996). After the Great Depression, the "child-saving" movement went into decline. SPCCs were supported by private philanthropy dollars, in shorter supply after many lost their fortunes (Nelson, 1986).

In addition to the child-saving movement, another social change was underway in the 19th century with important implications for child welfare. The Settlement House movement established community hubs where the poor and recently immigrated could receive housing, food, social services, and education. The most famous settlement houses include Toynbee Hall in London (established 1884) and Hull House in Chicago (established 1889). These early settlement houses demonstrated new services for children and families and worked for social reform and strengthening local communities as environments for families. Direct services for families, research on social conditions, and political work were combined to create positive change for families at a neighborhood as well as broader societal level (Halpern, 1995).

It is important to note that African American children and other children of color were not the focus of these child-saving efforts. During the period following the Civil War and emancipation (1877–1900), the question of formal care for dependent African American children arose. African American children were excluded from most orphanages, with a few exceptions. Mutual aid organizations and voluntary associations such as churches provided the dominant form of formal care immediately following emancipation and beyond. Child welfare services offered by voluntary associations formed by African American women expanded in the early decades of the 20th century, fulfilling one of the directives of the National Association for Colored Women. Services decreased after the Great Depression and again after World War II, supplanted by institutionalized social welfare arrangements (Peebles-Wilkins, 1995). Although African American children were fully integrated into the child welfare system after the mid-1940s, this population has continued to experience disproportionate rates of child maltreatment reports, investigations, and placement in foster care, which many would argue stems at least in part from institutional racism (Hill, 2004).

Child maltreatment fell off the public and governmental agenda for several decades, until scientific research brought it back to the fore. In 1962, C. Henry Kempe and colleagues published an article on "The Battered-Child Syndrome" in the *Journal of the American Medical Association*. These researchers found that cases identified as accidental injury among children were very often the result of child abuse. The diagnosis of "battered child syndrome" was established for certain clinical indicators of child maltreatment. This article is often credited with leading to greater public awareness of the existence and scope of child maltreatment, both in the United States and internationally, as well as attention to child maltreatment as a topic of academic inquiry (Nelson, 1986).

Kempe and other physicians were crucial in the passage of state and federal legislation on child maltreatment. By 1967, five years after Kempe's article was published, every state had adopted child abuse reporting laws, mandating certain professionals to report suspected abuse, and many states set up 24-hour hotlines to facilitate the reporting of suspected abuse by the public. Six years later, in 1973, the Child Abuse Prevention and Treatment Act was introduced in Congress and passed easily through both houses. This act authorized funds for the prevention and treatment of child abuse, the establishment of the National Center on Child Abuse and Neglect, and research and demonstration projects. It also provided the first national definition of child abuse. After several rounds of reauthorization and amendments, the act continues to play a guiding role in child welfare intervention and policy today (Pecora et al., 2000).

Following the "rediscovery" of child maltreatment and the implementation of mandated reporter laws, the number of children in care skyrocketed—from 245,000 in 1960 to 502,000 in 1977. The period of the 1970s to the 1990s marked a time of reform efforts and exposés. A report by Henry Maas and Richard Engler in 1959, "Children in Need of Parents," revealed that many children languished in foster care and experienced multiple moves, in a phenomenon labeled "foster care drift." This report, and others that followed, instigated a professional controversy over the balance between the interests of parents and children and whether these interests were in opposition. On one side was the perspective that if only abusive and neglectful parents would relinquish their parental rights, adoptive parents would be found who would give children what they require. The opposing side believed that the child welfare system removed children unnecessarily and insisted on greater efforts to support biological families. Tensions between these poles are evident in two major pieces of federal legislation. Developed in response to concerns that too many children were being removed from their families, the 1980 Adoption Assistance and Child Welfare Act promoted preservation of family ties by requiring agencies to make a "reasonable effort" to prevent child maltreatment and provide services to facilitate family reunification. Perceptions that the pendulum had swung too far on the side of family preservation and that children were kept in potentially unsafe families or were remaining too long in foster care lead to the passage of the 1997 Adoption and Safe Families Act, which established expedited timelines for family reunification or termination of parental rights (Murray & Gesiriech, n.d).

The mission of the American child welfare system today continues to focus on the needs of children reported as abused, neglected, or at risk of being maltreated, with foster care or residential services provided for those children who are deemed to be unsafe in their homes (Pecora, 2008). In 2007, child welfare agencies across the countries received around 3.2 million referrals for alleged maltreatment of approximately 5.8 million children. Investigations were made on behalf of roughly 3.5 million children (US DHHS, 2009). About 800,000 children per year are looked after in the U.S. foster care system—about half a million on any given day (Pecora, 2008). Placement types vary. Family foster care by nonrelatives is most common, with 46% of children in this form of care nationally in 2006 (US DHHS, 2008). Foster care by relatives (kinship care) is the second most popular placement type, accounting for 24% of foster care in 2006 (US DHHS, 2008); this care option has increased in popularity since the mid-1980s, when federal reimbursement parity was established for kin caregivers (Hegar & Scannapieco, 1998). Residential care is primarily intended for children and youth who need specialized services that cannot be provided in the context of a family setting (Child Welfare League of America, 2004); 10% of children were cared for in an institution and 7% in a group home in 2006 (US DHHS, 2008). Children of ethnic and racial minorities are more highly represented in the child welfare system—at the level of report, investigation, and placement—than they are in the general population (Pecora, 2008).

Some have suggested that the mentality of Progressive era social policies lingers on in the modern American child welfare system that it created. One example is the dependency dynamic established between social workers and clients (Rappaport, 1981). Another is a common experience of CPS services as victimizing and exclusionary, in a system of services designed without attention to possible loss of rights (Hegar & Hunzeker, 1988; Rappaport, 1981). Yet another is the narrow focus of child welfare on parenting domains and the persistence of labeling child abuse as a purely personal failing, without accounting for societal contributions to the problem (Belsky, 1980; Garbarino, 1977). In addition to these criticisms, the American child welfare system has been described as perpetuating the disadvantaged position of minority children, particularly African American children, by removing them from their families and placing them in damaging state-run care (Roberts, 2002). The narrow child protection approach to child welfare services that predominates in Anglo-American countries has simply failed all too many children and families. A new approach that builds the capacities of families and communities to better care for children is called for.

The Developmental Approach to Child Welfare

The developmental approach to child welfare is exemplified by programs that promote early childhood care and development, involve communities and the extended family, and enable families and youth to accumulate assets. In many parts of the world, such efforts are often a reaction against ineffectual remedial approaches to child protection that fail to address problems of poverty, stress, and social isolation at the root of child maltreatment. Many countries in the developing world have long recognized that a child protection orientation based on the Western model is ineffective for dealing with social problems in societies marked by poverty and deprivation. The conventional child protection approach—reactive rather than proactive, focused on urban areas, and limited to problems of child abuse and neglect—does not fit in contexts where issues like infant death and malnutrition are more pressing (Midgley & Livermore, 2004). This section considers conceptual models and programmatic examples in the areas of early childhood care and development, community and extended family involvement, and asset building, and how these approaches can build the capacities of families and communities to better protect and care for children. As backdrop to considering these developmental interventions, this section first lays out the underlying principles of a developmental approach—namely, an emphasis on prevention, attention to poverty alleviation, and acknowledgment of human rights, particularly as expressed by the 1989 U.N. Convention on the Rights of the Child.

Underlying Principles: Prevention, Poverty Alleviation, and
Children's Rights

The importance of prevention in social work has been recognized for many decades but unfortunately has not been given priority in social work practice or, indeed, more generally in the social services field. Social work's predominant use of direct practice with individuals and families facing serious challenges has focused professional intervention on problem solving rather than prevention. Although many social workers in clinical practice do recognize the need for prevention, they seldom have the time to promote preventive programs. Similarly, prevention is often seen as peripheral for child welfare workers, whose time and efforts are primarily concentrated on child safety and permanency. Preventive functions are often assumed to be the purview of schools, churches, youth clubs, and various other community-based institutions. Although social workers used to provide organized educational and recreational activities for children through the Settlement Houses, to promote socialization and foster social integration of poor children into community life, these activities were eventually separated from professional social work, as the field became largely concerned with clinical practice. Even in community social work practice, prevention is not always given as much emphasis as local community social services planning and the mobilization of local residents for social action.

In view of the large numbers of children in the formal child welfare system today, prevention needs to be given much more attention by social workers seeking to address the problems of child maltreatment. This goal is compatible with the basic ideal of the developmental model, which is concerned with improving the well-being of all children and families and not focusing exclusively on those children who are neglected or abused. To reduce the numbers of children in the statutory child welfare system, social workers involved in child welfare need to engage much more proactively in prevention activities.

Another key factor in addressing the problem of child maltreatment, which was referred to earlier in this chapter, is the high number of children in the child welfare system that come from poor families or who live in poor communities. There is a strong correlation between the incidence of child maltreatment and poverty that cannot be attributed solely to biases among mandated reporters. Higher rates of child maltreatment among the poor have been identified in studies based on the reported rates of child maltreatment as well as the population-based National Incidence Studies. Moreover, studies of child homicides have consistently identified a pattern of victims coming predominately from poor families (Pelton, 1994). The relationship between poverty and child welfare involvement is particularly strong for infants, with children born into poor family more likely to be placed into foster care than non-poor infants (Wulczyn, 1994; Barth et al., 2005). Disproportionate representation of children of color in the child welfare system appears to be partially associated with minority overrepresentation among the deeply poor (Pelton, 1994). If the incidence of child maltreatment is to be reduced, child welfare policies need to be more proactively linked with poverty alleviation strategies.

Legal recognition of children's rights can provide a constitutional basis for ensuring that children are protected from harm and their best interests promoted through prevention efforts. A distinction can be made between "moral" rights, generally understood as basic human rights, and "legal" rights, encompassing constitutional, political, or civil rights enforced by the judicial system. As young humans, universal human rights apply to children as they do to adults. In terms of legal rights, however, a distinction is made between children and adults; children grow into the full complement of adult rights when they reach maturity. During the period of childhood, children depend on others to meet their needs and provide protection. Parents hold primary responsibility for these roles, unless it can be demonstrated that the "best interests of the child" are not being met, in which case the state has the authority to intervene under the English common law doctrine of *parens patriae*, or parent of the country. This doctrine is the underlying justification for state intervention in cases of child maltreatment, custody and visitation, as well as other matters pertaining to children and families (Staller, 2008).

Human rights and legal rights for children merged in a document called the Convention on the Rights of the Child, adopted unanimously by the UN General Assembly on November 20, 1989 and currently ratified by 193 countries (United Nations Children's Fund [UNICEF], 2009). This document emphasized that children have human rights and need special protections beyond those provided to adults (UNICEF, 2008). Three types of rights are recognized: protection rights, which guard against harm; provision rights, which guarantee basic needs; and participation rights, which enable children to have a voice (Staller, 2008). The Convention is legally binding on those countries that have ratified it. After Somalia recently announced plans to ratify the Convention (Reuters, 2009), United States remains the sole U.N. member nation that has not ratified the document, ostensibly because it only considers one human rights treaty at a time, and the Convention on the Elimination of All Forms of Discrimination against Women currently holds priority (UNICEF, 2008). The Convention has supporters and detractors in the United States, both of which acknowledge that the chances of ratification are greater under an Obama administration than in the previous 20 years since its development. Supporters argue that U.S. ratification of this document would provide guidance to domestic policies related to children as well as lend the Convention greater weight internationally. Detractors worry that it would undermine parental authority, and a movement is underway to add an amendment to the U.S. Constitution recognizing the right of parents to make decisions related to their children's education and upbringing (Crary, 2009). Although the Convention is not currently implemented in the United States, it is nevertheless a major document of historical importance that informs a developmental approach to child welfare by suggesting a broader scope for child welfare, one ensuring that society provide the conditions that children need to flourish (Clifton & Hodgson, 1997).

Prevention, poverty alleviation, and children's rights goals can be advanced by a more effective system of collaboration with the community resources such as schools, churches, and other governmental agencies. It is a major deficiency of the

child protection system that partnerships with other community-based organizations and even other social services agencies are limited. Social workers in child
welfare need to be out in the community meeting and establishing relationships
with these organizations, and they should be actively engaged in promoting a more
effective coordination of services. Too often, child protection functions in isolation
from these services. Developmental child welfare must be community-based and
must involve local people and local organizations. Although the settlement houses,
which were well-positioned to provide services of this kind, no longer on function
on an appreciable scale in their original form, they have been replaced by community or neighborhood centers that are actively involved in building community
strengths and providing services that have a prevention function. A recent study of
17 such neighborhood centers in San Francisco and Vancouver (Yan, Lauer, & Sin,
2009) found that they are actively involved in outreach providing a variety of services to all age groups in the community. These include early childhood programs,
educational and recreational activities, parenting classes, and cultural events that
serve to promote community integration, coordinate local services, and involve
local people more actively in community life. Similar centers exist in many other
parts of Canada and the United States. They provide a viable opportunity for child
welfare social workers to work closely with center staff to promote prevention.

Recently, the British government recognized the limitations of the child protection approach by introducing legislation designed specifically to improve prevention services. Although earlier legislation, such as the 1989 Children's Act, made
provision for early intervention services, only children who were judged to be at
high risk were actually targeted, with the result that many moderate- and low-risk
children subsequently came into contact with the child protection system. Following
several high-profile cases in which children died as a result of systematic abuse,
steps were taken to expand prevention services. The 2005 Children's Act introduced new requirements, including the preparation of strategic plans at the city
and county level to address local problems and promote prevention services. These
plans were developed by partnerships between child welfare agencies and various
nonprofits and community organizations. In addition, funds specifically allocated
to prevention services were made available to local communities to allow them to
contract with nonprofit organizations engaged in preventive work. The legislation
also required child welfare agencies to work collaboratively with other statutory
providers such as schools, clinics, and hospitals and to ensure better service integration and coordination at the local level. New provisions were also made to promote service integration at the national level. This is exemplified by the integration
of the central government departments responsible for child welfare and education
in 2007. Although much more needs to be done to promote prevention within
child welfare, it appears that the government's policies are having some effect
(Morris, Barnes, & Mason, 2009).

The developmental interventions discussed in the following sections of this
chapter show how child welfare programs can be concerned with both prevention
and poverty alleviation strategies, based on a foundation of children's rights.

Community-based early childhood care programs such as Head Start in United States and the Integrated Child Development Scheme in India have multiple functions ranging from preschool education to the creation of group environments for the socialization of small children, but it will become clear that they also have an important prevention role. Because of the high incidence of malnutrition among poor children, the prevention of malnutrition through daily lunch programs is given high priority in the India program. Similarly, by weighing children regularly, it is possible to identify early cases of neglect. These programs also contribute to poverty alleviation by fostering human capital development at an early age and creating opportunities for children from poor communities to attend primary and secondary school and realize their potential. Similarly, the child savings accounts discussed later have a direct antipoverty effect.

Early Childhood Care and Development

Early childhood is a time of hope for many families and a prime opportunity to provide families with support to prevent child maltreatment. Formal child care settings offer a natural source of assistance to families. The dramatic rise in female workforce participation in the latter decades of the 20th century has been associated with a concomitant increase in reliance on nonrelative childcare, both in the United States and globally. Nonrelative child care has traditionally met three important goals: substitute care for children during hours of parental employment, learning opportunities to stimulate social–emotional and cognitive development, and compensatory services for poor and disadvantaged children (Scarr & Eisenberg, 1993). Two programs, one from an industrial country (Head Start in the United States) and one from a developing country (Integrated Child Development Scheme in India), that serve all three of these purposes will now be described, with an emphasis on how such programs can be combined with child protection.

Part of the Johnson administration War on Poverty, the United States Head Start program was "designed to help break the cycle of poverty" by addressing the psychological, nutritional, social, health, and emotional needs of poor children (Child Care Resource Center, 2008). The program is open to all 3- and 4-year-old children below a certain income threshold, although only about one-third of those eligible receive services as the funding allocated by Congress have never been not sufficient to meet the total need (Garces, Thomas, & Currie, 2000). Head Start has a "whole-child" approach to services that recognizes the interrelatedness of children's development across a range of domains and how that interacts with supporting and involving parents to help children and families meet their full potential (Westat, Xtria, & The CDM Group, 2003). Each Head Start center employs one or more paraprofessional "family advocates," who provide families with social support, information on community services, and, in some cases, ongoing case management when needed. Parents are also invited to workshops geared to fit their interests as well as informal fun activities. Many parents take an even more active role in their Head Start program: During 2003 to 2004, 27% of Head Start staff were parents of current or former participants, and over 880,000 parents contributed volunteer time in their local program (Administration for Children and Families, 2006). The next example has some parallels with Head Start, with its focus on parental and community involvement in early childhood care and education.

The Integrated Child Development Scheme in India, created in 1975, provides comprehensive services through community-based centers for children under age 6 years, pregnant and nursing mothers, and, more recently, adolescent girls. Programs are primarily implemented in rural and tribal areas, with urban slum areas as a secondary geographical focus. The ultimate goal is to promote the survival and health of young children. Six core services are "integrated" through delivery at local "Anganwadi" Centers: supplementary nutrition, immunizations, health check-ups, referrals for medical treatment, preschool education, and nutrition and health education (Ministry of Women and Child Development, N.D.) Local programs are staffed by volunteers who are paid a small honorarium. These Anganwadi workers build relationships with local entities, such as village councils, to ensure that the program can be sustained with minimal government assistance and integrated into community life (Sonty, 1992).

These two programs share a focus on prevention and developing human and social capital and may therefore be more cost-effective than reactive child protective approaches, which rely on investigation and remediation (Midgley & Livermore, 2004). Childcare centers can provide disadvantaged children with a safe and stimulating place to learn and develop, within the context of supportive relationships with caregivers. If a child appears to be mistreated (e.g., arriving with bruises or without being fed), the childcare setting can monitor the problem and decide how to intervene. Pre-existing relationships between parent and childcare provider, or between parent and other parents, can provide a safety net for families at risk of maltreating their children. These relationships can be used to provide families with respite care, emotional support, and information about community resources. Bringing together child protection with early childhood care and education can effectively combine a developmental and preventative function with a remedial approach, to protect children while promoting their well-being. With the majority of children in the United States and many other countries enrolled in formal childcare, partnerships between child welfare and childcare providers may provide a fruitful avenue for nonreactive child protection.

Community and Extended Family Involvement

There is a consensus in field of child welfare that at-risk families all too frequently lack positive support from their communities. Lack of social support or negative social support appears to be associated with child maltreatment (Kotelchuck, 1982; Polansky et al., 1981; Polansky, Ammons, & Gaudin, 1985). Relationships of both a personal and professional nature can provide social support. Family and friends are often a naturally occurring, informal source of support. More formal supports include groups and organizations within a community and individuals such as professionals and paraprofessionals in the medical and mental health fields (Hogan, Linden, & Najarian, 2002). Studies have consistently found that people express preference for informal over formal support and desire professional help only when other forms of support are not available (Finfgeld-Connett, 2005). Child welfare agencies are beginning to recognize that they shared responsibility for child protection with community and extended family. This realization is reflected in the current emphasis on family group decision making, first developed for the Maori people of New Zealand, and efforts to promote community involvement, such as Family-to-Family in the United States.

Until the passage of legislative reforms in the 1980s, the history of child welfare practice in New Zealand followed the Anglo-American child protection model, with greater emphasis on investigation and alternative placement than support for children's birth and extended families. Unfavorable studies as well as the scandal of a child's death lead to awareness that the system of foster and institutional care did not provide optimal care for children, particularly Maori children. Ensuing legislation called the Children, Young Persons and their Families Act of 1989 recognized the family and larger community as the primary caregivers of children and young persons and delineated a secondary role for the child welfare system as facilitators of a process that encourages family and community responsibility. This process is formalized in family group conferences, a practice based on methods of traditional Maori decision-making. Family group conferences are invoked for reported cases of children in need of care and protection. A Care and Protection Coordinator is assigned to convene the child's birth and extended family, as well as community members and professionals involved in the child and family's lives. The family group conference has three phases: information sharing, which entails a frank discussion of the reasons for the referral; the private family deliberation, an opportunity for families to discuss the issues and possible solutions without professionals and other parties in the room, if they so choose; and the reaching of agreement, when the families take the lead in developing plans to ensure the child's appropriate care and safety (Connolly, 1994). Family group decision making, as well as related practices that have developed in countries including the United Kingdom, Ireland, and the United States (Merkel-Holguin, Nixon & Burford, 2003), are more than simply additional tools in the child welfare toolkit—they represent a fundamental shift away from the paternalistic model in which the professional assesses problems and prescribes solutions, to an empowerment model in which families confront their challenges and claim responsibility for children's safety by using their existing resources and support networks as well as creating new relationships with informal sources of support and formal service providers (Merkel-Holguin, 2004).

The Family-to-Family Initiative, sponsored by the Annie E. Casey Foundation, similarly harnesses communities' interests in protecting their children. Family-to-Family provides child welfare agencies and neighborhoods with tools and strategies for reforming some of the more troubled elements of the child welfare system, including the lack of foster families residing in the neighborhoods from which children are removed from their birth families (Mattingly, 1998: Omang & Bonk, 1999). Beginning with five states and three additional counties in 1993 (Omang & Bonk, 1999), the initiative spread to 18 states and more than 80 sites across the United States by 2009 (Annie E. Casey Foundation, 2009). Embracing a Family-to-Family approach means child welfare agencies must change their attitudes and behaviors toward birth families, foster families, and communities. Part of this is recognizing that neighborhoods with high placement rates can also support families at-risk of child placement—that is, these neighborhoods have strengths as well as challenges. Child welfare agencies utilizing the Family-to-Family approach engage with community leaders, asking them to play roles such as recruiting foster families and providing birth and foster families with needed services. Another strategy for including the community is Team Decision Making, a process much like Family Group Conferencing that invites community and extended family involvement in case planning for children (Fiester, 2008). Keeping children in their communities enables relationships to form between the birth families and foster families. Foster families are expected to encourage visitation and work with birth families toward reunification. After reunification, children may continue to have ongoing relationships with their foster parents. As such, family is redefined: "The child's family is in effect enlarged to include new caregivers, rather than torn asunder" (Omang & Bonk, 1999, p. 21). In sites where it is implemented, Family-to-Family is enabling more children to remain within their neighborhoods of origin and experience a greater sense of stability and community.

Family group decision making and Family-to-Family are emblematic of shift toward family-centered and strengths-based practices that encourage partnerships with extended families and communities to protect children and support families (Merkel-Holguin, 1998; Kempe et al., 2005). These efforts reflect a growing recognition that the job of child protection is simply too big for a child welfare agencies to do alone. The social work model of remediation and focus on deficiency has been criticized by authors such as John McKnight (1995) for eroding social bonds and self-sufficiency, creating dependence on professionals and the government rather than interdependence of communities and families. A more appropriate role is to build collective concern about children and the capacity of communities to support children and families (Barter, 2001). Efforts to include extended family and community members in supporting families can reduce their social isolation and build social capital. Social capital gives families access to the tangible and intangible resources of others through networks of relationships (Lin, 2001). Helping families recognize, reach out to, and possibly build or rebuild their social networks is a way that child welfare agencies can increase the likelihood that families will receive the support they need for the long-term.

Asset Development for Children and Youth

Extended family and community are not alone in their abilities to support vulnerable families—given the right tools, families are also capable of helping themselves.

The same is true for youth who may be transitioning out of the child welfare system to independence. However, a significant barrier that families and youth face in meeting their needs is poverty. Although connection between child maltreatment and poverty is axiomatic in the field of child welfare (Pelton, 1994), families are rarely provided with assistance that would enable them or their children to escape poverty; at best, they are likely to be offered help with finding a job or signing up for income transfers that will only maintain the family in poverty. Youth transitioning out of the foster care system often are even more vulnerable, as they generally lack resources that will enable them to pay for higher education or vocational training that would lead to economic self-sufficiency. There is a growing interest on the part of policymakers around the world in developing universal Child Savings Accounts, as well as asset development programs targeted to vulnerable populations.

National Child Savings Accounts may take different forms, but there are a few common design characteristics (Butrica et al., 2008). First, these savings and investment accounts are often established at birth (New America Foundation, 2008). Countries that provide a savings and investment account to newborns include Canada (*learn*$ave), the United Kingdom (Child Trust Accounts), and Singapore (Baby Bonus Scheme) (New America Foundation, 2006). Second, accounts are generally restricted for use toward paying for higher education or accumulating major assets like a first home (New America Foundation, 2008); some, however, can be used for costs associated with child rearing, such as Singapore's Baby Bonus Scheme (Loke & Sherraden, 1997). Third, governments can encourage asset accumulation through different types of subsidies, including seed funding, matching private contributions, and treating grants and interest as tax free (Butrica et al., 2008). Child Savings Accounts are often progressively funded, with greater public investments for children in lower-income households (New America Foundation, 2008). In addition to the financial benefits that accumulated assets bestow, there is evidence that assets can also have psychological and social effects. These include fostering a greater sense of control over one's life, orientation toward planning for the future, and participation in family and civic activities (Friedman & Sherraden, 2001).

Although the United States has yet to implement Child Savings Accounts as national policy, despite the introduction of legislation in the 109th session of Congress (New America Foundation, 2006), some jurisdictions in the United States have created asset development programs to improve the life chances of transitional age foster youth. Study after study has found that youth who "age out" of the child welfare system at age 18 years are more likely than nonfoster youth peers to experience a range of negative outcomes, including unemployment, homelessness, and welfare dependency (Child Trends, 2002). Although preventing these dire outcomes is complex, providing youth with opportunities for economic success is one approach endorsed by research, statements of former foster youth, and common sense (Foster Care Work Group, 2003). This a major goal of Connected by 25, an initiative supported by the Youth Transitions Funders Group that has been implemented in a number of states across the country, including Oregon, Florida, and California (Youth Transitions Funders Group, 2009). One of the strategies endorsed by the initiative is encouraging transitional age youth to save and accumulate assets. This is primarily accomplished by setting up savings accounts (Youth Individual Development Accounts), which offer a matched contribution for any contributions made by youth. The average match provided is 2:1, although match rates range from 1:1 to 4:1. Total cap on matched funds also vary, from a low of $250 to a high of $4,000. Savings may be used for a range of purposes, including preparing youth for economic self-sufficiency through higher education or vocational training, supplying material assets such as a first car or a computer, or setting them up for life on their own with a rental housing deposit or down payment for a home. Youth IDA programs often provide other support services to youth, such as adult mentors, financial literacy training, and employment assistance. Above and beyond financial uses, accumulated assets are expected to help youth think about their futures differently with more positive aspirations and less predilection to engage in risky behaviors (Foster Care Work Group, 2003).

A developmental approach to child welfare promises greater attention to child well-being, a goal that is seen as important yet illusive for many child welfare systems, like the United States (Wulcyzn, 2005). One key way to achieve this is to ensure that children, youth, and families have the economic resources that they need. Although Individual Development Accounts have not been explicitly linked prevention or reunification services in child welfare systems, such a marriage would offer numerous benefits. The type of flexibility provided by the Singapore Baby Bonus Scheme may make most sense for families involved with the child welfare system. This flexibility would enable families to use assets for child rearing expenditures, such as childcare and child mental health, which are major costs burdens. Indeed, the cost of child mental health services can be so burdensome that it forces families to relinquish their children to the child welfare system so that they can get the needed services (CWLA, 2006). Local, state, or federal governments could spur savings by providing a high match rate or cap on matching grants for child welfare-involved families, recognizing the depth of poverty that predominates among this population and the challenges they face in accumulating savings. In essence, these accounts could provide poor families with a subsidy for childcare and other child needs. Providing Individual Development Accounts as part of a developmental approach to child welfare is quite the opposite of a traditional child protection approach: it is investment-oriented, rather than residual; empowering, rather than paternalistic; and strengths-based, rather than problem-focused.

The Role of Social Work

The conventional approach to child protection, which involves removing children from families, placing children in foster or residential care, and arranging for adoptions, is so fundamental to child welfare and the field of social work that embracing a developmental approach would require a radical shift in thinking within social work, as well as by society and policymakers. Paradigm shifts, whereby a professional field transcends previous formulations of looking at a phenomenon and embraces a new way of thinking, can occur (Heller et al., 1984). Indeed, a developmental approach requires this kind of paradigm shift. A major challenge is changing the predominant mindset toward families, away from the paternalistic view that focuses on parental deficiencies to one that recognizes the difficulties of parenting and provides support that empowers families and communities to care for children. Another challenge is making structural changes that enable the widespread adoption of developmental social work practices, including ensuring flexible use of funds and eliminating categorical restrictions that tie funding levels to foster and residential care placement rates. Perhaps most crucial is recognizing the inevitable failure of a crisis-oriented child welfare system and shifting to a system that recognizes children's inalienable rights to protection from harm through prevention efforts. Until transformative work is done to change biases against families and restructure failing bureaucracies, simply introducing new types of interventions is bound to fail. It is encouraging that the chorus of voices encouraging change in public child welfare systems dominated by a child protection orientation is growing ever louder.

All the developmental approaches to child welfare that have been described in this chapter can be combined with each other or with conventional approaches to child protection. For example, a community childcare center can be a site for recruiting families into an asset-development scheme, thereby building upon and reinforcing the bonds between families and sources of informal and formal support. The increased informal support created by efforts to encourage ties with extended family and community or mutual support among families can be used to gently intervene with families who appear at-risk of maltreating their children. It is difficult to imagine that the conventional child protection approach can be completely banished from the child welfare system, and indeed, this approach may be most appropriate for some families who are not ready to change behaviors that endanger children. However, many families are ill-served by the narrow child protection approach. Examples such as the Family-to-Family program suggest ways in which a developmental approach to child welfare can be combined with a child protection approach.

The roles of social workers under a developmental approach to child welfare will vary significantly from the traditional approach. For example, rather than waiting for a mandated reporter to make a call about a family, conducting an investigation, and removing a children from her family and community, a developmental child welfare worker would place greater attention to supporting families before they reach a state of crisis. This would require a more visible presence in the community and a proactive engagement of families into preventative services, such as early childhood programs. It would also entail collaboration with formal and informal community resources, including nonprofit organizations and neighborhood groups. In practice, this might look like the British "patch" model of locating child welfare workers within neighborhoods and building stronger links between the child welfare system and service providers related to health, employment, housing, and other family needs. This model has already been adopted in some jurisdictions in the United States, including Iowa (Waldfogel, 1998) and Massachusetts (Administration for Children and Families, 2007).

With past experience suggesting that the number of children and families involved in the child welfare system increases in times of economic difficulty (St. George & Dvorak, 2008), it is more important than ever before that the child welfare system offer assistance to families that enhances their abilities to care for their children. As child advocate Marian Wright Edelman has pointed out, the United States, with its child protection orientation, ". . .[is] willing to spend the least amount of money to keep a kid at home, more to put him in a foster home and the most to institutionalize him." The harm this approaches does to children, families, and communities is evident. It is time for a developmental approach.

REFERENCES

Administration for Children and Families, U.S. Department of Health and Human Services (N.D.). *NIS-4 Description*. Available at https://www.nis4.org/nis4.asp (Accessed February 27, 2009).

Administration for Children and Families, U.S. Department of Health and Human Services (2007, December). *Promising approaches in child welfare by state.* Available at http://www.acf.hhs.gov/programs/cb/cwmonitoring/promise/states.htm (Accessed May 3, 2009).

Annie E. Casey Foundation (2009). *Family to Family.*Available at http://www.aecf.org/MajorInitiatives/Family%20to%20Family/SitesAndContacts.aspx (Accessed February 27, 2009).

Bagnell K. (1980). *The little immigrants.* Toronto: MacMillan of Canada.

Barter, K. (2001). Building Community: A conceptual framework for child protection. Child *Child Abuse Review* 10: 262–278.

Belsky, J. (1980). Child maltreatment: An ecological integration. *American Psychologist.* 35(4): 320–335.

Butrica, B.A., Carasso, A., Steuerle, C.E., Toohey, D.J. (2008). *Children's savings accounts: Why design matters.* Washington, D.C.: The Urban Institute. Available at http://www.urban.org/publications/411677.html (Accessed March 30, 2009).

Cameron, G., Coady, N., & Adams, G. (2007). *Towards positive systems of child and family welfare: Current issues and future directions.* Waterloo, ON: Wilfrid Laurier University Press.

Child Trends, (December 2002). *Youth Who "age out" of foster care: Troubled lives, troubling prospects,* Child Trends Research Brief.

Child Care Resource Center (2008). *Project Head Start background and mission.* CCRC:Available at http://www.ccrcla.org/home/index.asp?page=147 (Accessed October 8, 2008).

Child Welfare League of America. (2004). *CWLA standards of excellence for residential services.* Washington, DC: Child Welfare League of America.

Clifton, J. & Hodgson, D. (1997). Rethinking practice through a children's rights perspective, in Cannan C. & Warren C. (Eds.) *Social action with children and families.* London: Routledge, pp. 43–65.

Cook, J.F. (1995). A history of placing-out: The orphan trains. *Child Welfare.* 74(1): 181–197.

Connolly, M. (1994). An act of empowerment: The Children, Young Persons, and Their Families Act (1989), *British Journal of Social Work*, 24(1): 87–100.

Costin, L.B. (1991). Unraveling the Mary Ellen legend: Origins of the "Cruelty" Movement. *The Social Service Review*, 65 (2): 203–223.

Costin, L.B., Karger, H.J., & Stoesz, D. (1996). *The politics of child abuse in America.* New York: Oxford University Press.

Crary, D. (2009, May 2). Children's rights treaty stirs debate: U.N. accord bring calls for amendment to U.S. Constitution. *The Atlanta-Journal Constitution.* Available at http://www.ajc.com/services/content/printedition/2009/05/02/currents0502.html (Accessed May 3, 2009).

D'Cruz, H. (2004). The social construction of child maltreatment: The role of medical practitioners, *Journal of Social Work.* 4 (1): 99–123.

English, D.J. (1998, Spring). The extent and consequences of child maltreatment. *The Future of Children*, 8 (1): 39–53.

Fiester, L. (2008). *The story of Family to Family: The early years 1992–2006, An initiative to improve child welfare systems.* Available at http://www.aecf.org/KnowledgeCenter/Publications.aspx?pubguid=%7B3496A32B-229E-452E-B5BE-951C321AD51E%7D (Accessed April 18, 2009).

Finfgeld-Connett, D. (2005, March). Clarification of social support. *Journal of Nursing Scholarship*, 37(1): 4–9.

Foster Care Work Group (2003). *Connected by 21: A plan for investing in successful futures for foster youth.* Available at http://www.aecf.org/upload/publicationfiles/connected%20by%2025.pdf (Accessed April 18, 2009).

Freymond, N. & Cameron, G. (2006). *Towards positive systems of child and family welfare: International comparisons of child protection, family service, and community care models.* Toronto: University of Toronto Press.

Friedman, R.E. & Sherraden, M. (2001). Asset-based policy in the United States, in S. Regan & W. Paxton (Eds.) *Asset-based welfare: International experiences.* London, England: Institute for Public Policy Research.

Garbarino, J. (1977). The human ecology of child maltreatment: A conceptual model for research. *Journal of Marriage and the Family*, 39(4): 721–735.

Garces, E., Thomas, D., Currie, J. (2002). Longer-term effects of Head Start. *American Economic Review*, 92 (Sep): 999–1012.

Gilbert, N. (Ed.)(1997). *Combating child abuse: International perspectives and trends.* Oxford: Oxford University Press.

Gordon, J. (1997). Discourses of child protection and child welfare. *The British Journal of Social Work*, 27(5): 659–678.

Hacsi, T. (1995). From indenture to family foster care: A brief history of child placing. *Child Welfare.* 74(1): 162–180.

Halpern, R. (1995). *Rebuilding the inner city.* New York: Columbia University Press.

Hegar, R.L. & Hunzeker, J.M. (1988). Moving toward empowerment-based practice in public child welfare. *Social Work.* 33(6): 499–502.

Hegar, R. & Scannapieco, M. (Eds.) (1998). *Kinship foster care: Practice, policy, and research.* New York: Oxford University Press.

Hill, R.B. (2004). Institutional racism in child welfare, in J. Everett, S. Chipungu, & B. Leashore (Eds.) *Child welfare revisited* New Brunswick, NJ: Rutgers University Press, pp. 57–76.

Hogan, B.E., Linden, W. & Najarian, B. (2002). Social support interventions: Do they work? *Clinical Psychology Review*, 22: 381–440.

The International Society for the Prevention of Child Abuse and Neglect (ISPCAN). *World perspectives on child abuse: An international resource book*, 8th ed. Available at http://www.ispcan.org/publications/documents/WorldPerspectives2008.pdf (Accessed November 30, 2009)

Jalongo, M.R. (2006). The Story of Mary Ellen Wilson: Tracing the origins of child protection in America. *Early Childhood Education Journal*, 34(1): 1–4.

Kemp, S.P., Allen-Eckard, K., Ackroyd, A., Becker, M.F., & Burke, T.K. (2005). Engaging families and communities: The use of family team conferences to promote safety, permanency, and well-being in child welfare services, in: Mallon, G.P. & Hess P.M. (Eds.) *Child welfare for the 21st century.* New York City, NY: Columbia University Press.

Kotelchuck, M. (1982). Child abuse and neglect: Prediction and misclassification, in Starr R. (Ed.) *Child abuse prediction* Cambridge, MA: Ballinger, pp. 67–104.

Lawerence-Karski, R. (1999). Key decisions in child protective services: Report investigation and court referral. *Children and Youth Services Review.* 21(8): 643–656.

Lin, N. (2001). *Social capital: A theory of social structure and action.* New York: Cambridge University Press.

Loke, V. & Sherraden, M. (1997). *Building children's assets in Singapore: The post-secondary education account policy.* CSD Publication No. 07-36. Available at http://csd.wustl.edu/Publications/Documents/PB07-36.pdf (Accessed February 27, 2009).

Lubeck, S. & Garrett, P. (1990). The social construction of the 'at-risk' child *British Journal of Sociology of Education*, 11(3): 327–340.

Mattingly, J.B. (1998). Family to Family: Reconstructing foster care in the US. *Children & Society*, 12: 180–184.

May-Chahal, C. & Cawson, P. (2005). Measuring child maltreatment in the United Kingdom: A study of the prevalence of child abuse and neglect. *Child Abuse & Neglect.* 29: 969–984.

McKnight, J. (1995). *The careless society: Community and its counterfeits.* New York: Basic Books.

Merkel-Holguin, L. (1998). Implementation of family group decision making in the U.S.: Policies and practices in transition. *Protecting Children*, 14(4): 4–10.

Merkel-Holguin, L. (2004). Sharing power with the people: Family group conferencing as a democratic experiment. *Journal of Sociology & Social Welfare*, 31: 155–173.

Merkel-Holguin, L., Nixon, P., & Burford, G. (2003). Learning with families: A synopsis of FGDM research and evaluation in child welfare. *Protecting Children*, 18(1–2): 2–11.

Midgley, J. and Livermore, M. (2004). Social Development: Lessons from the Global South, in Hokenstad, M. C. & Midgley, J. (Eds.) *Lessons from Abroad: Adapting International Social Welfare Innovations*, Washington, DC: NASW Press, pp. 117–135.

Ministry of Women and Child Development, Government of India (N.D.) *Integrated Child Development Scheme.* Available at http://wcd.nic.in/icds.htm (Accessed March 5, 2009).

Morris, K., Barnes, M., & Mason, P. (2009). *Children, families and social exclusion: New approaches to prevention.* Bristol: Policy Press.

Murray, K. O. & Gesiriech, S. (n.d). *A brief legislative history of the child welfare system.* The Pew Commission on Children in Foster Care Available at http://pewfostercare. org/research/docs/Legislative.pdf. (Accessed February 24, 2009).

Nelson, B.J. (1986). *Making an issue of child abuse: Political agenda setting for social problems.* Chicago: University of Chicago Press.

New America Foundation (2006). *Savings accounts at birth and other children's savings accounts proposals.* Available at http://www.newamerica.net/files/ CSA%20two%20pager.pdf. (Accessed April 18, 2009).

New America Foundation (2008). *Child savings accounts: A primer.* Available at http:// www.newamerica.net/files/CSA%20Primer.pdf (Accessed March 27, 2009).

North American Council of Adoptable Child (March 2007). *Child welfare financing 101* Available at http://www.pewtrusts.org/uploadedFiles/wwwpewtrustsorg/Reports/ Foster_care_reform/NACAC_CWFinancing1010307.pdf (Accessed November 30, 2009).

Omang, J. & Bonk, K. (1999). Family to Family: Building bridges for child welfare with families, neighborhoods, and communities. *Policy & Practice of Public Human Services,* 57: 15–21.

Parton, N., Thorpe, D., & Wattam, C. (1997). *Child protection, risk and the moral order.* Basingstoke: Macmillan.

Pecora, P. (2008). Child welfare: An overview, in Mizrahi, T. & Davis, L.E. (Eds.) *Encyclopedia of Social Work, Volume I,* (20th ed.). Washington, DC: National Association of Social Workers, pp. 270–277.

Pecora, P. J., Whittaker, J. K., Maluccio, A. N., Barth, R. P., with Poltnick, R. D. (2000). *The child welfare challenge: Policy, practice and research* (2nd Ed.). New York: Aldine de Gruyter.

Peebles-Wilkins, W. (1995). Janie Porter Barrett and the Virginia Industrial School for Colored Girls: Community response to the needs of African American children. *Child Welfare.* 74(1): 143–167.

Pelton, L. (1994) The role of material factors in child abuse and neglect, in Melton, G.B. & Barry, F.D. (Eds.) *Protecting children from abuse and neglect: Foundations for a new national strategy.* New York, NY: Guilford Press, pp. 131–181.

Polansky, N. A., Ammons, P. W., & Gaudin, J. M. (1985). Loneliness and isolation in child neglect. *Social Casework: The Journal of Contemporary Social Work,* 6: 38–47.

Polansky, N. A., Chalmers, M. A., Buttenwieser, E., & Williams, D. P. (1981). *Damaged parents.* Chicago, IL: The University of Chicago Press.

Rappaport, J. (1981). In praise of paradox: A social policy of empowerment over prevention. *American Journal of Community Psychology,* 9(1): 1–25.

Reuters (2009, November 20). *Somalia to join child rights pact: UN.* Available at http://af. reuters.com/article/topNews/idAFJOE5AJ0IT20091120 (Accessed November 30, 2009).

Roberts, D. (2002). *Shattered bonds: The color of child welfare.* New York: Basic Books.

Sedlak, A. J. (2001). *A history of the National incidence study of child abuse and neglect.* Available at https://www.nis4.org/NIS_History.pdf (Available February 27, 2009).

Sedlak, A. J. & Broadhurst, D. D. (1996). *Executive summary of the third National Incidence Study of Child Abuse and Neglect.* Available at http://www.childwelfare.gov/pubs/ statsinfo/nis3.cfm (Accessed February 27, 2009).

Scarr, S. & Eisenberg, M. (1993). Child care research: Issues, perspectives, and results. *Annual Review of Psychology.* 44: 613–644.

Sonty, N. (1992). A multimodal approach to prevention: A review of India's Integrated Child Development Scheme, in Albee, G.W., Bond, L.A., & Cook Monsey, T.V. (Eds.) *Improving children's lives*. Newbury Park: Sage Publications, Inc, pp. 191–199.

St. George, D. & Dvorak, P. (2008, Dec. 29). Child neglect cases multiply as economic woes spread: Lost jobs and homes exacerbate family stress across region. *Washington Post*, B01.

Staller, K. M. (2008). Children's Rights. In: Mizrahi T. & Davis L.E. (Eds) *Encyclopedia of Social Work Volume I*, (20th ed.). Washington, D.C.: National Association of Social Workers, pp. 265–268.

Trocmé, N., MacLaurin, B., Fallon, B., et al. (2001). *Canadian incidence study of reported child abuse and neglect: Final Report*. Ottawa, Ontario: Minister of Public Works and Government Services Canada.

United Nations Children's Fund [UNICEF] (2008, August). *Convention on the Rights of the Child*. Available at http://www.unicef.org/crc/index_30160.html (Accessed May 3, 2009).

United Nations Children's Fund [UNICEF] (2009, November). *UNICEF and partners commemorate 20 years of Convention on the Rights of the Child*. Available at http://www.unicef.org/policyanalysis/index_51872.html (Accessed November 30, 2009).

U.S. Department of Health and Human Services, Administration on Children, Youth and Families [US DHHS] (2008). *The AFCARS report: Preliminary FY 2006 Estimates as of January 2008*. Available at http://www.acf.hhs.gov/programs/cb/stats_research/afcars/tar/report14.pdf

U.S. Department of Health and Human Services, Administration on Children, Youth and Families [US DHHS]. (2009). *Child Maltreatment 2007* (Washington, DC: U.S. Government Printing Office, 2009).

Waldfogel, J. (1998). *The future of child protection: How to break the cycle of abuse and neglect*. Cambridge: Harvard University Press.

Westat (n.d.) *NIS-4 Description*. Available at https://www.nis4.org/nis4.asp (Accessed March 3, 2009).

Westat, Xtria, & The CDM Group, Inc. (2003). *Head Start FACES 2000: A whole-child perspective on program performance*. Available at http://www.acf.hhs.gov/programs/opre/hs/faces/reports/faces00_4thprogress/faces00_4thprogress.pdf (Accessed February 27, 2009).

Wulczyn, F., Barth, R., Yuang, Y., Jones Harden, B. & Landsverk, J. (2005). *Beyond common sense: Child welfare, child well-being, and the evidence for policy reform*. New Brunswick, NJ: Aldine Transaction.

Wulczyn, F. (1994). Status at birth and infant foster care placement in New York City, in R.P. Barth, J.D. Berrick & N. Gilbert (Eds.) *Child Welfare Research Review*. New York City: Columbia University Press, pp. 146–184.

Youth Transitions Funders Group (2009). *Overview*. Available at http://www.ytfg.org/about_mission.html (Accessed April 18, 2009).

Yan, M. C., Lauer, S., & Sin, R. (2009). Issues in community rebuilding: The task of settlement houses in two cities. *Social Development Issue*,. 3131(1): 39–54.

3

Productive Aging and Social Development

NANCY GIUNTA

The aging of the worldwide population has associated demographic, economic, and sociocultural implications. Over the next several decades, the population will continue to be comprised of increasingly larger proportions of older adults. Although they have benefited from various policies and programs, older adults and their caregivers are still at risk of income insecurity, isolation, and unmet health and social service needs. Many traditional social work approaches in the field of aging have consisted of disparate interventions addressing individual needs without considering the larger social, physical, or economic context of an aging society. Moreover, traditional approaches neglect to recognize potential strengths and resources older adults may offer society.

The concept of productive aging provides a framework for discussing social work interventions that may utilize tactics similar to those in the area of social development to capitalize on the strengths and resources of older adults. The term *productive aging*, coined by Butler in 1982, has been more recently defined by Caro, Bass and Chen (1993) as "any activity by an older individual that produces goods or services, or develops the capacity to produce them whether they are paid or not" (p. 6). Recent theoretical contributions to the concept of productive aging have recognized that productivity may be defined not only as the economic value of an individual's actions, but also in terms of social or civic contributions (Kaye, 2005). As the demographic shift of an aging population occurs, accepting a broader definition of productive aging and implementing innovative interventions that embrace a social development approach will have much to offer.

This chapter discusses several innovative approaches to gerontological social work that parallel the tactics used in social development. It begins by providing a demographic, economic, and sociocultural context of aging in the United States and other developed countries. Next, the concept of productive aging is described and used as a framework to discuss conventional social work interventions designed to address issues related to older adults. Then, the framework is used to present current innovations in gerontological social work that promote productive aging. Four areas of gerontological social work are highlighted: employment and retirement; volunteerism and civic engagement; informal caregiving; and investment in local, cross-sector planning and collaborative community development. Finally, implications and future directions for practice, research, and education in gerontological social work are suggested.

An Aging World

There is no doubt that the global population is aging. Decreased fertility and mortality rates, particularly in developed countries, have led to the global phenomenon of an aging population. In developed regions of the world, 15.5% of the population is age 65 years or older and this figure is projected to grow at a rate of 2.6% per year (United Nations, 2007). In the United States, one in eight Americans was over age 65 years in 2000, and by 2030, the projection is one in five. By 2050 in the United States, there will be three times the number of people over age 60 years than children below age 4 years (Roszak, 2001). In developing regions of the world, the proportion of older adults in the population is expected to double by mid-century from 8% to nearly 20% (United Nations, 2007). This rapid growth is cause for concern because social and economic infrastructures may not have sufficient time to address changing needs.

In addition to the growing size of the older adult population, the ethnic and racial diversity of older adults of all ages is increasing. The United States Census Bureau projects current ethnic and racial minorities to reach majority status by 2042, with substantial growth among Hispanic and Asian populations (U.S. Census Bureau, 2008). In 1990, older adults of color represented 13% of the U.S. population over age 65 years. In 2000 this proportion increased to 17%, and by 2050, older adults of color are expected to account for 35% of the older adult population. During the first half of the 21st century, it is expected that among older adults of color, the Latino population will triple from 5% to 16%, comprising the largest group among ethnic/racial minorities (Himes, 2002). European countries are facing their lowest fertility rates in history, leading to shrinking native populations with a rapidly increasing median age (Muenz, 2007). In the United Kingdom, the proportion of minority ethnic groups is growing (Harrop & Jopling, 2009).

This relatively rapid growth in the absolute numbers, proportion, and diversity of older adults in the population has economic and social implications not only for older adults themselves but also for the field of social welfare, as current social policies are not designed to meet the needs of older adults. Indeed, the looming retirement of the 76 million Baby Boomers, the first of whom turn age 65 years in the year 2011, brings the issue of aging and social development to the forefront of gerontological social work research, policy, and practice.

Although older adults have benefited from policies and programs, resulting in lower rates of poverty and disability, economic disparities prevail. Women, racial or ethnic minorities, and immigrants are more likely to live in poverty or not have access to public pension benefits. Opportunities for older adults to participate in the workforce are limited, placing economic risk on older adults who cannot afford to retire (Toder et al., 2008). Similarly, opportunities for full-time workers to phase into retirement by scaling back to part-time work with the same employer are rare (Hutchens & Martin, 2006). Coupled with limited employment or partial retirement opportunities for older workers, the ratio of number of workers for every retired person is expected to fall from 3.2 to 2.2 between 2010 and 2030 (Toder et al., 2008). In the United States, for example, it is projected that the Social Security system will begin paying out more in benefits than it collects in tax revenue by as early as 2017 (or as late as 2041).

There is substantial evidence that economic disparity has an adverse impact on health among older adults (Bowen & Gonzalez, 2008; Brown & Prus, 2003; Subramanian & Kawachi, 2006). Dunlop and colleagues (2002) identified significant gender and ethnic/racial disparities in health care and dental service utilization among Medicare beneficiaries. Their findings suggest that although gender and ethnic disparities are influenced by economic access in dental care utilization, economic access does not account for all gender and ethnic/racial disparities in health-care use (Dunlop et al., 2002). This suggests the need to explore factors related to the sociocultural context of health among older adults.

In social and cultural terms, older adults face an increased risk of isolation and dependency. Indeed, one of the predictors of institutionalization is whether an older adult has access to family or friends for informal assistance. Compared with Scandinavian countries, older adults in the United States rely more heavily on informal networks for support in the home than formal assistance (Davey et al., 2005). Family members and friends providing informal care to older adults are also at risk of decreased physical, mental, and financial well-being. The risk is compounded for ethnic and racial minorities in the United States, perhaps by cultural norms surrounding familial obligation and use of formal assistance for elder care (Scharlach et al., 2008; Scharlach et al., 2006).

Social workers can play a key role in assisting older adults and their families with accessing needed services. However, there continues to be a significant shortage of social workers in the field of gerontology. This shortage may be exacerbated by the medicalization of aging, where the workforce serving older adults places less emphasis on social needs and more emphasis on medical models of care or crisis intervention, both of which take a paternalistic approach. Although social workers are obviously needed to provide these services, they fail to meet the wider needs of older adults and indeed those of an aging society. In addition, institutionally based services in the form of assisted living and nursing home care is still favored by public funding when community-based care is urgently needed. If public funding were redistributed away from institutional care and toward community-based services, many elderly people in institutional care could live and receive support in their homes. Such redistribution has begun in a small number of U.S. states under the label of rebalancing long-term care financing. A developmental perspective can help support productive aging and further the efforts of rebalancing long-term care financing through advocacy work. As noted in Chapter 1, social work needs to transcend its conventional and limited remedial role and adopt a developmental perspective that recognizes the resiliency and strengths of clients and facilitates their integration into the community. The concept of productive aging is highly compatible with the developmental social work approach and can inform a renewed commitment by the profession to improve the lives of older adults today.

Incorporating a productive aging perspective into social work practice considers the value orientation of older adults in society and reconsiders the concepts of dependency and assistance, especially across cultures. Older adults and their caregivers may offer valuable informal exchanges that could be considered "productive" in a broad sense. In an effort to contribute to what she refers to as the largely atheoretical concept of successful aging across cultures, Torres (1999) presents a theoretical framework that incorporates value orientation of older adults to further understand productive aging within culturally relevant contexts. Cultural differences in placing value on the contribution of elders themselves and the status gained by providing care offers positive implications to the role of older adults in an aging population. The question now becomes: What are the implications to the field of social welfare, particularly in addressing the need to support productive aging within the economic and sociocultural context of an aging population?

Historical Context of Productive Aging

As Achenbaum (2001) eloquently noted, despite the fact that the term *productive aging* has only recently been introduced to the gerontological literature, older adults have been compelled to remain productive for most of history. This section discusses the development of the concept of productive aging by briefly presenting how older adults became viewed as not productive. Then, productive aging is explored through its conception among conventional social work approaches.

Throughout history, the perceived value of older adults in society has varied. Achenbaum described the perception of older adults as indispensable in offering "a lifetime of experience" (p. 10) and knowledge about longevity, virtue, and productivity. During the industrial revolution, older adults were viewed as less able to perform the demanding physical labor necessary for production. Early social policies in the United States, such as Social Security, were introduced with this worldview. Indeed, the life expectancy of citizens in the United States at the time was only about 59 years for men and 63 years for women. Since then, as life expectancy has increased (as did the occurrence of both public and private pension benefits), the experience of retirement from the workforce has become more commonplace. Workers are expected to leave the workforce altogether when reaching the somewhat arbitrarily defined retirement age of 65 years.

After World War II, as a result of advances in medical technology, life expectancy began to rise more rapidly, causing more people to survive beyond retirement age. During these post-war years, an unprecedented baby boom continued from 1946 until 1964. This created a large cohort, the "Baby Boomers," who essentially changed how public and private programs negotiated every stage of the life course: more hospital beds were needed as they were born; more primary and secondary schools were needed as they were educated; increasing demand and competition for higher education led to significant growth in that sector; and finally, as young adults, the Baby Boomers had significant influence on the labor and housing markets. Social movements such as the Civil Rights and anti-war movements had historical significance because of this cohort. Today, as the Baby Boomers are reaching retirement age and expected to live well beyond it, they are faced with redefining yet a new stage of the life course. Coupled with the increases in longevity, a decrease in fertility following the baby boom in the second half of the 20th century has brought about the phenomenon of our population aging.

The decrease in fertility that followed the mid-century baby boom was not only a trend in the United States. Population aging is indeed a worldwide trend. Many developed nations, particularly in the European Union and Japan, are faced with similar trends of the aging Baby Boom generation compounded by increasing longevity and decreasing fertility rates (Zaidi, 2008). Developing countries are similarly faced with demographic challenges and opportunities resulting from the rapid growth of aging populations, but what differs in these countries is that the majority of older adults live in rural areas. In developed countries, the majority of older adults live in urban areas.

Traditionally, old age has been viewed as a stage of life in which people become increasingly dependent and burdensome on industrial and post-industrial society. In 1965, the Older Americans Act, Medicare, and Medicaid were introduced in the United States to address the economic, social, and medical needs of the elderly. By the end of the 20th century, the age-based social policies introduced throughout the century were attributed to increased health and decreased poverty rates among older adults. More recently, however, increasing disparities in well-being among older adults has raised questions of whether policies and programs should be more targeted based on need.

Also in the 1960s, gerontologists began to recognize the value of the knowledge and experience older workers brought to the labor market (Riley & Foner, 1968, cited in Achenbaum, 2001). Nearly two decades later, the term *productive aging* surfaced in the literature when it was coined by Dr. Robert Butler, the first director of the National Institute of Aging. Following the introduction of this term, empirical evidence increasingly showed that older adults were contributing to the welfare of their families and communities well into old age and that older workers were breaking stereotypes with the emerging evidence that regarded them as more loyal, productive, and reliable than their younger counterparts.

Since the 1980s, the literature on productive aging has flourished and similar concepts surrounding productive aging have been introduced, all suggesting more positive contributions or experiences of older adults. The term *successful aging*, introduced by Rowe and Kahn (1987) suggested that it is possible for older adults to be free from disease and have higher levels of cognitive and physical functioning. Although both "successful" and "productive" aging capture a positive experience of later life, the former emphasizes individual psychological and physiological indicators, and the latter encompasses the interaction between the older adult and society. At the same time, evidence has clearly shown that older adults with decreased social engagement face a higher risk of cognitive decline than their more socially integrated counterparts, thus supporting the need for interventions designed to promote some concept of "productive" or "successful" aging (Bassuk, Glass, & Berkman, 1999; Fried et al., 2004; Fratiglioni et al., 2000).

The concept of productive aging began to gain traction in the field of gerontological social work within a broader context of a growing independent living movement described by Knapp and Midgley in Chapter 5. Also within the context of social policy, devolution of federal policy to the state level was underway. This helped fuel a paradigm shift in the fields of social gerontology and social work and helped introduce approaches to tap resources of the older adult population, particularly around supporting post-retirement employment and caregiver support. More recently, interventions designed to engage older adults to help build social and human capital within communities have been introduced.

Hooyman (2005) aptly relates the concept of productive aging as an inherent context for social exchange theory in that various strengths and resources are exchanged across generations. Additionally, old age brings with it the opportunity for people to reconstruct the traditional experience of aging and retirement (Hooyman, 2005). Older adults have the capacity to help build a community's social and economic capital through various means outside of the traditional labor market. Within the field of gerontological social work, tactics for promoting productive aging are similar to those of social development. Social development and investment through promotion of productive aging may help us capitalize on the valuable contributions older adults can potentially make to the social capital of a community.

Estes and Mahakian (2001) critique the concept of productive aging from the perspective of critical theory and the political economy of aging. As they and others point out, economic status as well as race, ethnicity, and gender all have an overriding impact on the aging experience, and perhaps the term *productive aging* refers to placing a purely economic, albeit uncompensated, value on the contributions during this stage of the life course. They note that informal caregivers are a particularly vulnerable population, providing unpaid labor being labeled as "productive." As discussed further in the remaining sections of this chapter, a social investment approach may help us redefine the concept of productive aging and steer it away from its economic roots, eliminating barriers to productivity through various mechanisms such as leadership development, among others.

Indeed, growth in the support of productive aging can be illustrated with examples ranging from informal arrangements within support networks to more formal and institutionalized policies. In the next section of this chapter, four examples are presented to illustrate the intersection of productive aging and social investment. These examples are drawn from the following areas of gerontological social work: employment and retirement; volunteerism and civic engagement; informal caregiver support; and multidisciplinary investment for "age-friendly" communities.

Productive Aging, Social Work, and Social Investment

The Madrid International Plan of Action on Ageing (MIPPA) was published in 2002 as an effort to assist countries worldwide in collaboration around addressing issues related to an aging population. The United Nations Principles for Older Persons carried the Madrid Plan further by presenting specific principles for governments to incorporate into public policy, grouped into the following five general areas: independence, participation, care, self-fulfillment, and dignity.

The principles of independence suggest, among other things, that older adults should have the right to participate in and retire from the labor force at their own discretion and have access to appropriate training and education to do so. In the United States, the 1978 Age Discrimination in Employment Act limited mandatory retirement in most jobs; however, in other countries, mandatory retirement prevails. The principles related to participation suggest that older adults have the right to be active in their community through civic engagement and volunteer opportunities and have the right to participate in planning policy that directly affects their lives. In the area of care, the United Nations principles support that older adults have the right to informal and formal means of care in the community and institutionally in a way that respects dignity and cultural norms. This also suggests that family caregivers be supported in their role in providing unpaid care to family members in need. Finally, the principles of self-fulfillment and dignity support older adults' rights to access spiritual, recreational, or cultural activities and to be free from abuse or other unfair treatment based on age.

Four areas in which productive aging is supported are discussed in this section. Each of these areas demonstrates how the Madrid Plan and the U.N. principles may be implemented through macro-social work practice. The four areas in which productive aging is supported include: employment and retirement initiatives; volunteerism and civic engagement; long-term caregiving; and local, cross-sector planning and collaborative community development.

Employment and Retirement Initiatives

There is a growing body of research on the employment needs of Baby Boomers. We know that most intend to work in some capacity. Although they plan to work well into retirement age, they are doing so for different reasons. Those facing vulnerable economic situations must remain in the labor market, whereas others choose employment to satisfy emotional or intellectual needs. The decreased value of private 401(K) plans and other retirement investments during economic recessions often cause older adults to postpone retirement plans. This problem is particularly acute in the current recession, as the value of investments has fallen rapidly. The current economic recession has also put older workers at risk of unemployment because of increased likelihood of cutbacks by employers. Three trends among initiatives that support productive aging within the context of employment and retirement include: the reconceptualization of the traditional retirement experience, support for the economic security of the Baby Boomers, and recognizing the needs of an intergenerational workplace.

The experience of retirement will no doubt be reshaped by the Baby Boomers just as they have redefined nearly all stages of the life course. Freedman's (2008) popular book, *Encore: Finding Work that Matters in the Second Half of Life*, presents alternatives to the traditional concept of retirement by describing the concept of the "encore" career. Despite the target audience of this book seemingly being the less economically vulnerable than the usual focus of social work interventions, it is important to recognize that a diverse pool of older workers in the labor force is needed to protect national economic security. Older workers are contributing to the Social Security fund, their retirement savings remain in private investments, and if they all retired en masse, a significant labor shortage and decrease in investment funds would occur. Therefore, alternatives to traditional retirement are necessary (*see* Toder, 2008).

The New York Academy of Medicine (2008) has recently reported that more than three of four older adults in New York City identify employment opportunities as essential to their well being. One-third of older workers in the same sample have "little confidence" that they will have resources to live comfortably in retirement, and many are working past the age at which they had planned to retire. Civic Ventures is a nonprofit think tank and business incubator founded by Freedman to develop opportunities for older adults to combine social change with workforce participation. As described on their website and in their policy papers, their work aims to "define the second half of adult life as a time of individual and social renewal" (Civic Ventures, 2008) and "to engage millions of baby boomers as a vital workforce for social change" (Greenya & Golin, 2008). Civic Ventures administers several initiatives promoting workforce participation, volunteering, and civic engagement.

Three examples of programs that engage a diverse population of older workers to contribute to community well-being are the Senior Community Service Employment Program (SCSEP), the Colorado Experience Bank, and the ReServe program. The SCSEP is the oldest training and employment program for older workers in the country. Introduced by President John F. Kennedy and incorporated into the Older Americans Act in 1965, it enables low-income older adults to receive job skills training and stipends in exchange for work in the area of community service.

The Colorado Experience Bank is a website connecting job seekers and employers. Because it was implemented recently (May, 2008), evidence of its outcomes is not yet available. It is particularly noteworthy that the site was developed by Baby Boomers through a public/private partnership between the state of Colorado and private industry, which may make replication of the intervention feasible in other geographic regions.

The ReServe program serves two functions. Primarily, it provides retired older adults opportunities to work at nonprofit and public agencies in exchange for a fixed hourly stipend. Second, the program educates potential partner organizations about the benefits of hiring "ReServists." The ReServe program is one example of a collection of organizations recognized by Civic Ventures and the MetLife Foundation's BreakThrough Award for engaging adults over age 50 years in the workforce through the spirit of service.

Volunteerism and Civic Engagement

In addition to choosing more civically minded encore careers, some older adults are leaving the workforce to join the growing ranks of the retired. As discussed earlier in this chapter, the Baby Boomer generation is expected to change the traditional experience of retirement. Volunteering and civic engagement during retirement is becoming more popular as the Baby Boomer generation reaches retirement age. The body of evidence is growing that volunteering in late life is related to positive health outcomes that are sustained over the long term (Fried et al., 2004; Tan, et al., 2009). The Volunteerism Information and Coordination Center (VOICE) in Sri Lanka (2008) proposes a conceptual framework to link volunteerism with civic engagement and social mobilization. According to this framework, volunteering fosters empowerment among elders.

In addition to their workforce initiatives described above, Civic Ventures has initiated several programs to recognize and foster the experience older adults share with their communities through volunteer work and civic engagement. One initiative, the Purpose Prize, awards up to $100,000 to individuals identified as social innovators who create new programs to deal with complex challenges in their communities. In 2008, the award was given to, among many others, a retired language professor who developed a mentoring program for newly arrived immigrants in Fargo, North Dakota; a retired marketing executive who developed a program to reduce prison recidivism rates among young men; and a retired state government employee who helps African American farmers in the South participate in the growing green economy through the Greening of Black America initiative.

Other volunteer programs match older adults to specific volunteer roles in the community. Experience Corps, also supported by Civic Ventures, is an evidence-based program that places older adults in schools to tutor and mentor elementary school students. The program is offered in 23 cities throughout the United States. Programs supported by federal funds are administered by the Corporation for National and Community Service (CNCS) to support low-income volunteers.

Programs within the Corporation include the Retired Senior Volunteer Program and the National Senior Volunteer Corps.

Current literature on civic engagement and volunteering among older adults has been criticized for its focus on white, non-Latino elders, thus not promoting an understanding of the diverse population of older adults (Delgado, 2009). Hinterlong and Williamson (2006) warn that as expectations of productive aging through civic engagement become more common, some older adults may not have the resources to contribute in traditionally valued ways and thus may face being undervalued in society. Older adults of color historically have been excluded from civic participation and therefore face various barriers that limit their engagement. Such barriers can be as basic as lack of transportation options or as complex as structural oppression of communities of color. These barriers will need to be eliminated for civic engagement opportunities to be fully accessible to them.

Long-Term Caregiving

The majority of long-term care received by older adults in the United States is provided by unpaid family members or friends. Although this unpaid care saves significant public resources, it is not provided without substantial social costs. It is well-known that although caregivers provide much needed care for elders, they face financial, emotional, and physical health risks. They sometimes cut back on paid work or leave the workforce completely, pay for elder care-related costs out of their own pocket, and are often expected to meet multiple demands of caring for both elders and children or grandchildren. Many face isolation and burden, which leads to depression. Because most informal care is provided by women, caregiving is fundamentally a women's issue. A paradigm shift has begun in which informal caregivers are being recognized not only as valuable providers of long-term care services but also as clients in need of supportive services for themselves. In the United States, two federal policies have been introduced to support caregivers in the productive role they play in this scenario (Giunta & Scharlach, 2009).

The Family and Medical Leave Act (FMLA) of 1993 has provided employees of some companies unpaid leave to care for a child, spouse, or parent. Although well-intended, this national policy does not cover all workers, and it only provides unpaid leave, which many middle- or low-income caregivers cannot afford to take. Some states have introduced more generous policies that include paid family leave. The National Family Caregiver Support Program (NFCSP) was introduced in the United States in 2000 as an amendment to the Older Americans Act. The purpose of this entitlement is to provide five types of services to caregivers through a network of 56 State Units on Aging, 655 local Area Agencies on Aging (AAAs), and 243 Indian Tribal and Native Hawaiian Organizations (ITNHOs) nationwide. These five services are: information; assistance with access; respite; education, counseling, and support groups; and supplemental services. Caregivers of all income levels are eligible for services if they are providing care to someone over age 60 years. People age 55 years and older who provide care to children are also eligible for support services under the National Family Caregiver Support Program. Individuals with greatest social or economic need receive priority in planning programs.

Although much has been achieved, it is clear that more resources will be needed if older adults with health and related needs are to be supported in the community. As shown in Chapter 1, developmental social work avoids the use of residential services whenever possible and is committed to community-based care. The costs of residential care are prohibitive, but providing proper community care also requires financial and other resources. Nevertheless, it is a worthwhile investment if older adults are to live in their homes and participate fully in the life of the community.

Cross-Sector Planning Efforts

A fourth area in the field of aging parallels the strategies of the social investment approach. Support for local cross-sector planning has been used in an effort to improve community "age-friendliness" and to promote opportunities for healthy aging. Such collaborative efforts are increasingly receiving attention in the United States as well as internationally, both in the academic literature and the popular media. Development initiatives of this type come under the purview of creating "elder-friendly" or "lifelong" communities (also called aging-friendly, communities for a lifetime, communities for life, and livable communities). The World Health Organization's Global Age-friendly Cities project recently released an active aging framework for cities to frame their planning efforts to prepare for the increasing proportions of older adults residing in cities worldwide (World Health Organization, 2007). The framework presents six determinants of active aging: social, economic, health and social services, behavioral, personal, and the physical environment. Thirty-five cities have joined the Global Age-friendly Cities project to analyze their community needs by using the active aging framework, which diverges from traditional city planning approaches of identifying needs and incorporates more of a social justice approach by identifying rights and opportunities for maintaining health. The Age-friendly project also supports the developmental goal of ensuring that older adults are able to live in their communities and become an integral part of these communities.

At a more local level, community development initiatives vary in their methods but likely include the creation of local partnerships to meet the long-term care needs of the rapidly growing older adult populations. Similarly to social investment strategies, these efforts are multidisciplinary and inclusionary in practice. Two particularly noteworthy initiatives in the United States are the Robert Wood Johnson Foundation's Community Partnerships for Older Adults (CPFOA) Program and the AdvantAge Initiative, developed by the Center for Homecare Policy and Research.

The Community Partnerships for Older Adults Program provides support for communities to decide together how best to meet the needs of the older adult population. Sixteen multidisciplinary community partnerships have received funding to develop and implement individualized strategic plans consisting of innovative solutions to help older adults live full, rich lives. The partnerships funded by this initiative primarily address fragmentation of health and social service systems, pilot innovative initiatives, and strengthen local cross-sector networks. In Atlanta, GA, local aging service planners and providers have worked with older adults to spearhead a successful effort to change housing and zoning laws across the region to incorporate mixed housing types and services within neighborhoods where older adults live. Collaboration with urban and regional planners and policymakers has aided the success of this effort. In Maui, HI, one of the objectives of the Community Partnership Program was to prevent nursing home placement of the island's *kupuna* (elderly) by retrofitting their houses. Through collaborative work with aging service planners and providers and the local high school's building and trades program, high school students learn home improvement skills while making elders' houses more accessible. Research into this program shows that it is cost-effective and has reduced nursing home utilization (Pang, 2007). The partnership in Milwaukee, WI, brought together 125 partnership members from diverse organizations, including corporate, labor unions, older adults, and aging service providers and planners in an effort to identify community assets to help older adults stay connected to their neighborhoods and receive the support they need. This partnership, known as "Connecting Caring Communities," implemented several successful neighborhood-based programs to increase safety, reduce isolation among older residents, and provide information about existing services.

The AdvantAge approach is participatory and data-driven. Each community conducts a survey with a representative sample of its members to assess its "age-friendliness" using the AdvantAge framework. Community members decide how to utilize the survey results to make their community more supportive for older adults. The framework was initiated at a local level and most recently has been adapted to state-level planning in the United States. The first state to utilize this strategy was Indiana.

An international collaborative endeavor designed to support elder-friendly community development known as the Elder Friendly Communities Program (EFCP) was launched in Alberta, Canada and simultaneously in Southern Australia. This program was initiated by a partnership between the City of Calgary and faculty at the University of Calgary School of Social Work in 2000 as a demonstration project (Austin et al., 2005). It was then replicated by the University of South Australia's School of Social Work and Policy. The project, similar to the AdvantAge initiative, conducts an assessment of the community from a representative sample of its members and then presents the data to the community for interpretation and planning purposes. Community members then decide on priority areas on which to act.

Other approaches not discussed in this chapter but worthy of mention are the human capital investment programs that include service learning, community college or other "lifelong learning" initiatives, and educational travel such as the Elder Hostel and Road Scholar programs. Although the community college initiatives are beginning to address the need for elder employment, other lifelong learning initiatives have targeted the upper socio-economic categories.

The Role of Social Work

Similarly to the trends described in other chapters in this book, the fields of gerontology and social work seemed to become less connected during the 1980s and 1990s as services for older adults became increasingly medicalized and privatized. Particularly missing from gerontological social work is community development and social investment programs that solicit elder participation. The 21st century brings opportunities to reconnect social work and the wider field of gerontology. Morrow-Howell and her colleagues (2004) discuss the need to move the social development and aging research agenda from focusing on the individual to focusing on the interactions between social institutions and the individuals who are affected by them. Hooyman (2005) and others argue that programs and policies are needed to help shape institutional and structural factors that facilitate opportunities for older adults to engage in productive activities.

Drawing on the practice illustrations discussed in this chapter, the role of social work can be viewed at both the micro- and macro-levels. Conducting an assessment of informal caregivers while determining the needs of their elder care recipients acknowledges the productive role that caregivers assume in the provision of long-term care. This assessment may lead to supportive programs to sustain caregiver health.

To re-envision retirement and possibly design policies that support productive aging, further understanding of the motivation behind volunteering and civic engagement is needed, as is a method for better tapping the strengths that older adults bring to their communities. Whereas Mutchler, Burr, and Caro (2003) developed a measure of motivation for productive activity among older people, Kivnick and Murray (2001) presented an interview guide for assessing strengths of older adults. Social workers may find these helpful to assist older adults in defining encore careers or in developing meaningful volunteer and other civic activities.

Social workers practicing at the macro-level can utilize community organization and policy planning to increase civic engagement and facilitate cross-sector planning that solicits input from a variety of organizations and older adults. Cross-sector partnerships in community development initiatives will create opportunities for healthy aging and minimize the economic, social, and physical health risks currently faced by older adults in their communities. The increased popularity of community organizing caused by the recent election of a former community organizer to the United States presidency may provide increased opportunities for older adults to have a stronger voice in local and regional planning efforts that affect their daily lives.

Finally, the inclusion of culturally sensitive social investment and gerontological content in social work educational programs is necessary to promote productive aging and social development among racially and ethnically diverse elders. Although they did not target gerontological social workers, Yee, Wong, and Janczur (2006) examined organizational and individual barriers experienced by visible minority social workers within predominantly white social service agencies. Their research findings resulted in a series of recommendations to make agencies more culturally sensitive to employees of color, thus promoting an anti-racist strategy for serving clients. Such a strategy should be considered in the recruitment of social workers who serve communities of color (Yee & Wong, 2006). The Hartford Foundation's Gerontological Social Work initiative is an excellent illustration of efforts to build awareness and interest of gerontology in curricula of schools of social work (Hooyman, 2005). Since 1999, the multipronged Gerontological Social Work initiative has funded programs to train faculty, support doctoral student research, increase gerontological content in social work graduate curricula, and fund student stipends for field placements that introduce social work students to the field of aging.

Throughout this chapter, four areas of gerontological social work have been discussed using productive aging as a framework: employment and retirement; volunteerism and civic engagement; informal caregiving; and investment in local, cross-sector planning and collaborative community development. Social workers can play a major role in promoting social investment through micro- and macro-level gerontological initiatives that support older adults in each of these productive endeavors. To that end, social workers can help alleviate significant challenges and create great opportunities for an aging global population.

REFERENCES

Achenbaum, A. (1978). *Old Age in the New Land: The American Experience since 1790.* Baltimore, MD: Johns Hopkins University Press.

Achenbaum, A. (2001). Productive aging in historical perspective, in Morrow-Howell, Hinterlong, J. & Sherraden, M. (Eds.) *Productive Aging: Concepts and Challenges.* Baltimore, MD: Johns Hopkins University Press.

Austin, C., Des Camp, E., Flux, D., McClelland, R.W., & Sieppert, J. (2005). Community development with older adults in their neighborhoods: The Elder Friendly Communities program. *Families in Society*, 86(3): 401–409.

Caro, F. G., Bass, S. A., & Chen, Y. P. (1993). Introduction: Achieving a productive aging society, in S. A. Bass, F. G. Caro, & Y. P. Chen (Eds.) *Achieving a productive aging society*. Westport, CT: Auburn House, pp. 3–26.

Civic Ventures (2008). Available at http://www.civicventures.org. (Accessed October 15, 2008).

Bassuk, S. S., Glass T. A., & Berkman, L. F. (1999). Social disengagement and incident cognitive decline in community-dwelling elderly persons. *Annals of Internal Medicine*, 131: 165–173.

Bowen, M. E. & Gonzalez, H. M. (2008). Racial/Ethnic differences in the relationship between the use of health care services and functional disability: The Health and Retirement Study (1992-2004). *The Gerontologist*, 48: 659–667.

Brown, R. L. & Prus, S. G. (2003). Social transfers and income inequality, in old-age: A multi-national perspective. *Social and Economic Dimensions of an Aging Population Ontario.* Canada: (SEDAP).

Davey, A., Femia, E., Zarit, S., Shea, D., Sundstrom, G., Berg, S., Smyer, M., & Savla, J. (2005). Life on the Edge: Patterns of Formal and Informal Help to Older Adults in the United States and Sweden. *The Journals of Gerontology Series B: Psychological Sciences and Social Sciences,* 60: S281–S288.

Delgado, M. (2009). *Older Adult-Led Health Promotion in Urban Communities.* Lanham, MD: Rowman & Littlefield.

Dunlop, D. D., Manheim, L. M., Song, J., & Chang, R. W. (2002). Gender and ethnic/racial disparities in health care utilization among older adults. *Journal of Gerontology B Psychological Science, Social Science,* 57: S221–233.

Estes, C. & Mahakian, J. (2001). The political economy of productive aging, in N. Morrow-Howell, J. Hinterlong, & M. Sherraden, (Eds.) *Productive Aging: Concepts and Challenges.* Baltimore, MD: The Johns Hopkins University Press, pp. 197–213.

Fratiglioni, L., Wang, H., Ericsson, K., Maytan, M., & Winblad, B. (2000). Influence of social network on occurrence of dementia: A community-based longitudinal study. *Lancet,* 355: 1315–1319.

Freedman, M. (2008). *Encore: Finding Work that Matters in the Second Half of Life.* New York: PublicAffairs Press.

Fried, L. P., Carlson, M. C., Freedman, M., et al. (2004). A social model for health promotion for an aging population: Initial evidence on the Experience Corps model. *Journal of Urban Health,* 81: 64–78.

Giunta, N. & Scharlach, A. (2009). Caregiver services: Variations across states, in Qualls, S. & Zarit, S. (Eds.) *Aging Families and Caregiving: A Clinician's Guide to Research, Practice, and Technology.* Hoboken, NJ: Wiley Publishing.

Greenya, J. & Golin, I. (2008). *Building an Experience Dividend: State Governments Lead the Call to Engage Older Workers.* San Francisco, CA: Civic Ventures Policy Series.

Harrop, A. & Jopling, K. (2009). *One Voice: Shaping our Ageing Society.* London: Age Concern and Help the Aged.

Himes, C. L. (2002). Elderly Americans. *Population Bulletin,* 56(4): 1–40.

Hinterlong, J. & Williamson, A. (2006-07). The effects of civic engagement by current and future cohorts of older adults. *Generations,* XXX(4): 1–18.

Hooyman, N. (2005). Conceptualizing Productive Aging. *Perspectives on Productive Aging: Social Work with the New Aged.* Washington, DC: NASW Press, pp. 37–57.

Hutchens, R. & Grace-Martin, K. (2006). Employer willingness to permit phased retirement: Why are some more willing than others. *Industrial and Labor Relations Review,* 59(4): 525–546.

Kaye, L. (2005). The emergence of the new aged and a productive aging perspective. In L. Kaye (Ed.) *Perspectives on Productive Aging: Social Work with the New Aged.* Washington, DC: NASW Press, pp. 3–18.

Kivnick, H.Q. & Murray, S.V. (2001). Life strengths interview guide: Assessing elder clients' strengths. *Journal of Gerontological Social Work,* 34(4): 7–32.

Morrow-Howell, N., Sherraden, M., McBride, A., Hinterlong, J., Rozario, P., & Tang, F. (2004). *An Agenda for Productive Aging Research, Policy, and Practice.* St. Louis: Center for Social Development.

Muenz, R. (2007). *Aging and Demographic Change in Europe.* 2nd OECD Forum on Statistics, Knowledge, and Policy. Istanbul: June 28.

Mutchler, J. E., Burr, J. A., & Caro, F. G. (2003). From paid worker to volunteer: Leaving the paid workforce and volunteering in later life. *Soc Forces*, 81: 1267–1293.

New York Academy of Medicine (2008). *Toward an Age-Friendly New York City: A Findings Report.* New York: Author.

Pang, L. (2007). Cost Benefit considerations of preventing elderly falls through environmental modifications to homes in Hana, Maui. Paper presented at the Pacific Global Health Conference, Honolulu, HI.

Roszak, T. (2001). *Longevity Revolution: As Boomers Become Elders.* Berkeley, CA: Berkeley Hills Books.

Rowe J. W., Kahn R. L. (1987). Human ageing: Usual and successful. *Science, 237* (4811): 143–9.

Scharlach, A., Giunta, N., Chow, J., & Lehning, A. (2008). Racial and ethnic variations in caregiver service use. *Journal of Aging and Health*, 20(3): 326–346.

Scharlach, A., Kellam, R., Ong, N., Baskin, A., Goldstein, C., & Fox, P. (2006). Cultural attitudes and caregiver service use: Lessons from focus groups with racially and ethnically diverse family caregivers. *Journal of Gerontological Social Work*, 47: 133–156.

Subramanian, S. V., & Kawachi, I. (2006). Whose health is affected by income inequality? A multilevel interaction analysis of contemporaneous and lagged effects of state income inequality on individual self-rated health in the United States. *Health & Place*, 12(2): 141–156.

Tan, E., Rebok, G.W., Yu, Q., et al. (2009). The long-term relationship between high-intensity volunteering and physical activity in older African American women. *Journal of Gerontology: Social Sciences*, 64B(2): 304–311.

Toder, E. J., Johnson, R. W., Mermin, G. B., Lei, S. (2008). *Capitalizing on the Economic Value of Older Adults' Work: An Urban Institute Roundtable.* Washington, D.C.: Urban Institute.

Torres, S. (1999). A culturally-relevant theoretical framework for the study of successful ageing. *Ageing and Society*, 19: 33–51.

United Nations Department of Economic and Social Affairs (2007). *World Population Ageing* 1950–2050.

U.S. Census Bureau (2008). *An Older and More Diverse Nation by Midcentury.* U.S. Census Bureau News. Released August 14, 2008. Available at http://www.census.gov/ Press-Release/www/releases/archives/population/012496.html. (Accessed April 11, 2009).

Volunteerism Information and Coordination Center (2008). *Volunteerism in an ageing society: Linking social mobilization, civic engagement, and inter-generational solidarity.* Policy brief. Sri Lanka: Author.

World Health Organization (2007). *Global age-friendly cities: A guide.* Geneva: Author.

Yee, J. Y., Wong, H., & Janczur, A. (2006). *Examining Systemic and Individual Barriers Experienced by Visible Minority Social Workers in Mainstream Social Service Agencies.* Research Report, Toronto: Access Alliance Multicultural Community Health Centre.

Zaidi, A. (2008). *Features and Challenges of Population Ageing: The European Perspective.* Vienna: European Centre for Social Welfare Policy and Research.

4

Social Investment and Mental Health

The Role of Social Enterprise

MARY AGER CAPLAN

We are on the horizon of a new paradigm in the conceptualization, discourse, and treatment of mental health, and it centers on one word: recovery. Sparked by the advocacy of mental health consumers and grounded in the concepts of hope, relationship, meaningful activity, empowerment, self-determination, and education, recovery has become the buzzword in psychiatric and community mental health social work across the globe. Public mental health systems in the United States now actively focus efforts to transform policies and practices to become more recovery-oriented, and the United State's most influential consortium of mental health practitioners has as its primary goal the creation of a national mental health system in which recovery is fundamental (President's New Freedom Commission, 2003).

Whereas conventional social work approaches to mental health treatment tend toward individually based therapy and case management of there is growing evidence that an investment approach can be more effective at improving the quality of life for people who suffer from mental illness. The social investment approach to mental health social work practice provides opportunities for social inclusion for some of the most marginalized people in society, working with them to overcome the experiences of isolation and stigma that are often the most debilitating effects of mental illness. This chapter provides background on the nature and scope of mental illness, outlines conventional approaches to mental health care in the field of social work, highlights examples of the social investment approach, describes how emergent recovery-based services link with social investment approaches, and offers practical steps to integrate social investment into social work. In particular, the chapter highlights an innovative community mental health project known as

The Village, which incorporates the social enterprise approach as a central component to mental health services. This project not only embodies the social investment strategies discussed in the chapter but also has relevance for mental health policy in general.

The Nature and Scope of Mental Illness

What is "mental illness?" To succinctly define mental illness is challenging because there are a myriad of types of mental illnesses and a wide range in the severity and/or impairment of these conditions. In addition, the concept itself is subject to cultural construction and historical placement. In fact, the task is akin to defining "physical illness," as diagnoses, causes, and treatments can change wildly over time and place. For the purposes of this chapter, the definition from the *Dictionary of Social Work* published by the National Association of Social Workers will be used: "Impaired psychosocial or cognitive functioning due to disturbances in any one or more of the following processes: biological, chemical, physiological, genetic, psychological, or social" (Barker, 1999, p. 299). Of course, this definition is open to criticism. For example, it is unclear whether someone who is diagnosed with depression but not impaired in everyday life would be considered "mentally ill."

As with defining mental illness, it is essential to define its sister term, *mental health*, especially because the words are often incorrectly used interchangeably. There is an important distinction that points to a shifting paradigm in this field, one that focuses on strengths rather than weaknesses. Because there is no official definition of mental health, this chapter relies on one given by the World Health Organization, that it is: "a state of well-being in which every individual realizes his or her own potential, can cope with the normal stresses of life, can work productively and fruitfully, and [be] able to make a contribution to her or his community" (World Health Organization [WHO], 2009). According to this description, it is possible for a person to have a mental illness and experience mental health at the same time if they meet the above criteria.

Types of mental illnesses are generally categorized in three main groupings: mood disorders (such as depression or bipolar disorder), psychotic disorders (such as schizophrenia), and anxiety disorders (such as post-traumatic stress disorder; PTSD). There are numerous other conditions, such as personality disorders, mental retardation, and autism, that fall outside the main categories but can be disabling nonetheless. According to the Surgeon General's report (U.S. Department of Health and Human Services, 1999), half of people with a mental illness have two or more disorders, and these often include a substance abuse disorder.

Because of the variations of mental illnesses, it is not possible to identify a single cause, although efforts are made to categorize, understand, and develop etiologies of distinct mental illnesses. The "Diagnostic and Statistical Manual of Mental Disorder Criteria," the reference guide conventionally accepted as the authority on mental illness, outlines 374 mental disorders (American Psychiatric

Association [DSM-IV-TR], 2000). It provides detailed information on the causes, symptoms, prognosis, and statistics of particular mental health conditions and is used by psychiatrists, psychologists, social workers, and mental health counselors to assess someone seeking treatment. Every few years, the manual is updated, and the number of categorized mental disorders has risen nearly exponentially since the 1950s.

Mental illness is more widespread than is commonly understood. In the United States, the prevalence of mental illness is approximately 57.7 million people, or more than a quarter of the total population of people age 18 years and older (National Institute of Mental Health [NIMH], 2008). This, however, does not speak to severity or duration. For people with serious mental illness, it is estimated that the prevalence is 6% (NIMH, 2008). Impairment from mental illness is, in fact, the leading cause of disability in the United States and Canada for people ages 15 to 44 years, and 1.5% of people have a serious and persistent mental illness severe enough to need governmental disability support (U.S. Department of Health and Human Services, 1999).

In the United States, there are considerable disparities regarding mental health across ethnicities. People of color, generally speaking, have less access to mental health services, receive less services and services of poorer quality, and are inadequately represented in mental health research (U.S. Department of Health and Human Service, 2001). It is important to emphasize that the prevalence of mental illness is not drastically different between ethnic groups and that the disparities exist because of legacies of racism and discrimination, mistrust of the mental health system, and language, cultural, and communication barriers. Examples of these disparities include a suicide rate for Native American youth that is 50% higher than the national rate, greater risk for PTSD in refugees from Southeast Asian countries, higher rates of depression and anxiety for Latino youth than for other groups, and an overrepresentation of African Americans in populations that have higher rates of mental illness, such as the homeless, incarcerated, and youth in foster care (U.S. Department of Health and Human Services, 2001).

On a global level, the World Health Organization (WHO) asserts that the number of people affected by mental illness is estimated to be in the hundreds of millions and that there are 179 million people who suffer from depression and schizophrenia (WHO, 2009). The most recent WHO report, the Mental Health Atlas (2005), provides a survey of the most current information about global mental health issues, from policy to legislation to treatment capabilities. For example, only 62% of the 193 WHO member states have mental health policies, leaving nearly one-third of the world's population without a state-initiated mental health policy. This is notable because there is a strong association between state mental health policies and having other supports for people with mental illness, such as a state mental health programs, disability benefits, and community care facilities. Community care facilities exist for 83.3% of the world's population; however, in the African, Eastern Mediterranean, and Southeast Asian regions, only about half of countries have such facilities. Mental health legislation that ensures human rights of people with mental illness as well as regulations on care and facilities are present for only 69% of the world's population. Again, this differs by region, with European countries leading the pack (WHO, 2005). The disparities found in mental health infrastructure between various countries results in many people without support.

The disabling effects of mental illness can affect individuals in a multitude of ways, depending on the severity, duration, treatment, and the support structure of an individual. Unemployment, poverty, relationship issues, lack of housing, stigma and discrimination, and difficulty functioning in everyday life are just a few of the many common impairments that affect individuals and families. Communities are also affected by serious mental illness. Recently, as part of a law that was passed in the state of California to provide new funding to mental health systems, one community identified the top issues that resulted from untreated mental illness; these included homelessness, incarceration, and involuntary hospitalization (Berkeley Mental Health, 2005). The impact on societies in terms of "disease burden" (lost productivity caused by impairment from mental illness) is thought to be more than all cancers combined (NIMH, 2009). Moreover, it is argued that this disease burden on people of color in the United States is considerably worse than Whites because of disparities in access to and amount and quality of care (U.S. Department of Health and Human Services, 2001). But as with any discussion of disability, the question arises about which are more important contributors: environmental or individual factors. The Disability Rights Movement made great strides in identifying that the environment plays a significant role in causing impairment.

Over the past 25 years, the United States has experienced a growing focus on mental health like no other time in history. Mental health is no longer marginalized in comparison to other health concerns in the United States, as evidenced by the U.S. Surgeon General's report on Mental Health (U.S. Department of Health and Human Services, 1999) asserting that mental health is fundamental to overall health. Executive Order 13263 created the New Freedom Commission on Mental Health. This group was charged with addressing problems in the country's mental health system. The Mental Health Parity Act of 1996 ensures that for members of large health insurance groups, coverage is the same for both physical and mental health treatment.

The focus on mental health is a growing trend extending across the globe. According to the Atlas of Mental Health report, although 70% of countries have a national mental health program covering almost 91% of the global population, 61% of these countries have only developed it since the 1990s. Additionally, 85% of the countries with mental health policies have only developed them in the past 25 years (WHO, 2005). Although there is much that has been started, there is much yet to do to optimally promote mental health in the United States and beyond.

The Social Work Approach to Mental Illness

Social work practice in the area of mental health has transformed over time, from a medical model that emphasized institutionalization to a social model that develops strengths. These changes have reflected the dominant understanding of mental illness. Although this section focuses mainly on the history of mental health policy and practice in the United States with some global trends, the dominant paradigm of mental illness in any society at any given point will affect treatment, and that treatment will, in turn, be affected by the paradigm. Therefore, it is important to note how the conceptualization of mental illness, similarly to the conceptualization of disability, has changed toward a rights-based approach. Structural forces, science, new treatments, legal changes, and populist movements have all been major contributors. Although the conventional social work approach in the late 20th and early 21st century has been an expert-based clinical approach, the paradigm continues to shift to one of recovery, collaboration, and human rights.

Over the last 300 years, the conceptualization of mental illness has changed dramatically and so have treatment and policies. During the 17th century and some of the 18th century in Europe and North America, it was commonly believed that people with disabilities, including mental illness, were being morally punished for something they or their families had done (Rothman, 2003). People, therefore, were either removed from the community into poor houses or jails or lived with families. It has been said, however, that because conditions were so poor for most people during the Colonial time, those with mental illness were perhaps no worse off (Grob, 1973, cited in Trattner, 1999). Then, during the 19th and early 20th centuries, the conceptualization of mental illness shifted to the idea that it was caused by society. This new paradigm took hold during the Enlightenment, when individuals came to be regarded as having fundamental rights. As discussed in Chapter 5, in, one of the grandmothers of American social work, Dorothea Dix (1802–1887) responded by helping to create mental hospitals, also known as asylums, where it was believed that people could receive humane treatment. It is important to point out, however, that not everyone benefitted from this new paradigm. African Americans were frequently warehoused in public institutions, receiving grossly substandard care often for a mental illness diagnosis developed with racist bias (Jackson, 2003). An example is "drapetomania," a mental illness diagnosis concocted by American doctor Dr. Samuel Cartwright to describe slaves who escaped captivity.

These asylums were the norm until the mid-20th century, when the medical model became the dominant paradigm. This model posits that mental illness has biochemical or organic causes and as such can be treated and possibly cured. It was heavily influenced by several converging factors: scientific discoveries in brain chemistry, Sigmund Freud and the development of psychoanalysis, the emergence of psychotropic drugs, and the number of soldiers returning from World War I with "shell shock." These developments in turn influenced government and spawned successive waves of legislation in the United States. Two of the most notable are the National Mental Health Act (1946), which established the National Institute of Mental Health, and the National Community Mental Health Centers Act (1963), which helped to fund numerous outpatient treatment facilities in the country. The Americans with Disabilities Act of 1990 was another key piece of legislation because it incorporated mental illness into the range of disabilities covered. These statutes continued the trend of increasing the rights of people with mental illness.

A major setback to the forward progress that these laws embodied was President Reagan's Omnibus Budget Reconciliation Act in 1985, which had several unintended consequences. The law gave funding to states via block grants, which meant that states could use federal funding without constraints imposed by federal policy, thus effectively stripping away gains from earlier progressive policies. So, at the same time that people were being released from mental hospitals to receive care in their own communities (a movement known as *deinstitutionalization*), these communities lost the ability to serve them. The de jure policies of the 1960s and 1970s of providing quality care in a person's community environment became the *de facto* reality of a wave of homeless mentally ill in the 1980s.

Throughout these paradigmatic and policy changes in the 20 century, some people with mental illness publically protested abuses they had suffered in the mental health system. Known as the consumer or "ex-patient" movement, its roots can be traced back to the influential book *A Mind That Found Itself* (1908) by Clifford Beers, a psychiatric patient himself who found what is now known as the National Mental Health Association. The movement picked up momentum during civil rights efforts of the 1960s and 1970s, when more and more individuals came together to support each other, form self-help groups, and advocate for mental health reform. With parts of the movement having ties to the antipsychiatry movement in the 1970s, all consumers, regardless of political affiliation, demanded the end to stigma and involuntary institutionalization as well as the right to self-determination. Although it can be argued that there is much work yet to be done to transform the mental health system in the United States, the consumer movement has given voice to people who have been unjustly treated, and this voice has had major influence on national policy statements (President's New Freedom Commission, 2003).

Social Workers and Mental Health

The medical model of the past 50 years has resulted in a field dominated by professional clinical casework/psychotherapy and scientifically measured outcomes. Mental health is the largest area of practice in social work, and there are more social workers delivering mental health services in the United States than all other professions combined (SAMHSA, 2009). This statistic may be misleading, however, because the field has become saturated with licensed clinical social workers who conduct psychotherapy in private practice settings, serving a more affluent population than is served in public mental health services (Specht & Courtney, 1994). Similarly, on a global level, the number of social workers working in mental health varies considerably by how rich the country is. Most countries have an average of less than one social worker for each 100,000 people, but in the highest income group of countries, this ratio is nearly 16 to 100,000, and in poorest countries it is 0.4 to 100,000 (WHO, 2005).

There is a tension within the field regarding the optimal role for social workers in mental health. Whereas social work education in mental health encourages a wide range of roles for the social worker, such as community organizer, consultant, and job trainer, in practice the professional social worker in mental health is best known as a case manager or therapist (Bentley, 2002). In this role, interventions take place at the micro-level, using a variety of talk therapeutic techniques to reduce symptoms, set goals, monitor progress, and offer referrals to other psychiatric specialists. That said, some social workers themselves often find the medical model to be lacking in the ability to help people recover because the narrow focus on disease-based psychiatric treatment instead of working with the whole person has created a generation of specialist social workers (Jackson, 2001).

Finally, again reflecting the medical model, the current trend in mental health social work is what is known as "evidence-based practice." This approach to practice emphasizes the use of interventions that have scientific evidence suggesting success in meeting intended outcomes. It is used as a way to legitimize a given practice, and its popularity has steadily risen in the past 20 years as a response to mental health interventions whose outcomes were not measured or verified. Examples include Assertive Community Treatment, Functional Family Therapy, and Supported Employment (Drake et al., 2005).

A discussion of contemporary social work practice in mental health would not be complete without attention given to policy, as the two influence and are influenced by each other. Currently, the major policy in the United States that affects people disabled by mental illness is income maintenance, a policy that provides cash assistance in the United States in the form of Supplementary Security Income and Social Security Disability Insurance, depending on the severity and scope of the disability. Both programs are means-tested public income-maintenance programs comprised of monthly cash payments for people who are deemed mentally or physically disabled and unable to work. People over age 65 years, or blind or disabled people of any age, who are poor can qualify for Supplementary Security Income. Enrollment in Medicaid health insurance is automatic for recipients, guaranteeing a minimal level of health insurance coverage. Social Security Disability Insurance is social insurance program for people who have both a mental health or physical disability and a work history, and recipients are not automatically enrolled in Medicaid. Monthly payments in this program depend on the level of accrued contributions during the time that an individual worked. Although some people are eligible for both programs, recipients of either type of benefit are not eligible for Food Stamps (Social Security Administration, 2003).

Although it has been argued that introduction of income maintenance programs is responsible for the single biggest difference in improving the quality of lives of people with serious mental illness since 1950 (Frank & Glied, 2006), even with this help from the government, it is often not enough to make ends meet. For disabled people on Supplementary Security Income in California, for example, income payments currently range from $5,520 to $9,720 per year, depending on a number of factors, including receipt of other income, number in family, and type of residence. Income from Social Security Disability Insurance is about the same or less than the U.S. Poverty Threshold for one person, which was $9,573 in 2003. The Poverty Threshold is determined by the U.S. Department of Health and Human Services based on the theory that an individual or family will spend one-third of their after-tax money on food. A government-established "lowest-cost food plan" is then multiplied by three to determine the Poverty Threshold (Fisher, 1997). Based on this reasoning, recipients would be expected to spend between $151.80 and $270.00 on food alone, leaving $308.20 to $540.00 to spend on housing, utilities, clothes, personal hygiene items, and other goods and services such as laundry and transportation, which is clearly inadequate.

Recent qualitative research shows the effects poverty can have in mentally ill populations. A qualitative research study on 22 people with mental illness living in a residential treatment facility in Canada was conducted to assess how receiving government assistance (about $73.00 U.S. dollars/month) affects their lives (Wilton, 2003). Informants reported feeling economically deprived and that this condition made it difficult to meet daily needs, increased feelings of stigma, and interfered with social relationships and the ability to fully participate in society. Wilton concluded that because poverty plays such a defining role in the lives of people with mental illness, material resources need to be considered as a central element of mental health from practice and policy angles. Other studies have found that a majority of former mental hospital patients felt shameful and stigmatized receiving disability income (Estroff et al., 1997) and that most mentally ill respondents on disability income had insufficient money to participate in enjoyable activities (Elbogen et al., 2003).

Could there be another way to support people disabled by mental illness? As shown in the next section, mental health policy and practice can be expanded from this consumption-based model to one that is regenerative to both the individual and the community.

The Social Investment Approach to Mental Health

As described in detail in Chapter 1 and in chapters throughout this book, the key characteristics of the social investment approach are that economic development must promote social welfare and that social welfare interventions, in turn, must promote economic development, that interventions are not consumption-based but are productive and driven by consumers, and that human rights are at the forefront of all efforts. This section defines the emergent vision of recovery and how it is linked with the social investment approach and describes an innovative investment approach to mental health treatment called social enterprise, highlighting an example of this strategy in the United States.

The Vision of Recovery

Recovery, at its most basic level, is the concept that people can and do recover from mental illness to lead fulfilling and meaningful lives. Recovery does not necessarily mean the absence of illness; rather, it describes the ability to cope with symptoms of a mental illness and have a quality of life in whatever way is significant for the individual. This position views recovery as analogous to having a permanent physical injury: one can lead a fulfilling life despite the mental illness. Recovery can also be viewed as learning how to effectively cope with not only the symptoms of mental illness but overcoming the negative consequences of it as well (to which social stigma contributes considerably), such as homelessness, unemployment, or problems with primary relationships.

Recovery can be viewed as a personal vision as well as a vision for a mental health system, and definitions of recovery share common characteristics that are strikingly similar across the literature (SAMSHA, 2009; Anthony, 1993; President's New Freedom Commission, 2003). The fact that they are so alike shows that the recovery vision, initiated and articulated by consumers, seems to have become established and at least generally mutually agreed upon. The definitions include the following core concepts: self-direction, hope, empowerment, nonlinearity (i.e., recovery is a nonlinear process), involvement of supportive personal relationships, and having a meaningful role in society. For an individual, how recovery is defined as well as the journey one chooses to take can be intensely personal, but there are numerous commonly accepted strategies that can facilitate recovery, such as involvement with supportive caring people (professionals, peers, family, or friends), daily planning, involvement in meaningful activity, and gaining knowledge of one's symptoms and how to respond to them (Mead & Copeland, 2000). For a mental health system, the vision rests on how to transform the current system to a "recovery-based system" that espouses and holds central the main tenants of recovery. It has become a well-articulated goal in mental health systems across the United States since the 1990s (Jacobson, 2004). This is a shift in thinking from previous system transformations, where it has been argued that the focus was on how the physical buildings would change (i.e., mental institutions) instead of how people themselves would change (Anthony, 1993). Consumer involvement and leadership is a major concrete strategy in this campaign, and mental health plans across the country are asked to hire consumers in service, advocacy, policy, and planning roles (Subcommittee on Consumer Issues, President's New Freedom Commission, 2003).

Social Investment, Recovery, and Rights

The vision of recovery described above harmonizes with the social investment approach in several ways. First and perhaps foremost, both hold that human rights are central to advance each mission. A major violation of human rights is the stigma associated with mental illness (WHO, 2009). It is fueled in part by the media, which negatively influences public opinion about mental illness (Friedman, 2008). In addition to socially imposed difficulties at many levels, discrimination resulting from stigma prevents many people with serious mental illness from participating in everyday activities, such as having social contacts or having a job. Second, both assert that self-determination is a standard by which to operate any intervention aimed at increasing the welfare of a person. It is of utmost importance that a person has choices in their treatment, not to mention choices about how to participate in society. Self-determination can be achieved not just on the individual level but also on the collective level;–that is, consumers as a diverse but distinctive group should be included as equals in policy and services decisions. The recognition that each individual has unique talents that enable himself/herself to have a meaningful and productive role in society is the third similarity of both visions. Recovery and social investment honor the skills and knowledge that each individual possesses and encourages participation in education, community involvement, and employment to develop and ultimately share these talents. Finally, both approaches affirm the importance of the community or, simply put, connections with others. In the social investment approach, this is called social capital, the building of cohesive relationships between people for mutual benefit. In recovery, this can be achieved through mental health support groups that are organized by consumers themselves, also known as "peer support."

The Role of Social Enterprise

One compelling strategy that is aligned with the social investment approach to mental health care is *social enterprise*, an innovative way to ameliorate social and economic exclusion. It has widespread practice in Europe and is gaining popularity in Asia and the United States. The social enterprise approach builds on conventional social work practice in mental health such as psychosocial rehabilitation and supported employment, but it differs from these practices by its highly integrative composition.

Generally speaking, a social enterprise is a business that provides social services, produces goods and/or services, and purposefully employs people with disabilities as well as their nondisabled counterparts (Social Firms Europe, 2009). The main goal of a social enterprise is to break social isolation and exclusion using a market-driven business model. There are many terms for social enterprise across the world including: social firms, social cooperatives, community businesses, integration firms, solidarity firms, social-employment firms, and third-sector social economy. Although there are legal and operational variations between and within countries (Ducci et al., 2002), they share a social investment orientation—namely, that economic development for individuals and for the community are mutually inclusive. As opposed to a clinical intervention with an individual in a secluded office, social enterprise offers people opportunities to gain social, psychological, and practical skills in supportive working environments, a therapeutic experience that can do more than therapy alone (De Leonardis & Mauri, 1992). Social enterprises are supported in part by local governments through laws and subsidies, but they aim to be self-sustaining through generated revenue. In fact, profits from the social enterprise can be re-invested to create more opportunities for mental health consumers.

As mentioned previously, social isolation, poverty, and stigma are consequences of untreated serious mental illness, and social enterprise tackles these debilitating problems with a unique focus on promoting social and economic integration for people with mental health and other disabilities. It is known that social integration, the opposite of isolation, is vital to physical and psychological well-being (Ell, 1984). Formal job-related activities, such as training and labor, and informal activities, such as worker camaraderie, provide myriad of ways to build social capital. Economic integration is achieved by productive contribution in the labor force, an area where people with mental health disabilities have been either previously excluded or not supported sufficiently to maintain participation. Engagement in social enterprise effectively addresses stigma against people with mental illness, as a worker is a worker rather than a "disabled worker" or "mentally ill worker." His or her status may or may not be known, but the social enterprise is intentionally set up to be status-blind.

Researchers argue that the rise of social enterprise across the globe brings great promise to the promotion of mental health (Leff, 2001). These programs are widespread within Europe (Social Firms Europe, 2009). In Asia, a consortium of researchers and doctors has praised innovative programs that utilize social enterprise as "models of excellence," highlighting the benefits produced for both the consumer and the community. These projects provide a blend of services and employment to mental health consumers in rural India, Hong Kong, and Singapore (Akiyama et al. 2008).

The use of social enterprise has been well-documented in Italy, where there are over 5,000 social cooperatives (Ducci et al., 2002). Describing the history of social enterprise in Italy means first discussing their process of deinstitutionalization, because the resulting policies set the stage for social investment efforts. Unlike deinstitutionalization in the United States, the main goal of Italian deinstitutionalization was to transform the entire mental health system of the country to empower mental health consumers to be active in their treatment and recovery (De Leonardis & Mauri, 1992). New laws created and governed social enterprises (known in the country as "social cooperatives"), mandating that 30% of people employed in a social cooperative need to be considered disadvantaged in the workplace. Since then, social cooperatives in Italy have grown rapidly and today provide goods and services in many fields, most prominently in arts and crafts, cleaning, catering, agriculture, and the maintenance of buildings, parks, and other public spaces.

Social enterprise is a featured component in an innovative program in the United States that serves people with serious and persistent mental illness. In 1989, the California mental health system was formally challenged to develop innovative mental health programs, and the Mental Health Association of Los Angeles County designed the Village model. Based in the community, the project aims to prevent recidivism and hospitalization and promote quality of life. An individualized approach characterizes services with the assertion that every person is unique and that treatment should reflect this diversity. Each consumer, or "member," is part of a service team comprised of an employment specialist, money management and substance abuse specialists, as well as mental health practitioners who provide conventional psychosocial interventions. Using the improvement of quality of life as a guiding principal, services and support are available whenever and wherever they are needed (The Village Integrated Services, 2008; Levin, 1997).

Integral to the Village experience is employment in one of the agency's for-profit businesses, which include a credit union, mini-mart, and catering establishment. As members gain skills and confidence, they are placed in community jobs. In addition, many consumers work for the Village permanently in mental health, maintenance, or administrative support positions. Their Employment Department serves all members, not just those who have been referred or choose to participate. The guiding principles state the agency's belief that participation in work builds self-esteem and self-worth and that members can and should be integrated in work environments (Bender, 2006; The Village Integrated Services Agency, 2008).

The distinctive collaborative attributes and integrated approach of The Village are reflected in positive outcomes and commendations. Researchers have found that the Village's unique environment, where staff are perceived as supportive and there is significant peer leadership, has more of a positive effect on social integration than an individual's diagnosis or previous level of psychological, occupational, or social functioning (Levin & Brekke, 1993). A randomized control trial that assigned mental health consumers to either Village services or conventional county-based services showed that after 3 years, Village participants had significantly better financial stability, well-being, friendships, workforce participation, social support, and life satisfaction than members in the comparison group (Chandler et al., 1996). In a subsequent series of studies, it was found that members of the Village had nearly five times higher employment rates than a corresponding program (Chandler et al., 1997a), were less costly to serve than other "high users" of mental health treatment (Chandler et al., 1997b), and had lower hospitalization rates than a comparable cohort (Chandler et al., 1998). The national Substance Abuse and Mental Health Services Administration has honored the Village as an innovative program, and it serves as a training ground for other programs to replicate their model (The Village Integrated Services Agency, 2008).

The social investment approach builds on conventional mental health interventions—namely, psychosocial rehabilitation and supported employment that are already being practiced, although to a much lesser extent than clinical casework and therapy. Psychosocial rehabilitation is a modality that, like social enterprise, goes beyond individual therapy to build concrete skills in everyday living. It is practiced most often with an individual or group basis to develop skills with the aim of increasing the quality of life for the person with mental illness. Similarly, supported employment is another modality that takes mental health treatment out of the clinic and into the real world. It is a twofold approach of job development and job support, specifically, for people with mental health disabilities. The President's New Freedom Commission (2003) has recognized this as a model. Social enterprise takes these approaches several steps further by creating integration. Jobs are not sought out or designed for people disabled by mental illness but, rather, for a general population. Life skills are not taught in isolation but are learned experientially and practiced on the job. Social enterprise fits well with the vision of recovery because it respects the dignity of the person to use their abilities and capacities to create a meaningful life.

The Role of Social Work in the Social Investment Approach

Because of the large numbers of social workers involved in mental health, the field of social work has an important role to play in the development of social investment efforts. Making a shift from a clinical casework/psychotherapy model to a recovery, rights-based approach to social work mental health practice will require new skills and attitudes. Social workers can be influential on several levels: individual practice, community practice, and policy.

The new role of the social worker in an investment approach to mental health is one of generalist (not specialist), consultant, liaison, and job skills trainer. Practical skills required to carry out this new role include business plan development, financial management, resource acquisition, and team-based work. Valuing the principles of recovery is instrumental to the attitude of the social worker, as well as reframing the nature of professional social work in mental health from that of expert to that of consultant. It is also imperative that these roles be occupied by social workers who are ready, willing, and able to address and remedy the racial, ethnic, and cultural disparities that characterize access to mental health care and service delivery.

On the community level, social workers can work with mental health consumers as well as service organizations to encourage the building of social enterprises. The recommended recipe from social investment projects in Asia is the development of a business and financial management plan, acquisition of start-up money, training industry-specific skills, and identification of how to meet the larger community's needs with the goods and services provided by social enterprises (Akiyama et al., 2008).

There must be a commitment on the part of policymakers, fueled by social work advocacy on individual, organizational, and leadership levels, to create social enterprise firms similar to those in Europe—namely, businesses that require the hiring of disabled workers. As can be seen from the Italian example, established social enterprise is the result of the convergence of policy and practice. It will take both social work practitioners and social work policy advocates working together with governments to continue the work of recovery-based mental health reform.

There has been the call to individual social workers and the field of social work in general to shift professional orientation from that of expert psychotherapist to a role that better reflects the nature of social work as a field that should serve the most vulnerable and oppressed in society (Specht & Courtney, 1994). To be sure, there will always be a need for people who want it to get emotional and psychological support from others who are compassionate. When this does not happen through a natural helping system, such as with family members and friends, professional and paraprofessional social workers can be instrumental in helping people in dealing with complex social and interpersonal issues. The emphasis of social work in mental health is already securely oriented to this individual and consumptive way of working, and it is time to expand roles of social workers to adopt social investment strategies to help people with serious mental illness achieve the right to social and economic integration.

REFERENCES

Akiyama, T., Chandra, N., Chen, C., et al. (2008). Asian models of excellence in psychiatric care and rehabilitation. *International Review of Psychiatry*, 20(5): 445–451.

American Psychiatric Association. (2000). *Diagnostic and Statistical Manual of Mental Disorders* (Revised 4th ed.). Washington, DC.

Anthony, W. A. (1993). Recovery from mental illness: Guiding vision of the mental health service system in the 1990's. *Psychosocial Rehabilitation Journal*, 16(4): 11–23.

Barker, R. L. (1999). *The Social Work Dictionary*. Washington, D.C.: National Association of Social Workers Press.

Bender, E. (2006). Building community ties: It takes a village. *Psychiatric News*, 41(10): 12–13.

Bentley, K. J. (Ed.) (2002). *Social Work Practice in Mental Health: Contemporary Roles, Tasks, and Techniques*. Pacific Grove, CA: Brooks/Cole.

City of Berkeley, Department of Health and Human Services, Division of Mental Health (2009). *Community Services and Supports Plan, Mental Health Services Act*. Berkeley, CA.

Chandler, D. W., Meisel, J., Hu, T. W., McGowen, M., & Madison, K. (1998). A capitated model for a cross-section of severely mentally ill clients: Hospitalization. *Community Mental Health Journal*, 43(1): 13–26.

Chandler, D. W., Meisel, J., Hu, T. W., McGowen, M., & Madison, K. (1997a). A capitated model for a cross-section of severely mentally ill clients: Employment outcomes. *Community Mental Health Journal*, 33(6): 501–516.

Chandler, D. W., Meisel, J., Hu, T. W., McGowen, M., & Madison, K. (1997b). Mental health costs, other public costs, and family burden among mental health clients in capitated integrated service agencies. *Journal of Mental Health Administration*, 24(2): 178–188.

Chandler, D. W., Meisel, J., Hu, T. W., McGowen, M., & Madison, K. (1996). Client outcomes in a three-year controlled study of an integrated service agency model. *Psychiatric Services*, 47(12): 1337–1343.

De Leonardis, O. & Mauri, D. (1992). From deinstitutionalization to the social enterprise. *Social Policy*, 23(2): 50–54.

Drake, R., Merrens, M., & Lynde, D. (Eds.) (2005). *Evidence-Based Mental Health Practice*. New York: Norton.

Ducci, G., Stentella, C., & Vulterini, P. (2002). The Social Enterprise in Europe. *International Journal of Mental Health*, 31(3): 76–92.

Elbogen, E. B., Swanson, J. W., Swartz, M. S., & Wagner, H. R. (2003). Characteristics of third-party money management for persons with psychiatric disabilities. *Psychiatric Services*, 54: 1136–1141.

Ell, K. (1984). Social networks, social support, and health status: A Review. *Social Service Review*, 58(1): 133–149.

Estroff, S. E., Patrick, D. L., Zimmer, C. R., & Lachicotte, W. S. (1997). Pathways to disability income among persons with severe, persistent psychiatric disorders *The Millbank Quarterly*, 75(4): 495–532.

Fisher, G. M. (1997). The Development of the Orshansky Poverty Thresholds and their subsequent history as the official U.S. poverty measure. *Poverty Measurement Working Paper*. U.S.Census Bureau.

Frank, R. G., Glied, S. A. (2006). *Better But Not Well: Mental Health Policy in the United States Since 1950*. Baltimore, MD: The Johns Hopkins University Press.

Friedman, R. (2008). Media and madness. *Am Prospect*. July/August: A2–A4.

Grob, G. (1973). *Mental Institutions in America: Social Policy to 1875*. New York: Free Press.

Jackson, R. L. (2001). *The Clubhouse Model: Empowering Applications of Theory to Generalist Practice*. Belmont, CA: Wasdworth.

Jackson, V. (2003). *In Our Own Voices: African-American Stories of Oppression, Survival and Recovery in Mental Health Systems*. Available at http://www.mindfreedom.org/kb/mental-health-abuse/Racism/InOurOwnVoice/view. (Accessed September 3, 2009).

Jacobson, N. (2004). *In Recovery: The Making of Mental Health Policy*. Nashville, TN: Vanderbilt University Press.

Leff, J. (2001). Can we manage without the mental hospital? *Australian and New Zealand Journal of Psychiatry*, 35: 421–427.

Levin, S. J. (1997). Disease management in-depth: The Village Integrated Service Agency. *Behavioral Health Management*, 17(4): 32–33.

Levin, S. J. & Brekke, J. S. (1993). Factors relating to integrating persons with chronic mental illness into a Peer Social Milieu. *Community Mental Health Journal*, 29(1): 25–34.

Mead, S. & Copeland, M. E. (2000). *What Recovery Means To Us*. New York: Plenum Publishers.

National Institute of Mental Health. Website. Available at http://www.nimh.nih.gov (Accessed April 4, 2008).

President's New Freedom Commission on Mental Health (2003). *Achieving The Promise: Transforming Mental Health Care in America*. Available at http://www.mentalhealthcommission.gov/ (Accessed on April 4, 2008).

Social Enterprise Coalition. Website. Available at http://www.socialenterprise.org.uk/ (Accessed April 17, 2009).

Social Firms Europe. Website. Available at http://www.cefec.de/activities.html(Accessed April 17, 2009).

Social Security Administration (2003). *SSI in California*. Publication No. 05-11125. Washington D.C.: U.S. Government Printing Office.

Specht, H. & Courtney, M. E. (1994). *Unfaithful Angels*. New York: The Free Press.

Trattner, W. I. (1999). *From Poor Law to Welfare State: A history of Social Welfare in America*. (6th Edition). New York: The Free Press.

U.S. Department of Health and Human Services (1999). *Mental Health: A Report of the Surgeon General.* Rockville, MD: U.S. Department of Health and Human Services, Substance Abuse and Mental Health Services Administration, Center for Mental Health Services, National Institutes of Health, National Institute of Mental Health.

U.S. Department of Health and Human Services (2001). Mental Health: Culture, Race, and Ethnicity. *A Supplement to Mental Health: A Report of the Surgeon General.* Rockville, MD: U.S. Department of Health and Human Services, Substance Abuse and Mental Health Services Administration, Center for Mental Health Services, National Institutes of Health, National Institute of Mental Health.

Wilton, R. D. (2003). Poverty and mental health: A qualitative study of residential carefacility tenants. *Community Mental Health Journal*, 39 (2): 139–156.

World Health Organization Mental Health Atlas (2005). *Department of Mental Health and Substance Abuse.* Geneva.

World Health Organization. Website. Available at http://www.who.int/mental_health/en/ (Accessed April 17, 2009).

5

Developmental Social Work and People with Disabilities

JENNIFER KNAPP AND JAMES MIDGLEY

It has been estimated that approximately 10% of the world's population, or between 650 and 700 million people, are challenged by some form of disability. The great majority live in the developing countries of the Global South, and most are poor and have little if any opportunity to integrate into the mainstream of society. Many are maintained by their family members, often in seclusion, and few have access to education, employment, medical care, and income maintenance benefits. In the Western countries, medical, rehabilitative, income support, and other social services are much more extensive, but even in these countries people with disabilities continue to face many challenges.

Although social work has been involved in providing services to people with disabilities for many years, it cannot be claimed that the profession has given high priority to the field. A cursory review of leading, introductory social policy and social welfare textbooks reveals that disability issues are given very little prominence. Indeed, very few of these books even have chapters on the subject. Another problem is that social work has long relied on an "expert" model by which people with disabilities are seen as the passive recipients of care provided by professionals. This approach has now been challenged by people with disabilities who have vigorously advocated for their right to make decisions about their own welfare. They have also campaigned to be treated as citizens who have equal opportunities to education and employment so that they, like other members of society, can live productive lives.

As people with disabilities have increasingly taken charge of their own affairs, social work's traditional role in the field has changed. Today, more social workers recognize that people with disabilities have strengths and capabilities and they now use their professional knowledge and skills to collaborate with them to assist in advocating for services and opportunities. It is more widely recognized today that social workers should work closely with people with disabilities to facilitate their full integration into the social and economic life of the community. In addition to emphasizing disability rights, these services are developmental in that they mobilize investments that enhance the capabilities of people with disabilities to realize their goals. However, although this approach has now been more widely adopted, it cannot be claimed that social work with people with disabilities has completely abandoned the conventional, "expert-based" approach.

This chapter discusses the developmental approach to social work practice with people with disabilities. This approach is also known as the rights-based approach, largely because of the disability community has effectively utilized the discourse of rights in campaigns to secure their rights as citizens, to live normal lives in the community, and to participate actively in the productive economy. Increasingly, social work in the disability field—and this includes people with disabilities who have professional qualification in social work—are committed to promoting a rights-based developmental approach. As noted earlier, this is a collaborative approach in which social work professionals work closely with people with disabilities and their organizations. It emphasizes the rights of people with disabilities to be fully integrated into society and to have access to educational, transport, employment, and other opportunities that most people take for granted.

The Challenge of Disability

Of all the disadvantaged groups in the world, people with disabilities comprise one of the more diverse populations. The nature of their disability as well as their gender, culture, socio-economic status, sexual orientation, and other characteristics vary significantly. This complicates efforts to formulate a definition of the term *disability*. Obviously, people with visual, developmental, auditory, psychological, and physical disabilities view themselves very differently, and attempts to identify common features are difficult. Nevertheless, in 1976, the World Health Organization (WHO) formulated a comprehensive definition that differentiated between an impairment, a handicap, and a disability. An impairment was defined as "any loss or abnormality of psychological, physiological or anatomical structure or function," whereas a disability was viewed as a restriction or lack of ability resulting from an impairment "to perform an activity in the manner or within the range considered normal for a human being." A handicap was defined as "a disadvantage for a given individual, resulting from an impairment or a disability, that prevents the fulfillment of a role that is considered normal (depending on age, sex and social and cultural factors) for that individual."

This definition is controversial among disability rights activists who believe that the WHO's definition confuses "impairment" with "disability." They contend that impairment refers to the physical or cognitive limitations that individuals may have, such as the inability to walk or see, but that "disability" refers to socially imposed restrictions. It is largely the system of social constraints, they claim, that are imposed on those with impairments by the discriminatory practices of society that hamper their effective functioning.

The United Nations *Standard Rules for the Equalization of Opportunities for People with Disabilities* of 1993 recognizes that the concept of disability refers to the relationship between people with disabilities and their environment, and it emphasizes the shortcomings in the environment and the social institutions that prevent them from participating in society on equal terms with others. These shortcomings may relate, for example, to the lack of information, transportation, education, and opportunities available to people with disabilities. Subsequently, in 1980, the WHO revised its definition, and its *International Classification of Impairments, Disabilities, and Handicaps* now more clearly distinguishes between "impairment" and "disability." In 2001, after 5 years of consultation with disability advocates, it again revised this definition; in the *International Classification on Functioning, Disability, and Health*, it linked disability to the notion of peoples' abilities to function in society. It also placed greater emphasis on the way people with disabilities are defined by the wider community and on the obligations of the community to recognize their rights and capabilities. However, some critics still believe that the classification and its definition is excessively medical and too centered on the person with disability and the way this person adjusts to the expectations of society (Quinn & Degener, 2002).

Although it may appear that debates about definitions are semantic quibbles, it is important to use language that accurately captures the way people with disabilities define themselves and view their role in society. This is especially important when formulating policies that address the needs and aspirations of people with disabilities. Conventional approaches suggest that it is the responsibility of individuals and their families to adjust to the able-bodied world. However, by looking at the meaning of "disability" in the wider social context, disability advocates counter that the wider community has a responsibility to remove barriers and prejudices that impede the efforts of people with disabilities to live normal, productive lives. As will be shown, this idea is central to the rights-based, developmental approach to social work practice with people with disabilities.

The way the concept of disability is defined also has relevance to attempts to determine its prevalence. Studies have shown that the definition of disability varies widely from country to country. Some physical or psychological conditions are not recognized as disabilities in some countries, whereas in others, a more encompassing approach is used. Because of these factors, is difficult to find an internationally useful way of assessing the prevalence of disability (Mont, 2007). Accordingly, very different estimates of the incidence of disabilities in different nations have been made. As mentioned earlier, it has been estimated that there are about 650 to 700 million people in the world with disabilities. This number includes people facing physical, psychological, and developmental challenges. Generally, the incidence of disability is higher in the Western countries, and this is often attributed to differences in definition, the way information is collected, and a greater capacity to diagnose some disabling conditions. Other factors, such as having more elderly people and higher survival rates for people with disabilities, can also lead to higher rates of disability in these countries. So, for example, survey results show that the prevalence of disability ranges from under 1% in Kenya and Bangladesh to 20% in New Zealand (Seipel, 1994). In the United States, the Centers for Disease Control (CDC) estimates that approximately 18% of the population is challenged by a disability. However, the incidence varies between the different states. West Virginia has the highest incidence, with approximately 26% of the population having a disability.

These statistics provide some indication of the impact on disabilities on the lives of disabled people and their families. Although much of the social work literature focuses on the experiences of disabled people and the challenges they face, the wider community is also affected. For example, Metts (2000) at the World Bank estimates that the exclusion of people with disabilities from gainful employment comes at a staggering cost and may amount to an annual loss of almost $2 trillion in global gross domestic product. Obviously, disabling conditions and the way people with disabilities are perceived impede their ability to live productive lives. Klasing (2007) believes that in developing countries such as India, the biggest problem is the exclusion of people with disabilities from everyday life, employment, schools, politics, social gatherings, and even development projects. Often, people with disabilities are only recognized in their roles as beggars and supplicants. Widespread discrimination and the exclusion of people with disabilities from participating in everyday life poses a major challenge to disability policy in the developing world.

In the Western countries, the rights of people with disabilities to education and employment may be officially recognized but are not always valued. In the United States, for example, 34% of men and 33% of women with disabilities were employed in 1999, compared with 95% of men and 82% of women without disabilities (Bruyere, Erickson, & Ferrentino, 2003). Similar disparities exist in health and education. In Canada, nearly a half (43.5%) of people with disabilities had received less than 8 years of education, whereas only about one-fifth (20.6%) of the general population had received less than 8 years of education. Studies have also shown that people with disabilities have higher rates of diabetes, heart disease, depression, and other secondary conditions (Field, Jette, & Martin, 2006). These adversities must be linked to the common practice of discriminating against people with disabilities. Despite considerable progress over the years, people with disabilities are still viewed in negative terms by a significant proportion of the population, and popular stereotypes about the nature of disability remain widespread. These attitudes engender discriminatory practices, which, in the case of disabled people of color, are exacerbated by racist attitudes. Faced with these depressing realities, social workers need to contribute more effectively to ensuring that the challenges facing people with disabilities are fully addressed.

Social Work Approaches

It was suggested earlier that working with people with disabilities is not a priority social work practice field. Nevertheless, social workers together with other professionals have sought over many years to provide services to people with disabilities. Generally, their contribution has been valued. However, like other professionals, social workers are influenced by prevailing attitudes and professional beliefs, and as suggested earlier, many practice within an "expert" model. Although as Haden (2000) noted, professionals are usually motivated by altruism and a commitment to care for those in need, professionally managed programs are often based on the belief that experts know what is best for people with disabilities.

This attitude also characterizes the "medical" model, which as Rothman (2003) noted, has dominated services to people with disabilities for many years. In addition to relying on the opinions of experts, disabilities are medicalized and subject to treatments that are intended to "cure" the disability. The medical model also assigns people with disabilities into the passive role of patient. The aim of a medical approach is to make people with disabilities "normal," which of course implies that they are "abnormal." It also focuses on individuals and posits that people with disabilities need to change, rather than society or the wider social and physical environment. Sometimes, as in the case of President Franklin Delano Roosevelt, denying and concealing the disability promotes an image of the "cured cripple" rather than accepting the challenge of openly living a normal life (Fleischer & Zames, 2001).

Historically, altruism has often characterized popular responses to people with disabilities and has influenced what is known as the "charity" model (Miller & Ziegler, 2006). This approach casts people with disabilities in a tragic role and is meant to invoke pity from able-bodied people. This model has a very long history and has often motivated charitable giving. It has also been sanctioned by religious teaching over the centuries. Of course, it is still popular today and characterizes fundraising drives, such as Jerry Lewis's telethon for disabled children. However, it defines people with disabilities as passive recipients of aid and denies them the right to self-determination.

The charity approach has often been interwoven with what Rothman (2003) calls the "morality model." This approach attributes the cause of disabilities to the failings of individuals or their parents; it may also be viewed as the result of a lack of faith and religious observance or even of demonic possession. The morality model has found expression in many religions and cultures over the centuries. Unlike the charity model, it blames the victim and often evokes strong negative reactions from able-bodied people. Stigmatization and shame are common responses, and because of widespread ostracism, people with disabilities have often been secluded. Those who attempt to live normal lives in the community are often ridiculed and taunted and may even be subjected to physical abuse. Klasing (2007) has reported that this is still a common problem in India, where victims may even commit suicide out of despair. Of course, these attitudes and behaviors are also found in the Western countries. In earlier times, abusive and discriminatory practices were often institutionalized. In Chicago, for example, people with disabilities who were described as "diseased, maimed, mutilated or in any way deformed so as to be an unsightly or disgusting object" were prohibited from appearing in public places by a city ordinance of 1911. The ordinance was only repealed in 1974 (Fleischer & Zames, 2001). As is well-known, the immigration policies of the United States have long discriminated again people with disabilities.

These different approaches have not only influenced societal responses to people with disabilities but also have shaped services and professional interventions. Before the advent of formal services by governments and nonprofit organizations in the 19th and 20th centuries, families were expected to care for those with disabilities. In some cases, people with disabilities were taken into monasteries or convents, and among the wealthy, disabled relatives were often cared for by paid attendants. Because of widespread poverty and poor standards of health, few working people with disabilities reached even the low life expectancies that prevailed at the time. In addition, many died sooner because of willful neglect.

By the 19th century, many people with disabilities were incarcerated in almshouses and similar institutions, and in time, specialized residential institutions for different groups of people with disabilities were established. The use of residential services was considered to be an appropriate and humane response. In the mid-century, Dorothea Dix campaigned for the creation of mental hospitals where mentally ill homeless people and those who been incarcerated in jails and prisons could be cared for. Earlier in 1817, the first school for deaf people was established in Hartford, CT, to provide educational opportunities for hearing-impaired children. Specialized institutions for developmentally disabled people and other groups were also constructed. Institutions for people with disabilities were also established in many developing countries during the Colonial era either by governments or missionaries. However, they seldom catered for more than a small proportion of those needing services. With deinstitutionalization in the Western countries, the use of residential services has declined sharply but has not disappeared. Today, many commercially owned nursing homes continue to house people with disabilities. Similarly, charitable and religious organizations often prefer to provide residential care to people who could, with adequate support, live in their own homes in the community.

Social workers are employed by both public and nonprofit organizations providing services to people with disabilities. Although the numbers are not large, they can be found in residential institutions, sheltered workshops, and vocational rehabilitation centers. They also practice in medical settings and often specialize in counseling, referral, and case management. They are generally well-regarded for their ability to access a variety of services for their clients, such as income maintenance benefits, housing, transportation, and medical care. In more recent times, they have become increasingly responsive to the efforts of people with disabilities to define their own needs and campaign for services. As the limitations of the "expert model" have been recognized, more social workers are now transcending the traditional practice of viewing people with disabilities as passive "patients" or "clients" and instead now work with them on a collaborative basis.

Professional associations, such as the National Association of Social Workers in United States, have also questioned the expert model and now emphasize the role of social workers in securing the rights of people with disabilities to be accepted, educated, and employed and to be integrated into the mainstream of society. Although the expert model has not been abandoned, Mackelprang (2007) believes that more social workers in the Western countries today are embracing a developmental and rights-based approach. Nevertheless, much more needs to be done to transcend the limitations of conventional practice approaches. This is equally true in the Global South, where relatively few social workers are involved in the disability field. Although some are employed in hospitals and governmental agencies as well as in international nongovernmental disability organizations, they often operate within the context of limited and inappropriate services. As mentioned earlier, residential services are still commonly used but seldom cater for more than a fraction of those in need even though they consume sizable revenues that could be better spent on community services. Few developing countries provide income maintenance benefits to people with disabilities, and access to education and medical services are very uneven.

As Klasina (2007) reveals, the well-intentioned efforts of the government of India to meet the needs of people with disabilities falls short of its target. India is one of a small number of developing countries that provides cash benefits to people with disabilities, but the amounts are small and often people in rural areas are not covered. This is also true of rehabilitative services and of the provision of prosthetics and other aides. In South Africa, which is a middle-income country, services to people with disabilities were introduced many years ago, and as Gathiram (2008) reports, these involve an active partnership between government and the nonprofit sector. The South African government has affirmed its support for international disability rights instruments and has also explicitly recognized that disability is a key developmental concern. A range of services to people with disabilities have been introduced, and in addition, people with disabilities receive income maintenance benefits. The government has also adopted a *National Rehabilitation Policy*, which seeks to integrate people with disabilities in economic and social life. However, Gathiram notes that these policies are not matched by adequate budgetary allocations, and services do not reach all of those in need. In addition, administrative problems limit their effectiveness, with the result that millions of people with disabilities are still not adequately served.

The Rights-Based Developmental Approach

There is no doubt that a major shift has taken place in professional and policy thinking on disability. Despite the continued influence of the expert and medical models (as well as the charity and morality models), it is widely accepted today that disability must be viewed with reference to social attitudes, popular beliefs, and discriminatory and oppressive practices. Whereas previous conceptualizations focused on people with disabilities and their alleged deficits, the way they are defined and treated within the wider social context is now emphasized. This "social model," as it is often known (Rothman, 2003), emerged as a result of the efforts of people with disabilities to challenge prejudice and discriminatory practices themselves. Although the social model is concerned with the role of oppression and the attitudinal and institutional barriers that prevent disabled people from participating in the life of the community (Miller & Ziegler, 2006), it also stresses the positive dimensions of social integration. It emphasizes the strengths and capabilities of people with disabilities and their desire to have access to education, employment and other opportunities that will allow them to be active members of society.

The social model has also been called the disability rights or developmental model, but sometimes the social model is distinguished from the rights and developmental approaches. Whereas the social model offers a critique of oppressive practices, the rights approach stresses the role of legal instruments in protecting the well-being of people with disabilities. In turn, the developmental approach is associated with the integration of people with disabilities into the social and economic life of the community. On the other hand, many believe that these different facets form an integral part of an all-encompassing approach that recognizes the strengths of people with disabilities and their right to live productive lives in the community.

The key elements of the rights-based, developmental approach and its link with social development are readily apparent. First, this approach emphasizes the leadership of people with disabilities and their organizations in campaigning for rights, services, and opportunities. It also recognizes their right to self-determination and to be protected against discrimination. Second, a rights-based, developmental approach places emphasis on community living and seeks to normalize living arrangements of people with disabilities. Finally, to promote economic and social integration, it requires social investments that ensure the acquisition of educational qualifications and skills that facilitate the full participation of people with disabilities in the productive economy.

The Struggle for Rights

A rights-based, developmental approach is rooted in the idea that people with disabilities have the right to self-determination as well as the capabilities to achieve their goals. This idea is the antithesis of the models described earlier, which emphasize deficits rather than strengths and seek to address deficits through compassionate charity or medical treatment. The rights-based, developmental approach recognizes that people with disabilities face challenges, but its advocates, who obviously include people with disabilities themselves, believe that these challenges can be met through social investments and the abolition of discriminatory practices that maintain people with disabilities in a dependent, passive role.

People with disabilities have campaigned for self-determination for many decades. Although they have often been assisted by allies in the able-bodied community, it is largely through their own efforts that discriminatory and oppressive practices have been challenged. Their campaigns have a long history, and as Fleischer and Zames (2001) discuss in some detail, often have involved confrontation. Their struggles also encountered obstacles and reversals. For example, after the introduction of sign language in the early 19th century, educators in the United States successfully campaigned to have it banned and replaced with an oralist approach by which deaf children were taught to approximate speech. It was not until the 1960s that signing was reintroduced, largely as a result of the activism of deaf people themselves. In many cases, their campaigns were fueled by blatant examples of discrimination, such as when Florence Haskel, a leading disability rights campaigner in the early 20th century, was denied employment even though she was perfectly capable of working. Similarly, the League of the Physically Handicapped was established during the Great Depression years to challenge the routine practice of denying employment to people with disabilities on the grounds that priority had to be given to the able-bodied unemployed. Another example was the denial of admission to Ed Roberts by the University of California, Berkeley. Roberts, who had been severely disabled by polio, successfully sued the university, bringing about a complete overhaul of prevailing admissions policies not only at Berkeley but at colleges and universities throughout the country. His actions also contributed to the creation of the independent living movement.

In their struggle against discrimination and oppression, people with disabilities have often turned to the courts for redress, and they have also mobilized legislative support. Often, legislative campaigns have involved a long and protracted struggle. In the United States, after many years of campaigning, disability rights activists were disappointed that President Johnson's landmark Civil Rights Act of 1964 did not explicitly prohibit discrimination against people with disabilities. This decision was defended on the grounds that inclusion of disability rights might divert attention from the campaign against racism (Fleischer & Zames, 2001). Nevertheless, the struggle continued, and people with disabilities and their allies were able to include antidiscriminatory clauses in the Rehabilitation Act of 1973. Although President Nixon vetoed this legislation, a compromise was reached, and employment discrimination in the federal government and private firms contracting with the government was explicitly prohibited. The adoption of these provisions heartened the disability community and fueled further campaigns, which resulted in 1990 in the enactment of the Americans with Disabilities Act. This statute prohibits all forms of discrimination against people with disabilities and is regarded by many as the most comprehensive and significant disability rights provision in the United States (Hayden, 2000). The federal government plays an active role in ensuring compliance, and numerous judicial decisions, including rulings by the United States Supreme Court, have clarified the scope of the statute and the meaning of its provisions. On the other hand, the disability community has been disappointed by some decisions that they believe have not protected their rights. As Mallias (2007) reports, efforts are currently underway to amend the Act to clarify some of its provisions.

Most other Western countries also have laws designed to ensure that the civil and human rights of people with disabilities are protected. In Europe, the policies of individual countries have been augmented by several disability rights instruments adopted by the European Union (Traustadottir, 2008). Although many developing countries do not have statutory provisions of this kind, international efforts are underway to encourage their governments to adopt antidiscriminatory policies. The *Convention on the Rights of Persons with Disabilities*, which was adopted by the United Nations General assembly in December 2006, is now a part of international law and is enforceable at least among those countries that have ratified its provisions. The Convention requires member states to promote the interests of people with disabilities and to ensure that all existing laws, customs, and practices that discriminate against them are abolished. The Convention also recognizes their right to self-determination and to participate fully in social and economic life. It makes special provisions for the protection of women and children with disabilities who have historically been especially disadvantaged. Although the adoption of the Convention is a major achievement, it is recognized that the impediments to implementing its provisions must be addressed in both the Western and developing countries. As Klasing (1997) has noted, the Government of India enacted antidiscriminatory legislation in 1995 and also adopted affirmative action hiring policies, but discrimination against people with disabilities remains widespread. Unfortunately, a lack of enforcement characterizes disability rights policies and programs in many other countries as well.

Community Living

People with disabilities have historically been maintained by their families. Although some were able to move about in the local community, others were hidden and excluded. This was particularly true of people with severe disabilities who were often viewed with revulsion. Most faced serious medical and other challenges and few survived into old age. Therefore, it was with compassion that people with disabilities were cared for by the religious orders in the monasteries and hospitals. As mentioned earlier, this practice was widespread by the mid-19th century. In addition, people with disabilities were increasingly housed in residential facilities operated by governments. Unfortunately, as Hayden (2000) noted, the expansion of residential care was also accompanied by an increase in abuse and neglect. Also, the "warehousing" approach meant that people with disabilities were shunted aside, ignored, and hidden from the community. Overcrowding and poor nutrition and medical services often characterized life in the institutions. Although conditions in the mental asylums were particularly bad, the large chronic hospitals that were built to accommodate people with physical and developmental disabilities were also criticized.

By the mid-20th century, these criticisms attracted widespread public attention and gave rise to the proposal that people with disabilities should live in their own homes. The concept of "supported living" was popularized, and its advocates urged the provision of appropriately modified housing, adequate social assistance benefits, and a range of services that would make it possible for people with disabilities to live independent lives. Again, people with disabilities played a major role in promoting this idea. In 1958, Anne Emerman, who was a severely challenged wheelchair user, became the first resident of the Goldwater Memorial Hospital in New York to gain admission to a local college. She subsequently enrolled in Columbia University, where she trained as a social worker. Although it was assumed that those who had been hospitalized at Goldwater would never leave the institution, Emerman completed her professional education, found employment as a psychiatric social worker, married, had children, and was able to live an independent and productive life. She inspired many others, including those with serious disabilities, to leave the institutions and establish themselves in the community.

The promotion of community living owes much to disability activists such as Ed Roberts, who was mentioned earlier. In 1972, Roberts cofounded the Center for Independent Living in Berkeley, which has played a major role in promoting the integration of people with disabilities into the social and economic life of the community. At about this time, other activists were also promoting the notion of independent living, and governments in the Western countries eventually began to support these initiatives. Early legislative provisions built on the medical rehabilitation approach, which sought to promote independent functioning (usually through surgical procedures). Although critical of the limitations of this approach, disability activists realized that it could form the basis for their campaigns to obtain community services. In the United States, these campaigns initially secured funding for personal attendants who would provide home services and for transitional, supported housing. One of the country's first transitional housing programs was established in Ohio in 1974 to help those leaving institutions adjust to the challenges of independent living.

Funding was also secured to support the activities of the independent living centers that were being established in major cities. For example, in 1974, the Boston-based Center for Independent Living obtained funding from the state's rehabilitation agency to provide personal care attendant services, housing, assistive devices, counseling, medical, and other services. Of course, independent living centers also have a major advocacy function. In addition to campaigning for funding and improved services, they have challenged cases of housing and other forms of discrimination in the courts. They have also campaigned vigorously for improved accessibility to buildings and public spaces and for architectural innovations. One of these innovations is "adaptable design," which improves accessibility and mobility in private residences and allows for these homes to be readily adapted to meet the needs of people who might eventually require mobility assistance. This approach is compatible with the concept of "universal design," which seeks to ensure that all building and public spaces are accessible to people with disabilities.

By the 1960s and 1970s, deinstitutionalization was widely adopted as official government policy, and the numbers of people with disabilities (as well as those with mental illness) living in large institutions declined significantly. For example, Hayden (2000) has reported that the numbers of people with developmental disabilities living in large residential facilities fell by three quarters between 1970 and 1990. However, as is well-known, the transition from institutional to community living has been accompanied by a lack of community support, particularly for people with mental illness. Although people with physical disabilities have generally fared better, community services are often inadequate and threatened by frequent retrenchments in government expenditures.

As noted earlier, discrimination remains a major problem facing people with disabilities who wish to live normal lives in the community. Unfortunately, the view that people with disabilities should be confined to residential institutions is still widely held, and the idea that they should live in their own homes, be gainfully employed, and have access to local shops and amenities is not fully accepted. In particular, there is resistance to the idea that the cost of community care should be provided by local taxpayers. Children with disabilities face particular challenges when they attend local schools and seek to integrate fully into their curricular and extracurricular activities. Ridicule and blatant discrimination is not uncommon, and these children often have to deal with difficult and unpleasant reactions from some students. Disabled people of color are particularly disadvantaged, having to deal not only with their disabilities but with racist attitudes, which unfortunately remain widespread.

To live in the community, people with disabilities need to have a steady income. Although advocates of the developmental model are in favor of employment, the need for social assistance and other benefits that provide a secure income is also recognized. The governments of the Western countries have introduced income maintenance programs of this kind either through the social insurance system, which usually caters for those who have previously been employed, or through means-tested or universal tax-funded programs. The latter approach pays benefits to people with disabilities irrespective of their income or assets and is generally favored because it avoids the disincentive effect of phasing out means-tested benefits as income from employment increases. Many people with disabilities are eager to work but worried that they will be in financial difficulty if they lose their jobs or are unable to work.

A major issue in community-based living is access to public transportation. Obviously, if people with disabilities are to live normally in the community, they require access to shops and supermarkets, places of entertainment, recreational centers and the many other facilities that most people take for granted. In the United States, disability activists again took the lead by invoking the anti-discriminatory clause of the Rehabilitation Act of 1973 to campaign for access to buses and subways. In some parts of the United States, the municipal transportation authorities were cooperative and began to modify public transport services so that they could be used by people with disabilities, especially those using wheelchairs. In other places, such as New York, these proposals were resisted and resulted in various demonstrations as well as lawsuits that eventually resulted in appropriate modifications that now permit people with disabilities living in the community to travel with relative ease.

Education, Work, and Livelihoods

In addition to promoting the normalization of living arrangements for people with disabilities, advocates of the rights-based developmental approach urge the adoption of policies and programs that will secure their integration into the economic life of the community. Many people with disabilities wish to be economically productive, and for many, independent living is fully realized when they, like other people, have regular employment and can pursue their career goals. A generation ago, when many people with disabilities were still accommodated in residential facilities, the idea that they could be employed and participate in the productive economy would have been met with incredulity. But, as shown earlier, pioneers such as Anne Emerman and Ed Roberts demonstrated that this was possible.

Of the estimated 650 million people with disabilities in the world today, about 70% are of working age, but only a fraction are in regular employment in the formal economy (Seipel, 1994). As may be expected, employment rates are highest in the Western countries where antidiscriminatory legislation, affirmative action, and extensive educational and training opportunities have been created. Nevertheless, studies show that the proportion of people with disabilities who are employed in these countries is still quite low. As noted earlier, one study in the United States found that although about 70% of able-bodied people were in regular employment, only one-third of people with disabilities were employed (Bruyere, Erickson, & Ferrentino, 2003). In Europe, the proportion of people with disabilities in regular employment was somewhat higher at about 40%, but even here ". . . very few disabled individuals are actually able to leave benefits for paid work" (Traustadottir, 2008, p. 81).

In the Global South, the proportion of people with disabilities in regular employment is very small indeed. However, this does not mean that they do not work. Most are actively engaged in agriculture and work on family farms or as laborers for other farmers. Many also assist with household chores or work in small family enterprises. Klasing's (2007) research in India found that 65% were working in agriculture, whereas another 10% were employed in small businesses. About 4% worked as carpenters, potters, or weavers. Contrary to the widely held stereotype, only 2% engaged in begging. Klasing found only a handful of people with disabilities in government or commercial sector employment.

A range of policies designed to promote productive and remunerative employment among people with disabilities are now available, but implementation remains a major problem, particularly in the Global South where competition for formal sector jobs is intense. As has been noted already, many governments in the developing world have ratified the *Convention on the Rights of People with Disabilities* or have legislation that specifically prohibits employment discrimination. However, violations are widespread. Klasing (2007) reports that the civil service quotas created to employ people with disabilities in India have not been filled and that discrimination against disabled applicants for government jobs is widespread. In terms of the Persons with Disabilities Act of 1995, the Indian government is mandated to provide incentives to commercial firms so that at least 5% of their employees will be comprised of people with disabilities. However, a decade later, no steps have been taken to implement this legislation. The South African government has also enacted laws to prohibit employment discrimination among people with disabilities, and it has actively promoted their employment by commercial firms. However, Gathiram (2008) reveals that less than 1% of the workforce is disabled and that the vast majority of firms have no policies for hiring people with disabilities.

To promote employment, governments should more vigorously respond to incidents of blatant exploitation and discrimination. Practices such as such as requiring people with disabilities to work for lower wages than those paid to able-bodied workers maintain them in poverty and impede their ability to pursue career opportunities. The problem is aggravated when a disabled person seeking employment is a person of color or an immigrant. Compliance with antidiscriminatory legislation is generally greater in the Western countries, but even here incidents of blatant as well as subtle discrimination still occur. In addition, antidiscriminatory provisions are not always accompanied by affirmative action incentives. For example, in the United States, the Americans with Disabilities Act does not require affirmative action in hiring or promoting people with disabilities. Accordingly, the number of people with disabilities in regular employment has not increased significantly in recent years (Fleischer & Zames, 2001). Obviously, subsidies and tax incentives could encourage more commercial firms to employ people with disabilities.

More proactive policies that facilitate employment are needed. Traditionally, sheltered workshops have been used for this purpose, but their impact has often been limited. Many countries may have only one or two workshops of this kind with the result that they serve only a small proportion of people with disabilities. In addition, they often maintain their clients in inappropriate and unproductive subsidized work and few are adequately prepared for employment in the open job market. In India, most sheltered workshops are located in the urban areas and cater primarily for industrial employees who have been injured at work (Klasing, 2007). Although sheltered workshops in South Africa do provide people with disabilities a small income and companionship, their clients have little prospect of finding regular employment on the labor market (Gathiram, 2008).

In addition to promoting regular employment, economic participation can be enhanced through self-employment and particularly through cooperative self-employment. The disabled community and its organizations have a vital role to play in advocating for opportunities of this kind, and government should provide training, support, and financial subsidies. As noted in Chapter 1, the microenterprise approach has been widely used in many parts of the world, particularly to assist poor women in supplementing their incomes. Klasing (2007) believes that this approach has the potential to support people with disabilities who work in small family enterprises, many of which are operated from the home. Existing government programs for able-bodied homeworkers, such as traditional *beedi* or cigarette rollers, could be extended to assist people with disabilities who are engaged in similar occupations. Although there are challenges to using the micro-enterprise approach, it should be more widely used.

On the other hand, people with disabilities in some Western countries such as the United States have succeeded in establishing their own micro-enterprises even though they face many challenges, including a lack of support from government rehabilitation agencies. As the San Francisco-based nonprofit organization Supported Employment Education Designs notes, there is a need for start-up funds and technical support because self-employment is often a viable option for people with disabilities, particularly if they can work in their own homes and do not face the challenge of having to travel to an office and negotiate numerous architectural and other barriers. Although the numbers assisted by the California Department of Rehabilitation Services remains small, some people with disabilities have launched successful small businesses. They include a woman with Down syndrome who runs puppet shows at children's parties and at local street markets in the San Francisco Bay Area. Another successful entrepreneur is a wheelchair user who works from home as an ergonomic consultant (Brevetti, 2008). In addition, several nonprofit organizations promote self-employment for people with disabilities. One example is *Creativity Explored*, which provides opportunities for 125 developmentally disabled artists to work in two San Francisco studios. Apart from paying a small commission to the studio, artists retain the income realized from regular art exhibitions.

Although many countries have introduced income maintenance programs for people with disabilities, they are often poorly articulated with employment policies. The South African government has significantly increased the value of its means-tested disability benefit in recent years, but it has not modified its disincentive effect, with the result that benefits are terminated when people with disabilities secure employment. This has the unfortunate result that people with disabilities are maintained on income support even though many are eager to work (Gathiram, 2008). As suggested earlier, non-means-tested universal programs avoid this problem and should be more widely adopted. Instead of viewing income maintenance as a substitute for earnings, income maintenance programs should be used to compensate people with disabilities for the extra costs they incur as a result of disability. Although this principle has been accepted in a number of countries, means-tested programs are still widely used, even in countries that can afford to pay universal benefits, such as the United States .

The prospect of securing employment also depends on the acquisition of skills and educational credentials, and obviously employment policies need to be accompanied by appropriate human capital policies. This is a major field of advocacy among the disability community, which has long campaigned to provide educational opportunities. In the United States, where children with disabilities have historically been confined to segregated and often inferior special schools, advocacy for improved educational opportunities intensified in the 1970s when the disability rights movement gained momentum. As noted earlier, this was also the time when discriminatory university admissions policies were successfully challenged. As a result of these campaigns, two major statutes were enacted in 1975— the Developmental Disabilities and Bill of Rights Act and the All Handicapped Children Act. The second statute was amended and renamed the Individuals with Disabilities Education Act in 1990. This law is particularly noteworthy because it requires that children's educational needs be properly assessed and individualized educational plans be formulated. In addition, its "least restrictive environment requirement" specifies that children with disabilities should be educated with able-bodied children rather than in segregated special education schools or classes. Although this provision has not been welcomed by everyone or fully implemented, it has made a major contribution to mainstreaming children with disabilities and creating an environment in which their education is normalized. For many disability activists, this is another vital step in promoting the integration of people with disabilities into the community.

Social Work and Disability

As mentioned at the beginning of this chapter, social workers have been involved in disability services for many years, but this is not a major field of social work practice. Generally, they have worked in residential or medical settings and have provided counseling and case management services. They have also been responsible securing financial aid, prosthetics, and other services for people with disabilities. Many work in teams with medical, nursing, and other professionals and have been an integral part of the professional expert approach to service provision in the disability field.

With a growing emphasis on self-determination, rights, independent living, and full participation in the life of the community, the expert model has been challenged by people with disabilities themselves, with the result that social work's contribution has changed significantly in recent times. Instead of being the providers of services to passive recipients, more social workers now work together with people with disabilities as collaborators, allies, and advocates. This new approach provides exciting opportunities for social workers to utilize their skills and expand their involvement in the field.

Social work also has a vital role to play in advocating for the rights of people with disabilities. Although the social work profession has not been at the forefront of the struggle for disability rights, professional social work organizations should be much more active in supporting people with disabilities as they advocate for rights. Obviously, individual social workers who work with people with disabilities can also function effectively as advocates. In this regard, it is interesting that Ed Roberts was encouraged to apply for admission to the University of California, Berkeley by a social worker who, with the support of his mother, persuaded him of the benefits of obtaining a university education. Although probably not aware of the full implications of this advice, Robert's social worker made a major contribution to the ongoing struggle to normalize the lives of people with disabilities (Fleischer & Zames, 2001).

The shift from residential to community living also offers an opportunity for social workers to support and facilitate independent, community living. Social workers are highly skilled and experienced at accessing community services and, by utilizing the systems approach, are able to broker the services that people with disabilities need if they are to lead independent lives. Their skills in case management and in accessing community resources are particularly relevant to this task. They are also adept at counseling and advising people with disabilities on accessing services. They can be particularly beneficial to people with disabilities who live on their own and are also well-placed to protect them against abuse and exploitation. In addition, as Mackelprang (2008) suggests, they can provide culturally competent services and ensure the full participation of people with disabilities in all decisions that affect their lives.

A significant development in the struggle for a rights and community-based approach to disability is the increase in the number of people with disabilities who have enrolled in social work programs over the years and qualified as professional social workers. As mentioned earlier, Anne Emerman was one of the first to obtain a social work degree after many years of living in a residential facility. Today it is not uncommon to find people with disabilities enrolled on both undergraduate and graduate social work programs and in some cases, social work programs have been established within specialized higher education institutions such as Gallaudet University in Washington, D.C., which has graduated numerous deaf and hard-of-hearing students who are able to bring their special expertise to bear when working with the deaf community. Many social work graduates with disabilities find employment in organizations that provide services to people with disabilities, and in addition, many of these organizations are owned and managed by people with disabilities. This development obviously facilitates a closer integration between the social work profession and the disabled community and reinforces the notion that social work should support the efforts of people with disabilities to achieve their own goals. Social workers need to embrace people with disabilities as vital collaborators with the profession and in this way forge a closer and more effective partnership with the disability community. Through a closer collaboration of this kind, social work's role and contribution can be refined and strengthened.

REFERENCES

Bruyere, S. M., Erickson, W. A., & Ferrentino, J. T. (2003). Identity and disability in the workplace. *William and Mary Law Review*, 44(3), 1173+. Questia database, Available at http://www.questia.com/PM.qst?a=o&d=5001908661 (Accessed June 12, 2008)

Brevetti, F. (2007). Disabled entrepreneurs face uphill battle. *Contra Costa Times*, August 20, 2007.

Campbell, M. (2008). (Dis)continuity of care: Explicating the ruling relations of home support, in M. L. DeVault, (Ed.) *People at work: Life, power, and social inclusion in the new economy*. New York: New York University Press, pp. 223–247.

Field, M., Jette A., & Martin L. (Eds.) (2006). *Workshop of the committee on disability in america: A new look*. Washington, D.C: National Academies Press.

Fleischer, D. Z. & Zames, F. (2001). *The disability rights movement: From charity to confrontation*. Philadelphia, PA: Temple University Press.

Gathiram, N. (2008). A critical review of the developmental approach to disability in South Africa. *International Journal of Social Welfare*, 17(2): 146–155.

Hayden, M. F. Social policies for people with disabilities, in J. Midgley, M. B. Tracy, & M. Livermore. (Eds.) (2000). *Handbook of social policy*. Thousand Oaks, CA: Sage Publications, pp. 277–292.

Klasing, J. (2007). *Disability and social exclusion in rural India*. New Delhi: Rawat Publications.

Mackelprang, R. W. (2008). Disability: Overview, in T. Mizrahi & L. E. Davis. (Eds.) *Encyclopedia of social work*, 20th Edition. New York: Oxford University Press, pp. 36–43.

Mallias, A. H. (2007). *Focus on national disability policy*. New York: Novinka Books.

Metts, R. L. (2000). *Disability issues, trends and recommendations for the World Bank*. Washington, D.C.

Miller, U. & Ziegler, S. (2006). *Making PRSP inclusive*. Munich, Germany: Handicap International.

Mont, D. (2007). *Measuring disability prevalence*. World Bank. SP Discussion Paper No. 0706. Washington, D.C.

Quinn G. and Degener, T. (2002). *The current use and future potential of United Nations human rights instruments in the context of disability*. New York: United Nations Publications.

Ridzi, F. Exploring problematics of the personal responsibility welfare state, in M. L. DeVault, (Ed.) (2008). *People at work: Life, power, and social inclusion in the new economy*. New York: New York University Press, pp. 223–247.

Rothman, J. (2003). *Social work practice across disability*. Boston, MA: Allyn and Bacon.

Seipel, M. (1994). Disability: An emerging global challenge. *International Social Work*, 37 (2): 165–187.

Traustadottir, R. (2008). Work, Disability and Social Inclusion, in M. L. DeVault (Ed.) *People at work: Life, power, and social inclusion in the new economy*. New York: New York University Press, pp. 74–93.

6

Poverty, Social Assistance, and Social Investment

JAMES MIDGLEY

When social work first emerged as a profession in the late 19th century, social workers were actively involved in poor relief. Indeed, the profession's origins are often traced to the charities and particularly the Charity Organization Society, which provided emergency, short-term financial aid to those in need. As government social assistance programs expanded in the 20th century, social work's involvement also increased. For example, in the United States during the Great Depression, social workers were closely associated with the welfare services established in terms of the New Deal. However, in the latter half of the 20th century, they gradually withdrew from programs of this kind, and most gravitated toward specialized forms of practice that were not directly concerned with poor relief, such as child welfare, hospital social work, family welfare, and psychiatric social work. In addition, counseling and psychotherapeutic interventions became increasingly popular.

The disengagement of social work from social assistance is unfortunate not only because of social work's formative involvement in the field but because many of the people served by social workers live in poverty and deprivation. The persistence of poverty among these clients poses a major challenge to the profession. Social workers are ethically bound to serve the neediest and most vulnerable groups and to promote social well-being and social justice. By disengaging from social assistance, they have neglected poverty and deprivation and failed to meet this obligation. To be fair, it should be recognized that although few social workers in the United States are directly involved in the administration of social assistance, many still work with clients receiving social assistance benefits, by for example, providing

child welfare and mental health services. In addition, some have found employment as managers and supervisors of social assistance programs. However, as a
whole, the profession currently takes little interest in social assistance, and the subject is almost totally ignored at schools of social work in the United States.

On the other hand, social workers in some countries continue to be involved
in the management of social assistance programs. Although they are not always
concerned with the intricacies of determining eligibility, they play an active role in
supervising and managing social assistance programs; in several countries, they are
actively involved in policy formulation. As in the United States, they also work
closely with clients who receive social assistance benefits. Examples include countries as varied as Australia, Hong Kong, the Philippines, and South Africa. They
have also participated in formulating innovative approaches that offer new opportunities for social work to collaborate with others to address the problem of poverty. Known loosely as developmental social assistance, these programs promote
social investments that alleviate poverty and contribute positively to development.

This chapter seeks to show how social work can play an active role in developmental social assistance programs and contribution to poverty alleviation. It begins
by discussing the nature of social assistance and describing social work's involvement in the field. It distinguishes between the residual Poor Law approach and
more recent developmental innovations. Several examples are provided that illustrate how developmental social assistance has been used in different countries. The
chapter concludes by examining social work's role in implementing developmental
approaches. But first, the nature of social assistance and a brief overview of social
work's historical engagement with social assistance is discussed.

Social Assistance and Social Work

Social assistance forms a part of a larger category of governmental income maintenance programs that are also known in the international literature as "social
security," "income protection," or "social protection." Social assistance is a major
form of income maintenance. It is also known as "selective" or "targeted" programs
or as "cash transfers" or "minimum income" programs. In the United States, social
assistance is often referred to as "welfare." Similar to other income maintenance
programs, social assistance is established by legislation, managed by a governmental agency, and has clearly defined eligibility requirements and benefit provisions.
However, the use of the means test to determine need and eligibility distinguishes
social assistance from other income maintenance programs. The means test is used
to assess the income and assets of applicants and, provided they are below a prede-
termined level, benefits are paid. In addition to the means test, other eligibility
requirements such as citizenship, residence, age, disability, and gender may also be
imposed. Social assistance benefits usually take the form of cash payments, but
food rations, clothing, travel vouchers, prosthetics, access to housing, and medical
services may also be provided. In-kind benefits often take the form of vouchers that

are exchanged for goods and services. Social assistance programs either provide "general" assistance to individuals or families facing financial need or otherwise serve particular groups or "categories" of needy people, such as the elderly, children, or people with disabilities.

Social assistance programs are provided "as a right" to those who meet eligibility requirements. The notion of "right to benefit" is enshrined in many national statutes as well asn international treaties and human rights instruments and is vigorously championed by international agencies such as the International Labour Organization and the International Social Security Association. However, because of fiscal exigencies, administrative limitations, and ideological opposition, the right to receive social assistance is not always observed. Often, able-bodied adults— particularly able-bodied men of working age—are denied assistance. On the other hand, those who are unable to find employment may be assisted, usually on a temporary basis. In many countries, social assistance is only paid if claimants have no relatives who can support them.

Unfortunately, the payment of social assistance is often stigmatizing, and clients are frequently accused of being irresponsible, indolent, and "dependent" on government handouts. They are also often accused of abusing social assistance and even of obtaining benefits fraudulently. Social assistance and other social service programs targeted at poor people are a classic example of what Wilensky and Lebeaux (1965) called "residual" social welfare. Advocates of the residual welfare approach believe that governments should use the social services in a very limited way and only intervene when other sources of assistance are unavailable. Although residual social assistance may provide a modicum of aid to those in desperate financial circumstances, it fails to contribute to poverty alleviation at the community and societal levels.

Social Work's Historic Role in Social Assistance

Social assistance is the oldest form of statutory income maintenance. There are records of governments granting in-kind or cash benefits to needy people many centuries ago. For example, state-sponsored poor relief was provided by the Byzantian emperors to supplement religious charity provided by the Church, and during the time of the Islamic Caliphs, centralized public treasuries or *beit- ul-mal* were created to help those in need. However, state involvement in poor relief was uncommon, and poor people were usually aided through religious institutions such as temples, mosques, monasteries, and churches.

The evolution of statutory welfare provision in Northern Europe owed much to Christian teaching. de Schweinitz (1943) reported that the English monarchy first became involved in social assistance by enacting laws that imposed penalties on those who failed to pay tithes. These early medieval statutes also authorized the punishment of beggars and permitted the forcible repatriation of vagrants to their home parishes. As is well-known, the Elizabethan Poor Law of 1601 drew a sharp distinction between those who were unable to work and maintain themselves, and able-bodied applicants who were believed to be indolent and irresponsible. The former category was known as the "deserving poor," and they could expect to be helped. The latter category, which included beggars, vagrants, and the work-shy, were known as the "undeserving" poor and obviously were denied aid. This statute served as a model for many social assistance programs that were subsequently created in many other parts of the world.

With industrialization and urbanization in the 19th century, the numbers of people receiving social assistance increased, and in an attempt to discourage applications, harsh eligibility conditions were imposed. Those applying for aid were subjected to intrusive investigations, were required to appear at public hearings, and were often humiliated. In addition, many were consigned to residential facilities known as almshouses or workhouses where, as reformers reported, living conditions were appalling. These reformers, who included the founders of social work, campaigned to prevent the incarceration of the deserving poor. The reforming founders of social work were also concerned about the wider problem of poverty, deprivation, and exploitation in the rapidly growing industrial cities of Western Europe and North America. Many rural people and immigrants were drawn to the cities in the hope of earning cash wages and improving their living standards, but many lived in atrocious conditions in crowded tenement buildings and were exposed to disease, poor nutrition, and the exploitation of slum landlords.

Although social work's founders were committed to ameliorating these conditions, they had different opinions on how this should be done. The leaders of the Charity Organization Society emphasized the need for trained volunteer workers, known as friendly visitors, who could work directly with poor families, diagnose the causes of their need and help them to become self-sufficient. On the other hand, the founders of the settlements stressed the importance of community-based approaches that sought to improve local living conditions. They also advocated for social reforms that would address the root causes of poverty. They campaigned for improved working conditions, decent wages, education, and health care. They also advocated for the expansion of income maintenance programs, such as the Mother's Pensions, that were introduced by many state governments in the United States in the early 20th century.

These efforts intensified, and at the time of the New Deal, social workers played an important role in the administration and financing of the federal government's new social assistance programs. Their involvement was actively promoted by federal officials such as Harry Hopkins and Frances Perkins, who had been closely associated with the emerging social work profession. Hopkin's deputy, Josephine Brown, encouraged the schools of social work to prepare students to practice in the public sector, and she also arranged for incumbent civil servants to obtain a professional social work education. Following the enactment of the Social Security Act in 1935, Jane Hoey, who was a professionally qualified social worker, was appointed the first Director of the Bureau of Public Assistance. The Bureau was responsible for implementing the new Aid to Dependent Children (ADC) program, which had been established by the Act (Stadum, 1999). This program was subsequently renamed Aid to Families with Dependent Children (AFDC).

Hoey and other leading federal welfare administrators such as Charles Schottland, the Commissioner of Social Security, and Wilbur Cohen, Assistant Secretary at the Department of Health Education and Welfare (who had been a professor at the University of Michigan's School of Social Work) continued to promote social work's involvement in social assistance, largely by claiming that families receiving benefits faced various personal and social problems that were amenable to social work intervention. In 1956, Congress amended the Social Security Act to authorize the provision of "rehabilitative" social work services, and in 1962, during the Kennedy administration, the provision of social work services to social assistance clients was strengthened through what became known as the "service amendments" to the Act.

The amendments strengthen the role of social work services in income maintenance. Many schools of social work also benefited as more federal funds were allocated for professional education. In 1967, during the Johnson administration, additional amendments were passed. Despite these efforts, by the late 1960s, only a small proportion of the staff working directly with social assistance recipients had professional social work qualifications (Leighninger, 1999). In addition, critics questioned social work's effectiveness, noting that although additional funds had been allocated for intensive professional intervention, caseloads had continued to rise. They also claimed that professional social workers failed to help clients to find employment and become self-sufficient and that they were providing "soft" services rather than interventions that ended dependency (Gilbert, 1998). At the same time, many social workers were committed to welfare rights ideals and were reluctant to be associated with programs that sought to control the behavior of their clients.

In the 1980s, as social assistance programs were frequently pilloried in the media, public support for social assistance waned, and it was not surprising that the service amendments were repealed after President Reagan was elected to office. Reagan had been a vociferous critic of welfare, and with the enactment of the Omnibus Budget and Reconciliation Act (OBRA) in 1981, severe cuts were made to the AFDC program. Approximately 408,000 families were expelled from the system, and the benefits of another 299,000 were reduced (Stoesz, 2009). Stricter eligibility requirements were also imposed, and compliance monitoring was increased. In addition, funds for professional social work education were terminated.

Racist attitudes and stereotypes played a major role in undermining social assistance at this time. During the 1960s and 1970s, the numbers of African Americans and other minorities receiving social assistance benefits increased steadily. This fact did not escape the media's attention, which generally implied that the vast majority of AFDC recipients were African American women and other minorities. A number of well-publicized cases of fraud and abuse of the system by African American women resulted in the emergence of an image of the typical welfare recipient as an unmarried African American woman with numerous children who lived in relative comfort on AFDC, food stamps, and other social assistance benefits. The fact that White women had also been convicted of fraud and abuse was conveniently overlooked, as was the fact that the majority of AFDC recipients were not in fact people of color. In the 1980s, President Reagan himself exploited this stereotype in several campaign speeches where he made reference to the "welfare queen" who unashamedly exploited the welfare system. Although he avoided referring directly to race, White Americans understood the insinuation, and the welfare system was now inevitably racialized and gendered. This development also thrust welfare into the center of the political agenda and insured that it dominated electoral politics for many years to come. It also subtly discouraged social workers from playing a major role in social welfare.

Although the New Deal and the service amendments offered an opportunity for social workers to be involved in the American social assistance program, this opportunity was never fully realized. Few social work graduates were attracted to the field; rather, most sought employment in family counseling, mental health, child welfare, medical social work, and other more prestigious fields. The popularization of psychoanalysis and other psychotherapies also undermined social work's early commitment to address the poverty problem (Specht & Courtney, 1994; Lowe & Reid, 1999). At the same time, as social assistance and eligibility determination became more routinized and bureaucratic, the need for professional intervention was given little priority. By the 1990s, when welfare to work became a major issue in the United States, the social work profession was only marginally involved in national debates about the future of social assistance (Midgley, 2006).

Social Assistance and Social Investment

As in the United States, social workers in some parts of the world have also disengaged from social assistance. On the other hand, in some other countries, social workers have continued to be involved in social assistance; in some cases, they have participated in the formulation of new developmental approaches or even led these initiatives. As noted at the beginning of this chapter, these approaches transcend the residual Poor Law model by seeking to invest in people's capabilities, alleviate poverty, and promote development.

The following provides information about three types of developmental social assistance programs. These programs are developmental because they have an investment effect. The first comprises conditional cash transfer programs, which pay benefits to poor families provided that children attend school regularly and that other conditionalities, such as immunization and health checks, are met. The second is the employment activation or "welfare-to-work" approach, which is designed to promote the active participation of clients in the labor force through education and job training as well as employment referral and placement. A third type uses social assistance to subsidize the incomes of poor families through categorical programs. In addition to contributing to poverty alleviation, these programs have a social investment effect in that they contribute to improved nutrition and health and foster school attendance.

Human Capital Investment and Conditional Cash Transfers

The governments of the developing countries of the Global South have invested extensively in education since the 1950s, with positive results. Primary school enrollments and literacy rates have increased exponentially in many parts of the developing world. The contention that the developing countries needed to invest in human as well as physical capital if they were to experience economic modernization legitimized the rapid expansion of educational opportunities. Initially, human capital was narrowly defined as investments in education, but in time, the concept was broadened to include investments in health and nutrition. An efficient and productive labor force is not only well-educated but healthy and well-nourished (Schultz, 1981).

However, although improvements in education have been accompanied in some countries, such as Korea, Singapore, and Taiwan, with rapid employment growth and a significant decline in poverty, in others, employment growth has not been as successful, and many high school and college graduates cannot find work. In yet others, there has been little economic growth and poverty remains endemic.

Many factors are responsible for the persistence of poverty in the South. These include ineffective planning, inadequate investment, and limited access to global markets, but unfortunately, corruption, conflict, and dictatorship are also to blame. Another factor is the imposition of structural adjustment programs as a condition for debt relief by the International Monetary Fund and the World Bank in the 1980s and 1990s. These programs required massive public expenditure cuts, civil service layoffs, retrenchments in health and education programs, and the introduction of user fees by schools, health clinics, and hospitals. They had a serious impact on human capital development. In many countries where health, education, and other social service programs were retrenched, school attendance and health and nutritional standards declined. Faced with rising poverty rates and a deteriorating social situation, international agencies such as the World Bank supported the creation of what were known as "safety nets." These included social funds and food for work programs that replaced the governmental social assistance programs that had been abolished or retrenched because of structural adjustment programs (Hall & Midgley, 2004).

It was in this context that the governments of some Latin American countries introduced conditional cash transfer programs, which as noted earlier, pay benefits on the condition that poor families send their children to school regularly and comply with health and nutritional requirements. It was argued that this innovative use of social assistance would not only address the poverty problem but promote human capital investments, which would in turn contribute to economic development and have a durable, long-term impact on poverty (Morley & Coady, 2003).

The Mexican government is usually credited with taking the lead, and its program, which was originally known as *Progressa*, has been extensively discussed in both the academic literature and popular media. Concerned by the rise in poverty following the country's financial crisis of the 1990s, the government of President Ernesto Zedillo decided to use social assistance to augment the incomes of poor families with children and, at the same time, to promote human capital development through increased school attendance and the utilization of nutritional and maternal and child health services. It was believed that this would be more effective than the incremental "safety net" approach advocated by the World Bank. The program was launched in 1997 and, by the end of decade, was operating throughout the country. By 2005, approximately 5 million families (or almost all families living below the government's poverty line) were receiving benefits. During Vincente Fox's presidency, the program was renamed *Opportunidades* (Levy, 2006).

Similar programs have been established in many other Latin American countries, including Nicargua, Honduras, Chile, and Brazil, which now has the largest program of its kind in the world. The Brazilian program, which is known as *Bolsa Familia*, was based on an earlier program established by President Fernando Henrique Cardoso, but it has been significantly expanded and combined with other programs by his successor. Initially the program covered about 8.7 million families, and by 2007, 11.2 million families were receiving benefits. This figure is roughly equivalent to the numbers of families living below the country's poverty line. By 2005, the total cost of the program exceeded $3 billion (Silva, 2006).

A much smaller program, *Red de Proteccion Social* (RPS), has been operating in Nicaragua since 2000. This program pays a cash education grant equivalent to $15 every 2 months for each child enrolled in school as well as an annual $25 benefit to purchase school books and supplies. It also pays the equivalent of $42 per month per family in the form of food vouchers and a medical benefit of $90 per year that families can use to pay private providers for medical services (Bradshaw, 2008). Through the efforts on the World Bank and other international agencies, conditional cash transfer programs have now been introduced in other countries around the world as well.

Unlike the Poor Law approach, conditional cash transfer programs do not usually apply a strict individual means test to determine eligibility. Instead, a proactive, targeting approach is used through which the poorest neighborhoods or communities are identified and household eligibility is determined by proxy-targeting techniques, such as the condition of the family's home, the size of their agricultural holdings, and other indicators. In some cases, local committees comprised of community leaders determine eligibility. Some programs simply enroll all children at schools in poor communities, whereas others are demand-driven, in that families are encouraged to apply, but even here, the means test is not rigidly implemented. Cash benefits are usually paid, but vouchers for food, medical care, and other services are also used. Benefits are paid to mothers, who must produce documentary evidence, usually in the form of school attendance cards or other certified documents to confirm compliance. In many cases, benefits are paid on a designated day, and participating families are required to report in person to receive their benefits.

As will be appreciated, conditional cash transfer programs pay relatively small cash benefits, and their impact on the incidence of poverty may, therefore, be regarded as limited. On the other hand, a plethora of studies have shown that they have contributed to increased school enrollments and improvements in nutritional and health status in poor communities. In Mexico, school enrollments among program participants are reported to have increased from 7.2% to 9.3% for girls and from 3.5% to 5.8% for boys (Rawlings, 2005). In some rural areas, enrollment increases of up to 85% have been reported. However, because Mexico already has a high primary school enrollment rate, increases have been recorded largely at the intermediate and high school levels. In addition, it is claimed that the program has reduced the maternal mortality rate by 11% and that the nutritional and health status of children under age 3 years has improved significantly (Bradshaw, 2008). In Nicaragua, primary school enrollment among participants is reported to have increased by nearly 22%, but it should be noted that the initial enrollment rate was significantly lower than in Mexico (Rawlings, 2005). A 5% reduction in malnutrition among participants was also reported (Bradshaw, 2008). Similar positive outcomes have been recorded in Brazil (Hall, 2006).

Although conditional cash transfer programs are becoming popular, more rigorous evaluations are needed to assess their impact both in terms of their poverty alleviation and developmental effects. The programs are also faced with significant administrative and cost challenges. For example, in Nicaragua, the program currently serves only a small proportion of the poor population, and the cost of covering all of those in extreme poverty could be prohibitive (Bradshaw, 2008). Another problem is that it is difficult to measure compliance, especially in large programs where it is difficult to record school enrollments and attendance. It is equally difficult to monitor the use of medical and other social services. Another factor is whether local schools, clinics, maternal and child health centers, and other social services are able to provide quality services and whether increased utilization significantly improves the educational and health status of poor families and communities.

The effectiveness of these programs has also been questioned on gender grounds. Although they are targeted at women, conflicting assessments of their impact on gender equality have been produced. Their political ramifications have also been critically examined. As Hall (2006) reveals, the Brazilian program has been manipulated for electoral purposes and in some cases, families that do not support local politicians have been excluded. These problems obviously limit the effectiveness of these programs. Although many studies have shown that conditional cash transfer programs are well-targeted at the poorest groups, more needs to be done to ensure that they attain their goals, particularly in the poorest rural areas. Nevertheless, conditional cash transfers show that conventional, residual social assistance programs can be reconfigured so that they alleviate poverty, enhance human capital formation, and contribute positively to development.

Employment Activation and Welfare-to-Work

The employment activation or "welfare-to-work" approach is designed to help social assistance recipients find remunerative employment or engage in self-employment and, in this way, participate in the productive economy. Advocates of the activation approach believe that the vast majority of people meet their needs and those of their families through income derived from employment or self-employment. By engaging in work, they also contribute to economic development. Welfare-to-work proponents also believe that productive employment or self-employment offers a viable opportunity to escape from poverty.

However, this seemingly simple premise is complicated by a number of difficult issues. One issue is whether work should be required of those who receive social assistance benefits. Some contend that social assistance should embody social values such as altruism and a compassionate concern for the needy and that benefits should be provided unconditionally. On the other hand, many critics of social assistance believe that the payment of unconditional benefits to the poor fosters "welfare dependency," indolence, and other undesirable behaviors. These criticisms resulted in the imposition of increasingly stringent eligibility requirements on social assistance recipients in the United States and other countries in the 1980s and 1990s (Lodemal & Trickey, 2001; Midgley, 2008a; Peck, 2000).

The use of education and skills training as well as the provision of work supports is another relevant issue in the design of an effective welfare to work program. Generally, advocates of welfare-to-work believe that intensive job training, counseling, and employment referral and placement are essential for a successful transition to employment. They also believe that work supports such as child care and subsidized transport are needed. However, this position is challenged by advocates of the "work-first" approach such as Mead (1997), who argue that social assistance recipients should be placed in work immediately, irrespective of their educational level of job skills. Although the work-first approach was adopted in the United States with the creation of the Temporary Assistance for Needy Families (TANF) program in 1996, it has been heavily criticized and fortunately is not widely used in other countries.

A final issue is what type of welfare to work program should be adopted. Employment activation may involve job placement in the open labor market without supports, or it may involve placement in a supported environment where training and counseling are used. It may also utilize sheltered employment facilities where welfare recipients—particularly those with disabilities—are employed. A fairly novel development, at least in the Western countries, is self-employment. This approach has been pioneered in the Global South, where opportunities for the employment of social assistance recipients in the open labor market are very limited.

Many examples of these different approaches can be given, but to illustrate, only two are discussed here. The first, which comes from Britain, is the "New Deal" approach introduced by the Labour Government after its election in 1997. This approach is primarily concerned with moving long-term unemployed social assistance recipients into regular wage employment. It is similar to welfare-to-work programs in other European countries. The second comes from the Philippines, where the government helps social assistance recipients start and manage small businesses through providing microcredit and other supports. Although the TANF "welfare reform" program in the United States is widely cited internationally as an example of an effective welfare-to-work initiative, its coercive "work-first" philosophy, lack of social investments and political entanglements render it unsuitable for discussion in this chapter.

In 1998, the New Deal program was introduced by the Labour Government in Britain. The Labour Party was voted out of office some 18 years earlier and had lost several subsequent elections. Although the Party had historically championed the expansion of social programs, the claim that its welfare policies had contributed to the country's economic decline resonated with many voters. In response, the Party promised in its election manifesto that it would introduce a new welfare to work program that would, as the Party leadership put it, "provide work for those who can and security for those that cannot" (Evans, 2001, p. 260). Four different New Deal programs were introduced. The first is the New Deal for Young People that targets unemployed youth—particularly those who drop out of school. The second is the New Deal for the Long-Term Unemployed, which is concerned with adults over age 25 years who have been out of work for more than 2 years. The third, the New Deal for Lone Parents, assists single parents find employment. The next is the New Deal for Disabled People, which as its name suggests, targets people with disabilities. In addition to these core New Deal programs, programs for the spouses or partners of unemployed people and for unemployed people over age 50 years were also created.

These programs are administratively separated to provide tailor-made services and to ensure that clients receive specialized services. Nevertheless, they share common features. In each case, applicants are referred to one of the specialized New Deal programs mentioned earlier, where they are assigned a Personal Advisor who makes an assessment of their needs and circumstances and provides intensive counseling and support. After this initial "gateway" period, as it is known, a personal plan is prepared, and one of three options is chosen: First, clients may be referred to a full-time education and job training program; second, to regular employment (which is often subsidized); and third, to work in a voluntary or community setting that may range from a nonprofit agency or a municipal public works program. However, these programs are flexible and personal advisors are able to exercise considerable discretion in meeting the needs of their clients. Also, the use of sanctions varies with the different programs. Because the government has placed highest priority on addressing the problem of youth unemployment, intervention with this client group is intensive and firm.

Initial evaluations of the New Deal program were generally positive. Evans (2001) reported that the most successful were the New Deal for Young People and New Deal for the Long-Term Unemployed, which, as noted earlier, were given high priority. These two programs also provided the most intensive interventions.

Within 2 years of its inception, 490,000 young and 270,000 older unemployed people had enrolled in the program. However, although the proportion of young unemployed people who found regular employment was approximately 45%, only 19% of unemployed people over the age of 25 years were placed in regular employment. The proportions of those in the New Deal for Lone Parents and the New Deal for Disabled People who found regular employment were considerably lower. Whereas 23% of lone mothers who enrolled in the program found employment, the percentage for people with disabilities was only 5%.

A more recent government report on the achievements of the program (United Kingdom, 2008) stated that the number of long-term recipients of unemployment benefits had fallen from more than half a million in 1997 to about 125,000 in 2007. Similarly, the number of young people receiving long-term benefits had fallen from about 85,000 to fewer than 7,000 during the same period. The number of single parents receiving benefits had fallen by nearly 250,000. Drawing on a number of independent studies, the report claimed that the New Deal programs had contributed significantly to the decline in the country's overall unemployment rate and that it had benefited the economy by more than 500 million pounds sterling per annum (or about $750 million in 2009). Government spending on the New Deal programs produced a social rate of return of about 4%.

Although opinions on the outcomes of the New Deals differ, there is agreement that the program has reduced the incidence of poverty—particularly child poverty—largely because of employment activation, as reported by Evans and Millar (2006). However, many experts recognize that much more needs to be done to address the problem of poverty among ethnic minorities and immigrant families (McKay & Rowlingson, 2008). The current global recession and the steep rise in unemployment will undoubtedly exacerbate the problem. The Labour government was fortunate in that its welfare-to-work program and related antipoverty measures were implemented at the time of economic expansion and growing prosperity. These programs may be less effective in the current economic climate.

Whereas the British New Deal program is of relatively recent origin, the Philippines micro-enterprise program, which is known as the Self-Employment Assistance Program (SEAP), dates back to the 1970s. Earlier, small income-generating projects among needy people had been established with the help of UNICEF, and although these projects were limited in scope, their potential to augment the country's conventional social assistance program and have a wider poverty alleviation and developmental impact was soon recognized. In the early 1970s, this resulted in the introduction of several new social welfare programs that the government believed would have a significant developmental impact. In addition to the new SEAP, these included a nutritional program for preschool children, a community-based childcare program, and a commitment to promote family planning.

Originally, the SEAP provided small grants and loans to individual social assistance clients. Many were single women with children who had applied to the government's Social Welfare Department for emergency aid, but people with disabilities were also assisted. Vocational training and technical support was also provided.

By the mid-1980s, thousands of micro-enterprises had been established. Although the vending of cooked food, fruit, newspapers, candies, and soft drinks was popular, agricultural projects such as poultry raising, mushroom cultivation, and vegetable farming as well as the production of crafts, decorative household items, pottery, carpet and mat weaving, and basketry had also emerged. In the early days, the program was supported by private donors and nonprofit organizations, but as its achievements were recognized, the banks also became involved and government funds were also allocated.

An early study of the SEAP projects revealed that almost half were successful in that their owners reported increased incomes. 83%of participants reported that their consumption of food and clothing had increased, as had their utilization of schools and health clinics. Forty-five percent reported that they had learned new skills and improved their business acumen as a result of business skills training. Most of those who did not report improvement in skills were engaged in vending activities. Loan repayment rates were around 75%, but in the case of very small businesses, loans were often replaced by grants (Quieta et al., 2003).

Although most of the micro-enterprises were initially managed and operated by individual clients and their family members, cooperative enterprises were subsequently favored. This development was inspired in part by the success of the Grameen Bank in Bangladesh. Several demonstration projects were launched during the administration of President Fidel Ramos to test the cooperative model; this resulted in the creation of the Self-Employment Assistance–Kaunlaran Program (or SEA-K), which provides loans as well as training and technical assistance to cooperative enterprises consisting of between 20 and 30 members. As in micro-enterprise development projects in other countries, the majority of these members are women. Another development has been the gradual devolution of the program to the local government authorities so that the central government now has overall oversight and policymaking authority while the local governments are responsible for implementation. Quieta and colleagues (2003) reported that by 2001, cooperative SEA-K enterprises with more than 24,000 members were operating in many of the country's 42,000 barangays (which is the smallest unit of administration in the Philippines). Their study of the participants also revealed that 65% reported an increase in family income, and 75% reported that they were able to save some of their additional earnings. The majority also reported improvements in health and nutritional levels, especially among children. School attendance among the children of participating family members had also improved (Quieta et al., 2003).

The statistics reveal that micro-enterprise projects can serve as an alternative to conventional social assistance programs and that they have an investment function that enhances capabilities, raises standards of living, and contributes to economic development. However, the Philippine experience suggests that although self-employment has positive effects, it is not appropriate in all cases. As the statistics reveal, the SEAP program covers a relatively small proportion of needy people. In addition, a significant number of enterprises are not successful and either default on loan repayments or cease to operate. In many cases, micro-enterprises require hard work and generate small incomes. Although micro-enterprises are currently viewed as an effective antipoverty strategy by many development experts, their limitation should be recognized. Nevertheless, they have an important role to play in fostering a developmental approach to social assistance, particularly if linked to a wider poverty alleviation strategy (Midgley, 2008b).

Subsidizing the Incomes of Poor Families

Although social assistance has historically provided meager, short-term benefits to those in desperate financial need, many social assistance recipients actually require and receive long-term support. This tendency has become much more evident in recent times as the numbers of elderly poor people and people with disabilities receiving assistance has increased. Long-term social assistance receipt is also associated with the growing numbers of single parents who require aid while raising their children. The increasing utilization of social assistance by these groups has been observed in many different countries and accounts for the rise in social assistance receipt in many countries, particularly as the proportion of elderly people in the population has increased.

Long-term social assistance is provided in two ways. First, it may form a part of the government's general social assistance program; second, it may be provided through separate or dedicated "categorical" programs established specifically to pay benefits to particular groups of needy people such as the elderly. An example of the former is in Hong Kong, where the Comprehensive Social Security Assistance (CSSA) Program caters for all needy people, including those who require long-term support such as the elderly and disabled people. An example of the latter is South Africa where separate, categorical social assistance programs have been created. Here, needy elderly people are assisted through the State Old Age Pension (SOAP) program, and poor children receive benefits through a separate program known as the Child Support Grant (CSG). In turn, poor people with disabilities receive benefits through a separate Disability Grant program.

Because these programs are funded through public revenues and are usually administered by the same government agency, there may seem to be little need to administratively separate them. However, the use of categorical social assistance programs permits more effective targeting and addresses criticisms associated with the payment of social assistance to the unemployed and other allegedly "undeserving" groups. In Hong Kong, for example, criticisms of the CSSA Program have intensified in recent years as the numbers receiving benefits has increased (Tang, 2010). Although it is widely believed that the growth of the program has resulted from a rapid increase in work-shy immigrants and unemployed workers, these increases are largely the result of the number of needy elderly people requiring aid. If separate programs for different categories of needy people had been created, the true situation would be apparent. And, because needy elderly people are generally believed to be deserving of aid, the problem of stigma would be minimized.

The South African government has made particularly effective use of categorical social assistance programs to subsidize the incomes of poor families. In the mid-1990s, when the country made a successful transition from apartheid to democracy, the new government set about abolishing the racially discriminatory practice of paying different levels of benefit to different racial groups. In addition to addressing this problem, the government was also concerned about the country's high level of poverty, particularly among the rural African population. Although South Africa is a middle-income country, Patel and Trieghaardt (2008) report that about 10% of the population is below the World Bank's $1-a-day poverty line and that about a half fall below a more generous poverty line of about R 500 per month (or approximately $70 per month in 2008). Although the government implemented a vigorous economic development strategy in an attempt to create jobs and reduce the incidence of poverty, it was recognized that the country's social security system could be purposefully used to address the poverty problem.

The decision to use social assistance as a poverty alleviation strategy also came about because of the recommendations of the Lund Committee, which was appointed by the government in 1996 to review the country's Social Security programs. The Committee proposed that the social assistance system be reconfigured to target the poorest households, and it argued that it would be relatively easy to build on the program's existing infrastructure and increase the flow of benefits to the poorest pension recipients, the vast majority of whom are Africans living in poor rural areas. Their committee also recognized that the majority of pensioners live in extended families and that their benefits circulate within the household. By increasing their pensions, the household's income also increases. The committee also proposed that an existing social assistance program for lone mothers be replaced with a comprehensive child benefit program for poor children. The existing program was limited in scope and catered largely for young unmarried women with children. The Committee recommended that it be abolished and replaced with a Child Support Grant that would pay a flat rate benefit to all poor children up to age 6 years. Similarly to the old age assistance pension, it was likely that the additional income paid through the child benefit would circulate within the household income. The Committee also made recommendations about disability and other benefits, but its proposal that social assistance be deliberately used as a poverty alleviation strategy was particularly novel.

Following the adoption of the Lund Committee's recommendations, the numbers of poor elderly receiving the State Old Age Pension rose steadily, and by the end of the century, approximately 2.1 million were drawing benefits. The program is reasonably well-targeted and covers about 80% of those eligible for pensions. The benefit level is R 870 per month, which was equivalent to approximately $125 per month in 2008. Pensions are paid (subject to a means test) to men at age 65 years and women at age 60 years.

The Child Support Grant was launched in 1998. Initially, uptake was slow, but as the program became more widely known, the numbers of recipients increased steadily.

By 2005, approximately 70% of eligible children received the grant, and uptake was reported to be highest in the country's poorest provinces (Trieghaartd, 2005). By 2007, it reached approximately 7.9 million poor children (Patel & Trieghaartd, 2008). As the government recognized the program's role in poverty alleviation, the age of eligibility was increased from 6 years to 14 years. The benefit level is currently R 200 per month (or approximately $26 in 2008). Although comparatively low, the program injects cash into the incomes of very poor families. An added feature of the program is its integration with medical care and nutritional services for families with children under age 6 years. This is intended to augment the payment of cash benefits with improved health and nutritional status.

Although old age social assistance pensions and child support grants form the core components of the government's social assistance poverty alleviation strategy, other social assistance programs such as the Disability Grant and foster care grant have also contributed. The numbers receiving disability benefits rose from about 600,000 in the mid-1990s to 1.4 million in 2007 (Patel & Trieghaartd, 2008). The numbers of social assistance recipients who care for orphaned and abandoned or neglected children (such as relatives) has also increased.

The South African government's decision to use social assistance as a poverty alleviation strategy was not universally welcomed. In the mid-1990s when it took this decision, the tenets of neoliberal economics were generally accepted and few economists approved of the expansion of social programs. Many were convinced that social spending on the scale envisioned by the government would be counter-productive and have little impact on the incidence of poverty. The government's policies would, they claimed, divert sizable resources from economic development, increase public spending and borrowing, and have inflationary consequences (in the absence of real economic growth). Instead of allocating scare resources to "unproductive" welfare programs, the government was urged to adopt policies that lower taxes, liberalize trade, foster entrepreneurship, and create a dynamic free market economy.

Although the government was indeed committed to economic liberalization and greater international trade, it did not waver from its commitment to use the social security system to address the country's poverty problem and the numbers of social assistance recipients continued to rise. Several studies revealed that by 2004, the incidence of poverty had fallen not only because of higher rates of economic growth but because of the social assistance program (Patel & Trieghaardt, 2008). Research into the impact of social assistance on the incomes of recipients also showed that these programs were effectively targeted and that resources had been transferred to the country's poorest groups on a significant scale. The old age pension, disability grants, and child support grants were particularly effective in contributing to improved standards of living. Per capita incomes among recipients in the lowest two quintiles increased by about 30% as a result of social assistance subsidies.

In addition to alleviating poverty among social assistance recipients, the program also has an investment function. Studies have shown that with increased disposable income, children are less likely to work and more likely to be sent to school; obviously, this fosters human capital development (Edmonds, 2006). In addition, by intentionally linking families receiving benefits to health and nutritional services, the program promotes improved health and nutrition with positive implications for human capital development (Patel & Trieghaardt, 2008).

Another investment effect is an increase in local economic activities. Patel and Trieghaardt (2008) report that the injection of cash resources into the budgets of poor households stimulates trade and economic production, particularly in poor communities. With additional income, poor families are able to purchase extra food and other commodities they could not previously afford, and this has created higher demand and stimulated local small businesses. In addition, new forms of economic activity have emerged. Because few poor families have bank accounts, the government contracts with private firms to distribute benefits. This takes place on what are now colloquially known as "pension days," when benefit payments are made, usually in a central public place. In addition to receiving their benefits, social assistance recipients use the opportunity to buy and sell produce, livestock, and other commodities. In addition, recipients sell their own produce and other goods. Although social assistance is widely regarded as an unproductive, consumption-based program, the pension day markets that have emerged from the government's social assistance programs have clearly enhanced local economic activities (Patel & Trieghaardt, 2008).

Social Work's Contribution

Although social workers in the United States and some other countries have disengaged from social assistance, the emergence of developmental social assistance programs such as those described earlier provide a new opportunity for professional social workers to once again contribute positively to poverty alleviation. Fortunately this is being recognized. Some social work scholars in United States who have undertaken research into the implementation of the TANF program are persuaded that professionally qualified social workers are urgently needed to work with families who face serious challenges when seeking to comply with the program's mandates. For example, in an in-depth study of former social assistance recipients, Altman and Goldberg (2008) found that the need for professional services was overwhelming. Most of those interviewed had serious emotional, physical, and mental health problems and were challenged by poverty, low educational credentials and a lack of opportunities. Many also found it extremely difficult to cope with the demands of raising children and securing and maintaining regular employment. In addition, some agency managers and program administrators are beginning to make greater use of professional staff. In California, some county social services agencies have sought to integrate income maintenance and child welfare services through more effective use of professional social workers to help clients served by both child welfare and welfare-to-work programs (Berrick et al., 2006).

The multiple roles that social workers play in promoting developmental forms of social work discussed in Chapter 1 also apply to practice in the developmental social assistance field. Social workers can work directly with poor families applying for social assistance and help them to understand the complex rules that govern many social assistance programs. They can also help them to access needed services and provide counseling and other supports that address their emotional and personal problems. They can also work with groups of people such as the members of micro-enterprise cooperatives and motivate them to collaborate on successful ventures.

At the macro-level, social workers have an important contribution to make regarding administration, planning, and policymaking. It is encouraging that social workers have been at the forefront of the formulation of developmental approaches to social assistance in countries such as the Philippines and South Africa and that they play a key role in administering these programs. Social workers can also draw on their advocacy skills to lobby governments to introduce or redesign social assistance programs so that their effectiveness is enhanced. They can also serve as supervisors and managers and ensure that developmental social assistance programs are properly implemented. As professional social work services are being contracted out to nonprofit and commercial organizations, social workers can ensure that high-quality services are provided. Many nonprofit organizations are managed by social workers who can bring their professional social work skills and values to bear on the task of helping social assistance clients. Their research skills can also be used to evaluate the impact of these programs on the families they serve.

Because many developmental social assistance programs make use of paraprofessionals, social workers can also play an important role in motivating and supervising these staff. For example, in Mexico, the role of paraprofessional and village volunteer workers known as *promotoras*, who are responsible for the day-to-day implementation of the *Opportunidades* program, has been criticized (Luccisano, 2004). Arguably, the infusion of professional social work knowledge, skills, and values could improve the quality of the services they provide. In Chile, where the government's *Solidario* program provides intensive counseling and support services to very poor families, social workers have been used as program managers and supervisors, and in some cases, they also work directly with the program's participants. However, most of the staff are not professionally qualified, and most require extensive social work supervision to ensure the program's success (Saracosti, 2008).

However, many issues will need to be addressed if social work is to play a positive role in developmental social assistance. One of these concerns professional education. Many years ago, in a critical review of the Philippines Employment Assistance Program, Reidy (1981) noted that conventional social work curricula were not designed to prepare students to help clients establish and manage small businesses. Another issue is the need for a clearer definition of roles and responsibilities and the creation of appropriate career opportunities for professional staff. This issue needs to be addressed if graduates are to be attracted to the field.

Wider ideological issues also need to be debated. The neoliberal connotation that has been placed on welfare-to-work programs in many countries, including the United States, discourage social work involvement (Ehrenreich, 2002). This is true also of Australia, where social workers are employed in the country's welfare-to-work program, particularly as counselors (McDonald & Chenoweth, 2006). Also relevant is the disinclination of many social workers to engage in activities that have long been associated with residual social welfare and with a coercive approach that seeks to shape the behavior of poor people—particularly women. As Abramovitz (1988) and many other feminist writers have argued, the American welfare system has historically been used to regulate poor women.

On the other hand, there is an urgent need for social work to contribute positively to poverty alleviation, particularly at a time of global recession. As the problems of poverty and deprivation become more serious, developmental social assistance will have a vital role to play. Social workers should join with others to advocate for governmental intervention that responds to these problems and also enhances social investment and promotes development (Midgley, 2000). Hopefully, social workers will take a leadership role in ensuring that developmental strategies are effectively used to raise the standards of living of the world's poor.

REFERENCES

Abramovitz, M. (1988). *Regulating the Lives of Women: Social Welfare Policy from Colonial Times to the Present*. Boston, MA: South End Press.

Altman, J. C. & Goldberg, G. S. (2008). Rethinking social work's role in public assistance. *Journal of Sociology and Social Welfare*. 35 (4): 71–94.

Bradshaw, S. (2008). From Structural Adjustment to Social Adjustment: A Gendered Analysis of Conditional Cash Transfer Programmes in Mexico and Nicaragua. *Global Social Policy*, 8 (2): 167–187.

Berrick, J., Frame, L., Langs J. & Varchol, L. (2006). Working Together for Children and Families" Where TANF and Child Welfare Meet, in R. Hoefer and J. Midgley. (Eds.) *International Perspectives on Welfare to Work Policy*. New York: Haworth Press, pp. 27–42.

de Schweinitz, K. (1943). *England's Road to Social Security*. Philadelphia: University of Pennsylvania Press.

Edmonds, E. V. (2006). Child Labor and Schooling Responses to Anticipated Income in South Africa. *Journal of Development Economics*. 81 (2): 386–414.

Ehrenreich, B. (2002). Preface. In R. Albelda and A. Withorn (Eds.), *Lost Ground: Welfare Reform, Poverty, and Beyond*. Cambridge, MA: South End Press, pp. vii–x.

Evans, M. (2001). Britain: Moving Towards a Work and Opportunity-Focused Welfare State. *International Journal of Social Welfare*. 10 (4): 260–267.

Evans, M. & Millar, J. (2006). Welfare to Work in the United Kingdom. In R. Hoefer & J. Midgley (Eds.), *International Perspectives on Welfare to Work Policy*. New York: Haworth Press, 61–76.

Hall, A. (2006). From Fome Zero to Bolsa Familia: Social Policies and Poverty Alleviation under Lula.' *Journal of Latin American Studies*, 38 (4), 689–709.

Hall, A. & Midgley, J. (2004). *Social Policy for Development*. Thousand Oaks, CA: Sage Publications.

Gilbert, N. (1998). From Service to Social Control: Implications of Welfare Reform for Professional Practice in the United States. *European Journal of Social Work*. 1 (1): 101–108.

Leighninger, L. (1999). The Service Trap: Social Work and Public Welfare Policy in the 1960s. In G. R. Lowe & N. P. Reid (Eds.), *The Professionalization of Poverty: Social Work and the Poor in the Twentieth Century*. New York: Aldyne de Gruyter, pp. 63–88.

Levy, S. (2006). *Progress Against Poverty: Sustaining Mexico's Progresa-Opportunidades Program*. Washington, DC: Brookings Institution Press.

Lodemal, I. & Trickey, H. (2000). *An Offer You Can't Refuse: Workfare in International Perspective*. Bristol, Policy Press.

Lowe, G. R. & Reid, N. P. (Ed) (1999). *The Professionalization of Poverty: Social Work and the Poor in the Twentieth Century*. New York: Aldyne de Gruyter.

Luccisano, L. (2004). Mexico's Progressa Program (1997-2000): An Example of Neoliberal Poverty Alleviation Programs Concerned with Gender, Human Capital Development, Responsibility and Choice. In K. M. Kilty & E. A. Segal (Eds), *Poverty and Inequality in the Latin American-U.S. Borderlands*. New York: Haworth Press, pp. 31–57.

McDonald, C. & Chenoweth, L. (2006). Workfare Oz Style: Welfare to Work and Social Work in Australia. In R. Hoefer and J. Midgley. (Eds.) *International Perspectives on Welfare to Work Policy*. New York: Haworth Press, pp. 109–128.

McKay, S. & Rowlingson, K. (2008). Social Security and Welfare Reform. In M. Powell (Ed.), *Modernizing the Welfare State: The Blair Legacy*. Bristol: Policy Press, pp. 53–71.

Mead, L. (Ed.) (1997). *The New Paternalism: Supervisory Approaches to Poverty*. Washington, DC: Brookings Institution Press.

Midgley, J. (2000). Globalization, Capitalism and Social Welfare: A Social Development Perspective. *Canadian Journal of Social Work*. 2 (1): 13–28.

Midgley, J. (2006). Welfare and Welfare to Work in the United States: The Role of Social Work. In R. Hoefer & J. Midgley. (Eds.) *International Perspectives on Welfare to Work Policy*. New York: Haworth Press, 2006: pp. 7–26.

Midgley, J. (2008a). *Welfare Reform in the United States: Implications for British Social Policy*. (With commentaries by Kitty Stewart, David Piachaud and Howard Glennerster.) London: Centre for the Analysis of Social Exclusion, London School of Economics. CASEpaper 131, 2008.

Midgley, J. (2008b). Microenterprise, Global Poverty and Social Development. *International Social Work*. Vol 51 (4): pp. 1–13.

Morley, S. & Coady, S. (2003). *From Social Assistance to Social Development: Targeted Educational Subsidies in Developing Countries*. Washington, DC: Center for Global Development.

Patel, L. & Trieghaardt, J. (2008). South Africa, Social Security, Poverty Alleviation and Development. In J. Midgley & K. L. Tang (Eds.), *Social Security, the Economy and Development*. New York: Palgrave Macmillan, pp. 85–109.

Peck, J. (2001). *Workfare States*. New York: Guilford Press.

Quieta, R. et al. (2003). *Self-Employment Assistance Program: Three Decades of Enabling People to Help Themselves*. Quezon City: University of Philippines Press.

Rawlings, L. B. (2005). A New Approach to Social Assistance: Latin America's Experience with Conditional Cash Transfer Programmes. *International Social Security Review*. 58 (2/3): 133–162.

Reidy, A. (1981). Welfarists and the Market. *International Social Work*. 24 (1): 36–46.

Saracosti, M. (2008). The Chile Solidario Program: The Role of Social Work. *International Social Work*. 51(4), 566–572.

Schultz, T. W. (1981). *Investing in People*. Berkeley, CA: University of California Press.

Silva, M. O. da S. (2006). The Family Scholarship Program: Unification of Income Transfer Programs in Brazil's Social Protection System. *Social Development Issues*. 28 (3): 101–114.

Specht, H. & Courtney, M. (1994). *Unfaithful Angels: How Social Work has Abandoned its Mission*. New York: Free Press.

Stadum, B. (1999). The Uneasy Marriage of Professional Social Work and Public Relief, 1870-1940. In G. R. Lowe & N. P. Reid (Eds.), *The Professionalization of Poverty: Social Work and the Poor in the Twentieth Century*. New York: Aldyne de Gruyter, pp. 29–50.

Stoesz, D. (2009). Social Policy: Reagan and Beyond. In J. Midgley & M. Livermore (Eds.). *Handbook of Social Policy, Second Edition*. Thousand Oaks, CA: Sage Publications, 169–178.

Tang, K. L. (2010). Welfare to Work Reform in Hong Kong: Overview and Prospects. In J. Midgley and K. L. Tang (Eds.), *Social Policy and Poverty in East Asia: The Role of Social Security*. New York: Routledge.

Trieghaardt, J. (2005). The Child Support Grant in South Africa: A Social Policy for Poverty Alleviation. *International Journal of Social Welfare*. 14 (4): 249–255.

United Kingdom, Department of Work and Pensions. (2010). *Transforming Britain's Labour Market: Ten Years of the New Deal*. London.

Wilensky, H. & Lebeaux, C. (1965). *Industrial Society and Social Welfare*. New York: Free Press, 1965.

7

Crime, Social Development, and Correctional Social Work

WILL C. RAINFORD

The profession of social work has a long history of involvement in the criminal justice system of the United States. Although social work's origins are usually traced to the work of charities and settlement houses, the founders of social work were also involved with the State Boards of Charities and Corrections that had oversight over the emerging public social services and particularly with residential facilities operated by the state governments. Correctional facilities for both juveniles and adults were among the most important of these early social services. Although not as prominent in the early history of social work as the charities and settlements, a concern with criminal justice and with the development of appropriate services for those involved with the correctional system played an important role in the profession's evolution. In the late 19th century, social workers were actively involved in the National Conference of Charities and Correction and were leading participants in sessions on social work in prisons and jails. They contributed papers to the *Proceedings of the National Conference* and helped to shape the field. Soon, some graduates of the new social work schools found employment in the country's correctional system.

As social work's role in corrections grew in the 20th century, the focus of intervention was on individual defect— the prisoner as deviant— with an emphasis on the reform of character. With the advent of the mental health movement, correctional social work began to focus more on rehabilitation through treatment using a psychotherapeutic perspective. However, the economically turbulent 1970s, and dramatic increases in incarceration rates in the last three decades of the 20th century turned American correctional policy away from rehabilitation. Social workers did not participate in this neo-conservative prison movement to any great extent, and this, in turn, created uncertainty about what role social work should play in the field. In addition, social workers were often viewed with suspicion and criticized for failing to adopt a "get tough" approach with criminals.

As the prison population has now reached unprecedented levels, and as high recidivism rates have revealed the inadequacy of the incarceration approach, there is a renewed interest in social work's potential contribution to a more positive correctional policy focused on rehabilitation and the re-entry of people in prison into community life. This new approach to correctional policy is paying much more attention to education, employment, and job placement for former prisoners as well as the provision of adequate housing and community supports. Although this approach has not been widely implemented, growing disillusionment with imprisonment as a purportedly effective solution to the crime problem suggests that it will be more widely used in the future. This approach requires not only investments in community supports for former prisoners but also in the creation of effective programs within prisons that can prepare prisoners for re-entry. These developments create new opportunities for social workers to join with prison reformers and for correctional policymakers to implement an investment approach that can help achieve this goal.

Unfortunately, contemporarily or historically, correctional social workers have paid little attention to the role of investment interventions intended to provide access to economic opportunity either prior to or post-incarceration. However, as noted earlier, a small but growing movement has emerged that seeks to use social investment as a means of restoring prisoners to full participation in community life and the productive economy. Because a lack of economic participation is a major cause of recidivism, the role investments of this kind play is of critical importance.

This chapter describes several promising social investment programs currently being used to improve the chances of former prisoners and parolees to build sustainable, productive economic futures outside of prison, and it considers the role of social workers in achieving this goal. First, it provides a review of the demographics of who is incarcerated or paroled in the criminal justice system, with an examination of the over-representation of minorities and single mothers in prison as key issues. Next, the chapter details traditional responses by social workers to incarceration and parole. Examples of social investment programs that are being used in prisons are provided, and their implications for developmental social work practice are briefly discussed. The chapter is primarily concerned with investment programs within correctional facilities, but it should be recognized that counterpart community services are of equal importance in restoring people to full functioning in society.

Imprisoned America

Although the size of prison populations in many countries today is troubling, the incarceration rate in the United States is among the highest in the world. In no other Western country have so many people been imprisoned. Although the population of the United States is only 5% of the overall global population, it incarcerates 25% of all prisoners in the world (International Centre for Prison Studies, 2005). Resulting in large part from increased police enforcement on America's streets (Petersilia, 2001) and the "War on Drugs" (Travis & Petersilia, 2001) in the late 20th and early 21st centuries, the prison population in the United States has dramatically increased. More than 2 million adults are now imprisoned in the United States, nearly triple the rate in 1980. Prisoners serving sentences for violent crimes (such as murder, rape, robbery, and assault) more than tripled between 1980 and 2004 (from 200,000 to more than 600,000). Incarceration for crimes against property (such as burglary, larceny, and motor vehicle theft) nearly doubled (from approximately 100,000 to 200,000). Perhaps the most alarming increase was imprisonment for drug offenses (such as the possession, manufacture, and sale of narcotics), which hardly registered at all in 1980 (with fewer than 20,000 prisoners) but was more than 200,000 in 2004 (U.S. Department of Justice, 2006).

Not surprisingly, state spending on prisons jumped 145% between 1986 and 2001. In the last 10 years, the cost of incarceration increased by more than $5 billion. In 2008, the states spent over $30 billion for incarcerating prisoners (U.S. Department of Justice, 2008a). Further, in 1996, taxpayers paid $90 per capita toward prisons. By 2001, the cost had jumped to over $100 per capita. With inflation and the burgeoning prison population, the cost is expected to exceed $125 per capita in 2009. Although building new prisons accounts for a small fraction of the rise in costs (4% of state funding for corrections), the highest proportion stems from the costs of maintaining so many people in prison. Adjusting for inflation, states now pay approximately $65 per day to guard, house, feed, and medically care for each prisoner (U.S. Department of Justice, 2004a). Because of the high cost of imprisonment, programs that address recidivism have experienced severe budgetary retrenchment or have been totally eliminated (U.S. Department of Justice, 2004b).

Outside of prison, more than 5.5 million parolees and probationers are being supervised in the correctional system (U.S. Department of Justice, 2008b). Although some former inmates manage to reconstruct a productive post-incarceration life, or at least manage to avoid re-arrest, many more return to prison. In 2008, 53% of parolees were re-arrested. Furthermore, nearly 40% of prisoners in 2002 had three or more incarcerations prior to their current offense (U.S. Department of Justice, 2007). In addition to the cost of the crime, as well as costs of prosecution, trial, and re-incarceration, recidivism also represents loss of economic productivity for offenders, their families, and the community. With the majority of prisoners failing to maintain their lives outside of prison, traditional responses to rehabilitation and reform need to be augmented by other measures. There is a good deal of evidence to show that counterintuitively, harsher sentencing does not reduce recidivism rates. Although longer sentences obviously reduce the presence of criminals on the streets, studies show that when they are released, they are more likely to re-offend (Liang, Bellatty, & deHaan, 2008).

Of the more than 7 million people either incarcerated or paroled in the U.S. justice system (U.S. Department of Justice, 2008b), the majority are poor urban males. In particular, African American males are vastly over-represented (Mauer, 2006). Although African American males made up 12% of the overall U.S. population in 2007 (U.S. Bureau of the Census, 2008), they comprised 64% of the prison population (U.S. Department of Justice, 2008b). Similarly, men identifying themselves as Hispanic or Latino made up 15% of the overall population (U.S. Bureau of the Census, 2008), yet they comprised nearly 26% of the incarcerated population (U.S. Department of Justice, 2008b). In contrast, White males comprise only 10% of the prison population (U.S. Department of Justice, 2008b).

Understanding why African American males are three times more likely than Hispanic males and five times more likely than White males to be imprisoned (Schlesinger, 2008) is key to the discussion of providing access to economic opportunities through social investment programs for prisoners and parolees. On the one hand, the *differential involvement perspective* holds that minority males, and African American males in particular, actually commit more crimes than White males and accordingly are imprisoned at a higher rate (Pratt, 1998; Swain, 2002). The alternative *direct-impact perspective* contends that African American and other minority males do not commit crimes at a higher rate than White males but are more frequently prosecuted and experience higher incarceration rates, with longer prison sentences and lower parole rates (Loury, 2007; Pratt, 1998; Schlesinger, 2005; Steffenssmeier & Demuth, 2000). A third perspective, the *interactionist perspective*, posits that numerous social and economic factors lead to the over-representation of African American and other minority males in the criminal justice system. Economic inopportunity is seen in this perspective as a major force in the creation of the current racial imbalances in the justice system. African American males in the urban centers of America face very narrow economic opportunities across their lifespan and, in the absence of such opportunity, turn to criminal activity as both a rationale choice and out of happenstance (DeParle, 2005; Hannon & Defina, 2005; Rank, 2005; Wilson, 1996).

Despite media portrayal and popular belief to the contrary, there is no evidence that minority males commit more crimes than their White counterparts. For example, White males have the same prevalence rate of illicit drug use as African Americans (6% for both groups). Further, African American high-school seniors have lower rates for prevalence rates of drug use than their White counterparts (National Institute on Drug Abuse, 2003). In the transition from drug use to drug addiction, African Americans in urban areas do not suffer higher rates than Whites in suburban areas (Anthony, Warner, & Kessler, 1994; Ensminger, Anthony, & McCord, 1997). In raw numbers, then, White males outpace African American males in illicit drug use, and yet, African American males imprisoned for illicit drug use far outnumber White males. This is because African American males are more likely to be convicted and incarcerated for illicit drug use than Whites (Loury, 2007; Mosher, 2001).

The argument that African Americans commit more crimes against people and crimes against property is not true, either. By the Federal Bureau of Investigation's estimates, Whites account for nearly 70% of all arrests in America, 66% of arrests for crimes against property, and 66% of crimes against people (U.S. Department of Justice, 2008c); however, as noted, they only comprise 10% of the prison population. As discussed, the disparities between African Americans and Whites in prison (and thus eventual parole) as final disposition is more attributable to poverty, lack of economic opportunity, and *de facto* racism inherent in the justice system than it is by propensity of African Americans to commit crime.

Whereas the number of men in prison in the United States has grown rapidly, the number of incarcerated women has grown even faster (U.S. Department of Justice, 2008d). As with African American men and their White counterparts, African American women were much more likely to be incarcerated than White women (U.S. Department of Justice, 2008b). Alarmingly, two-thirds of women in prison are mothers who had custody of their children prior to sentencing (U.S. Department of Justice, 2000). With almost 115,000 women in prison (U.S. Department of Justice, 2008d), it is estimated that more than more than 200,000 children have mothers behind bars, and many more have mothers on parole. Effective programs that enable successful parole and prevent recidivism are vitally important, as having an imprisoned mother drastically increases the likelihood that the child will also become involved in crime (Hagan & Palonni, 1990). Given that poverty is the context within which women in prison lived their lives prior to incarceration, and poverty is likely to be the reality of their post-incarceration lives (*see* Carlen, 1988; Heimer & Kruttschnitt, 2005), social investment interventions that provide post-incarceration access to economic opportunities are urgently needed.

Social Work and Corrections

Because the Eighth Amendment to the U.S. Constitution prohibits cruel and unusual punishment, locking someone in prison for a lifetime is a very severe punishment. However, in recent decades, longer prison sentences with limited opportunities for parole have become the norm. And with the burgeoning size of prison populations in the last two decades, appropriate and judicious sentencing is a tool not only for the rehabilitation of criminals but for controlling the size of the incarcerated population. Nevertheless, most prisoners are eventually paroled. Nearly 70% of criminals in the corrections system are on parole or probation (U.S. Department of Justice, 2008b). As mentioned, two-thirds of former inmates will return to incarceration during their parole or probation. With both the budgetary costs and safety issues presented by recidivism, as well as loss of economic productivity and community instability, policymakers, public planners, and corrections administrators have come to realize that much more needs to be done to prevent recidivism (Bouffard & Bergeron, 2006). The issue, however, is how best to prepare prisoners for life outside of prison.

As correctional policymakers grapple with this question and as new interventions that contribute to the successful re-entry of prisoners are being formulated and tested (albeit on a limited scale), social workers have a major role to play. Social work, with its focus on the strengths perspective (Saleebey, 1992, 2000) is likely to contribute significantly to the implementation of new and effective strategies. Social workers have unique skills that can be used both within the prison setting and in the post-incarceration community setting to help former prisoners reintegrate into society and live productive and fulfilling lives. The investment strategies that form an integral part of this approach are well-suited to developmental social work.

As noted at the beginning of this chapter, social workers were actively involved in corrections in the late 19th century when reform and rehabilitation were key principles of correctional policy. They were not only involved in providing rehabilitative services within correctional facilities but with community-based services such as probation and parole. The founders of social work were greatly inspired by the 19th century reformer, John Augustus, who pleaded with judges for the release of prisoners he deemed to be candidates for reformation. Under Augustus' charge, these early probationers were supervised and employed. The modern probation and parole system has its origin in his pioneering work (Gumz, 2004). Social workers were also involved in the creation of the first Juvenile Court in Chicago in the 1890s, which provided an alternative to the adult courts and took the needs of children and their families into account. They also supported prison reform efforts, which resulted in the separation of incarcerated children from adults. They were also involved in crime and juvenile delinquency prevention, particularly through the work of the settlements that provided group work and recreational activities for youth living in poor communities. Unfortunately, social workers in the United States are no longer involved in probation or parole services to any great extent. However, community-based social work interventions are of critical importance for the effectiveness of re-entry strategies.

On the other hand, social workers have continued to find employment in correctional facilities. In the 20th century, with the popularization of psychotherapy in social work practice, mental health treatment became a major responsibility of correctional social work practitioners. Subsequently, as it was recognized that many prisoners had been convicted of drug offenses and many were addicted to drugs or alcohol, substance abuse treatment began to play a significant role in correctional social work.

Because there is strong evidence that drug abuse, crime, and recidivism are highly correlated, substance abuse treatment is an appropriate role for social work. It is estimated that more than 50% of all crime in the United States is drug-related. Approximately one-fifth of criminals report committing crimes to fund their drug habits. More than two-thirds of people arrested test positive for controlled substances at the point of arrest. In addition, 36% report being under the influence of alcohol at the time the crime was committed (U.S. Department of Justice, 2004c). High rates of substance use, abuse, and addiction among prisoners in the United States contributes to recidivism, and effective treatment can facilitate effective re-entry and reduce recidivism. There is evidence that treatment programs have modest success in reducing recidivism (Taxman, 1998). Treatment may be most effective for those who have relatively little criminal history and whose only current offense is drug-related (Petersilla, 1997).

Social work intervention in prisons in the form of substance abuse treatment is closely linked to mental health treatment. A substantial number of prisoners suffer from mental illness, including schizophrenia, clinical depression, bipolar disorder, and post-traumatic stress disorder. The rate of mental illness in prison is estimated to be two to three times higher than in the general population. Almost 16% of prisoners have one or more clinically diagnosable mental illnesses (Ditton, 1999). Further confounding rehabilitation and reduced recidivism rates is the co-occurrence of mental illness and drug addiction, which greatly complicates successful re-entry into society and presents significant obstacles to stable employment.

Today, social workers play a leading role in providing mental health treatment behind bars. Typically, they screen for mental health issues and offer mental health treatments. They work together with psychologists and psychiatrists to offer treatment that involves a mix of pharmacological interventions and counseling. Social workers in prisons are typically carrying out direct practice tasks such as intake, engagement, psychosocial assessment, and counseling. Most casework is targeted at behavioral change, resource brokering, and substance abuse recovery. Social workers may also support families of inmates in psychosocial counseling, social functioning, and economic maintenance (Gibelman, 2006). They also use traditional methods of social work intervention from relationship building to process-oriented interviewing to cognitive therapy (Farley, Smith, & Boyle, 2009).

However, there are huge disparities in the provision of mental health treatment in different parts of the country and in different correctional facilities. Local jails often provide no treatment at all, and in many cases, jails are used to incarcerate people with chronic mental illnesses, even though they have not committed crimes that warrant incarceration. This has become a major issue for the courts, which have mandated the provision of appropriate interventions.

Unfortunately, the numbers of professionally qualified correctional social workers—particularly graduate-level social workers in correctional practice—have declined over the years (Morales & Sheafor, 2002). In addition, just as there are fewer social workers practicing in the corrections system, there is limited information about the nature of social work interventions in prisons and jails today. Gumz (2004) notes that only two articles concerned with social work in corrections in the United States have been published in the last 10 years. Cnaan and colleagues (2008) go further and argue that social workers have abdicated their historic role as agents for rehabilitation and have allowed their role to be usurped by criminal justice and correctional staff, who are primarily concerned with safety and security issues. However, they do believe that it is possible for social workers to reclaim their traditional rehabilitative role and contribute positively to the task of promoting the re-entry of prisoners into society.

Social work practice has historically been constrained within the justice system, and this partly accounts for the declining numbers of social workers who opt for a career in corrections. Social workers celebrate values of inherent dignity of the person, self-determination, confidentiality, moral neutrality, and social justice (NASW, 2008). In contrast, the corrections system values order and control via punishment and supervision. Given the incongruence between the profession of social work and the corrections system, it is not surprising that less than 3% of social workers are currently employed in the prison system (Morales & Sheafor, 2002). Furthermore, in recent compilations of career trajectories for social work students, less than 1% of social work students identified their career path as corrections/criminal justice (Lennon, 2001; Gibelman, 2006).

Although therapeutic interventions certainly have their place in restoring prisoners to full functioning in society, increasing human capital, employability, and ability to productively build assets are fundamentally important factors in preventing recidivism (Przybylski, 2008). As will be seen, the use of social investment as a strategy of rehabilitation offers new opportunities for social work to contribute positively to rehabilitation and the re-entry of prisoners to community living. In this regard, it is important that social workers continue to advocate for progressive changes in sentencing policies as well as public attitudes that support the costly and largely ineffective incarceration of so many people today (Cnaan et al., 2008).

Social Investment Strategies in Correctional Facilities

The exponential growth of the prison population and the concomitant rise in the cost of incarcerating so many offenders has caused widespread concern, and there is a growing awareness that the continued use of imprisonment as a strategy for crime control is unsustainable. Although the use of prisons has in the past been politically popular, few politicians now aggressively promote imprisonment as an effective solution to the crime problem. In addition, the high recidivism rates following incarceration suggest that the policy of routinely imprisoning offenders is not effective. Although the advocacy of alternatives to imprisonment has previously been ridiculed and associated with "soft," liberal academics and social reformers, even conservative politicians realize that something needs to be done.

Although an awareness of the limitations of the imprisonment policy has encouraged new policy debates, it should be recognized that relatively little has been achieved. Traditional views about imprisonment remain popular, and many states are politically locked into perpetuating policies that rely on imprisonment. Nevertheless, more attention is now being given to crime prevention, and diversionary strategies such as probation and noncustodial sentences, drug treatment, and counseling for offenders are being more frequently used. It is in this context that the successful re-entry of prisoners into normal community living is being more widely advocated. Today, experimental re-entry programs that make extensive use of social investments are being implemented throughout the country and research into the effectiveness of these strategies is being undertaken (Manpower Demonstration Research Corporation, 2009). In addition, the enactment of the

Second Chance Act in 2008 authorized funding for state demonstration projects and for nonprofit organizations engaged in re-entry programs. Although the amount of funding is relatively small, this legislation demonstrates a commitment on the part of Congress and the Obama administration to promote successful prisoner re-entry.

Re-entry programs are designed to facilitate the rehabilitation and full re-integration of offenders into society. These programs rely on social investment strategies both within prisons and in the community and typically focus on education, skills training, job placement, substance abuse, and other forms of counseling and strengthening links between prisoners and their families and engagement in community activities such as civic and religious associations. They also involve a number of post-incarceration interventions, including support for reunification with families, job placement, access to affordable housing, participation in support groups, and similar interventions. These re-entry programs require much more than the usual parole services, which typically involve reporting to a parole officer on a regular basis. In addition to community supports in the post-incarceration stage, it is also being recognized that sentencing policies need to change. Although judges are limited in the use of discretion through mandatory sentencing requirements, severe pressures on public revenues in many states and localities around the country and a growing disquiet about the numbers being incarcerated suggests that new sentencing approaches may be adopted.

Although successful re-entry depends on a mix of pre-and post-incarceration interventions, this chapter will focus attention on the role of social investment strategies within the prison setting. However, it must be stressed that interventions behind bars are unlikely to succeed unless effectively harmonized and coordinated with community interventions such as those mentioned earlier. On the other hand, research suggests that post-incarceration community interventions are more likely to be effective if investments in education and skills development, job preparedness, micro-enterprise training, financial literacy, and economic asset development are made within prisons prior to prisoners being released (Seiter & Kadela, 2003). The interventions currently being used in re-entry programs are compatible with the social development principles and approaches discussed in the first chapter of this book. In particular, these strategies reflect the enterprise approach to social development (Rainford, 2001) that emphasizes the role of entrepreneurship, self-responsibility, and a commitment to succeed. Although this approach is not widely used in social development, it is appropriate to correctional policy and the culture of prisons, which often extol individualistic values.

Education and Employment Investment Strategies

It is well-known that prisoners who re-enter society struggle to obtain living wage jobs (Bernstein & Houston, 2000). This is attributable to many factors, including stigma, a lack of opportunity, and involvement with gangs and others engaged in crime; but limited education, employment skills, and job preparedness are also to blame. Few prisoners are afforded the opportunity to obtain job training and employment experience while in prison (Lynch & Sabol, 2001), leaving them without the necessary educational qualifications, job skills, and work experience (Becker, 1964). In addition, the longer prisoners stay behind bars, the less time they have spent in the workforce building up references, contacts, and reputation. Given a criminal history, a lack of human capital, and a lack of a social network, it is not surprising that employers are most reluctant to hire former prisoners (Holtzer, Raphael, & Stoll, 2001).

Low educational attainment is significantly correlated with recidivism, chiefly because it serves as a barrier to employment (Marano, 2003). Thus, it is of concern that more than 13% of parolees have less than an eighth grade education, whereas more than two-thirds of inmates do not have the literacy functioning necessary for normal functioning in society (Linacre, 1996). Further, more than 45% of prisoners in the United States have not yet obtained the equivalence of a high school degree (U.S. Department of Justice, 2000), but having such a degree increases earning potential by $10,000 per year (U.S. Census Bureau, 2008).

Harlow (2003) reports that prison educational programs reduce recidivism rates because of increased income, family stability, and increased employment. Harer (1995) has revealed that prison educational programs have converse negative correlations with recidivism. Further, one study found that having a high school degree reduces the likelihood of recidivism by almost 30% (Steurer, Smith, & Tracy, 2003). Unfortunately, although educational programs are relatively easy to implement and inexpensive to operate, they are not as widely used as they should be.

Although former prisoners do not fare well in the labor market post-incarceration, most did not fare well in the labor market before they were incarcerated either. Studies that track people through the corrections system from pre-arrest through parole suggest that incarceration itself may not be the confounding factor and that limited human capital and a lack of employment preparedness is a major reason for recidivism (Freeman, 2003). Providing social investment programs in prisons enables parolees to have the experience, knowledge, and skills necessary to land living-wage jobs post-incarceration. However, most prison employment programs are not designed for re-entry into society. The focus of employment training in prison typically focuses on earning money to repay fines, fees, and victim costs; earning money for the institution; or merely occupying the prisoner's time to reduce prison problems (Bushway, 2003). The proverbial mailbag sewing and other work activities used in correctional facilities do little, if anything, to prepare people for re-entry into productive employment in the community. On the other hand, where job training and employment-readiness programs are offered, recidivism rates after release do go down significantly (Gates, Flanagan, & Stewart, 2000). Successful employment does not merely provide a parolee with money. Employment provides structure, routine, obligation in relationship, and socially acceptable roles for former inmates. Nevertheless, it is higher wages, job stability, and career opportunities that reduce recidivism rates.

Social Investment Re-Entry Case Studies

The following section offers just some of the innovative interventions that are being used in correctional facilities today in an attempt to prepare prisoners for re-entry into the community. These interventions seek specifically to invest in the capabilities of those who are about to be returned to the community, and as shown earlier, they place emphasis on education, skill development, job training, and preparation for employment through meaningful and productive activities within correctional facilities. Although these initiatives are being used in limited ways and face many challenges, they are preferable to current practices and point the way to interventions that will, with proper funding, staffing, and commitment, do much to reduce crime in American society. The case studies briefly described below focus primarily on the education and skills development, job preparedness, asset accumulation, and the development of skills to establish and manage micro-enterprises. They are only some examples of the programs being used and, as noted earlier, are often linked to substance abuse and anger management counseling programs, family reunification interventions, and constructive recreation and sports. Although these interventions have been tried in a number of correctional facilities, they may not be successful everywhere and they should not be regarded as a quick and easy solutions to the problems caused by excessive incarceration. However, they clearly contribute to the formulation of a more effective rehabilitation and re-entry policy approach to corrections.

THE OPTIONS PROGRAM   One example of an employment-focused program is the *Options Program*, operated by the Lafayette Parish Correctional Center in Louisiana. In recognizing that crime and subsequent recidivism are multicausal, the program uses a multifaceted approach. Program participants, who self-select for entry, are provided traditional psychosocial assessment and counseling by professional counselors. At the same time, they enter into cognitive–behavioral training that provides them with life-skills training, including budgeting, credit management, parenting skills, interpersonal skills, and anger management. Participants are provided a skills/interest assessment to match them to potential job openings. In collaboration with Goodwill Industries, the program provides work-readiness training, including resume writing, interviewing, basic education (math and reading), and work maintenance skills. Louisiana Technical College provides prisoners in the program the opportunity to learn skills for high-paying jobs, such as air conditioner and refrigeration repair. The Lafayette Sheriff's Department provides training in forklift operations. The Louisiana Department of Motor Vehicles ensures that program participants have state identification cards, and local banks provide financial literacy training and checking and savings accounts. Prior to release, employers are invited into the correctional facility, where job interviews occur. An inmate in the program may not be released prior to having both housing and employment secured. Once released, the program administrator collaborates with probation and parole officers to ensure the participant is succeeding following incarceration. The first graduating class commenced in October, 2008. Eight men and three women are now in the process of entering society with jobs in-hand, housing secured, and access to banking. The program staff are optimistic that every one of the graduates will successfully retain their employment, build income and savings, and avoid returning to incarceration. Although evaluation of the program is just being implemented, the studies previously mentioned suggest that this expectation should be fulfilled.

San Quentin Prison's University Program   Going far beyond job readiness, San Quentin Prison, arguably one of the toughest prisons in the world, provides inmates college courses behind bars. Prisoners in the program are able to obtain a college degree, thereby not only providing them with post-incarceration career opportunities but also greatly improving their quality of life in prison. Currently, more than 70 faculty from the University of California-Berkeley, Stanford University, San Francisco State University, and other higher educational institutions in Northern California provide college courses to prisoners who possess a GED or high school education. The prison is affiliated with Patten University in Oakland, CA. More than 200 inmates participate in college courses, including the humanities, math, science, social sciences. A college preparatory course in math and English is also offered. College education is free to inmates, including the costs of materials and textbooks. To date, more than 74 inmates have completed an Associate of Arts degree. Many other former prisoners who participated in the program were paroled and completed their education in the community. Included in the program is an obligatory day-job in the prison, for which inmates earn $25 per month, thereby building both income and human capital. The Prison University Project is commencing a 5-year program evaluation to ascertain the effects of the program on students, family, and the community. The evaluation will focus on academic outcomes, social connectivity, health and mental health, employability and employment, substance abuse, housing stability, and recidivism.

Asset-Building Behind Bars

When prisoners re-enter society, they often do so with little or no money in their pocket, and their future economic opportunities are extremely limited. For example, in many states, prisoners are released back into society with very little "gate money," which is a cash grant issued by the prison. In some states, no financial aid of any kind is given. Yet, having funds for daily life is crucial for successful re-entry. Several states have initiated programs that not only help inmates save up their "walking money" but also help them save and invest toward future economic opportunities.

The State of Connecticut passed a law in 2002 requiring every inmate to have a savings account, with mandatory savings drawn from prisoner commissary accounts (which accrue either from money earned in prison or deposits made by family or friends). 10% of funds are transferred from the commissary account to the savings account. The funds continue to accumulate until $1,000 has been deposited. The money is then kept in the account until point of prisoner release. Unfortunately, the state does not provide incentive savings through matching funds, nor does it specify what the funds are to be used for post-release. However, prisoners will potentially, upon release, have enough for a deposit on a rental dwelling, which is a vast improvement over the former practice of merely releasing prisoners without any funds at all (Hartford Courant News, July 2, 2007).

In the State of Utah, a program that prepares inmates for release recognizes that a savings account is a valuable tool in preventing recidivism. In the *Your Parole Requires Extensive Preparation* (YPREP) program, participants set up a savings account and are allowed to send money home for future use. Once the inmate leaves the program, an Individual Development Account (IDA) is set up with matching funds to help leverage savings for special purposes. In one instance, a participant earning 30 cents a day sent $30 per month to her family. Not only did this help propel her toward release, but it helped stabilize her family relationships. The program also emphasizes education, job skills, and job searches. It currently has 37 bed spaces open because of the large success of transitioning participants ready for release into the community. This is a previously unheard-of success in the Utah Corrections System.

INDIVIDUAL DEVELOPMENT ACCOUNTS AND HOME OWNERSHIP   Another concern for prisoners re-entering society is housing. It is estimated that more than 10% of former inmates are homeless the month after being released (Langan & Lavin, 2002), with former inmates suffering from a mental illness facing an even higher chance of being homeless (Ditton, 1999). More alarming, in major urban centers, nearly half of all parolees and probationers may be homeless (California Department of Corrections, 1997). Even where homelessness is not a concern to parolees, finding and sustaining decent, affordable housing is often a major obstacle to successful life post-incarceration (Urban Institute, 2002). Arguably, if a former prisoner had the opportunity to be regularly employed and earn a decent income, then the purchase of a home could be a realistic goal. However, because of bad credit, instability and stigma, and lack of access to affordable housing—not to mention a lack of economic opportunity—home ownership is unachievable for most parolees.

Owning a home has been shown to have significant positive effects on people's lives. Home ownership provides a cache of economic security, is a springboard to future opportunities, increases civic engagement, and provides incentives for increased economic productivity (Sherraden, 1991). Individual Development Accounts (IDA), which are matched savings for low-income groups targeted at home purchase, coupled with affordable housing, are a reliable means of transforming low-income renters into homeowners over time (CFED, 2007). Although still in its infancy, the use of IDAs in prisons for the purpose of accumulating credit worthiness for home ownership should be strongly encouraged. However, to be effective, the accumulation of savings through IDAs and their potential use in securing a home ultimately depends on adequate supports being provided to prisoners on release. This is another example of the importance of linking developmental interventions within prisons with comprehensive social services to former prisoners in the community.

MICRO-ENTERPRISES One sure way of employing parolees is to provide them with the means to start their own business. Micro-enterprise and microcredit are now well-recognized ways of helping low-income people improve their standards of living. Although micro-enterprise first emerged in the developing countries of the Global South and has been popularized through the work of the Grameen Bank in Bangladesh, this approach has now become quite popular in the United States. One example of a micro-enterprise program behind bars is the *Women's Initiative for Self-Employment*. The program delivers business training, financing, and business support for low-income women seeking to start their own business. A central component of the program is microlending or microfinance. After an appropriate training within the correctional facility, former prisoners are helped to start their own businesses. The program helps women obtain leases for retail space through a one-time grant of $10,000 for the security deposit and the first month's rent. By participating in the program, clients who have bad credit create a relationship with the program, thereby enabling them to obtain credit in the community. Program evaluation over the last 10 years has shown very positive results. Annual household income increases twofold or more for participants 2 years into the program. Almost 70% of participants are in business within a year of training; 5 years later, most are still in business. The program estimates that business-owning clients hiring other workers will have created 1,000 new jobs in 2008. Average pay for these jobs is $16 per hour (WISP, 2009).

Social Work Roles

As mentioned earlier, social workers have a long association with corrections in the United States. They had been involved in a variety of community-based activities designed to prevent young people from being drawn into criminal activity, and in the profession's early days, they were also active in probation and parole. Social workers also found employment within correctional facilities for both juvenile and adult offenders. By the late 20th century, the numbers of social workers in the American correctional system had declined, but those who continue to work in the system are usually engaged in providing mental health and substance abuse treatment. In addition to using conventional therapeutic techniques, they also provide intake assessments, group sessions with prisoners, and prerelease planning.

Although these are worthwhile activities, social workers have an exciting opportunity to participate more actively in programs that use social investment strategies designed to prepare prisoners for successful re-entry into the community. As these new approaches are being more frequently implemented in the correctional system, social work, with its focus on the strengths perspective, can make a significant contribution to the growing emphasis on promoting a positive and successful transition for those being released into the community.

Social workers can also play a leading role in implementing and managing re-entry programs. Most correctional staff are concerned with security and the maintenance of order and discipline within correctional facilities and will not have the time or inclination to administer programs of this kind. Given current budget realities, it is unlikely that new staff will be hired specifically to implement these programs. This provides a good opportunity for social workers to volunteer to expand their conventional treatment services with innovative programs such as those described earlier. Of course, this will also require close collaboration with those engaged in educational programs within correctional settings and with external agencies willing to provide relevant services.

In many correctional facilities, social workers are often responsible for organizing groups designed to address the problems and challenges facing those who are incarcerated. These groups are concerned with issues such as anger management, group psychotherapy, and preparation for release. Social group work can also be used to facilitate the implementation of investment strategies. Participants need to be socialized into working together to attain common educational goals and to apply individual skills to cooperative enterprises. They also need to acquire the personal skills that will prepare them for community living. Social workers can work together with correctional staff to select those prisoners who are most suited to engage in these activities, and they can foster a wider culture of cooperation among those who participate in investment oriented re-entry programs.

Social workers and social work academics in particular also have a contribution to make by engaging in research and evaluation into effective re-entry outcomes. As evidence-based approaches become more widely used, more research into the effectiveness of re-entry programs will be needed. The National Association of Social Workers (2007) pointed out in its *Social Work Speaks* abstract on its website that: "it is already known that some practices to promote rehabilitation—such as helping prisoners maintain family ties and responsibilities—are effective. The social work profession should identify others through research (for example, other options for dispute resolution, alternatives to prison, and effective treatments within correctional settings)."

Because relatively few correctional facilities in the United States have wholeheartedly embraced re-entry investment strategies, social workers are well-placed to advocate for the adoption of these approaches. In some cases, this will involve collaborating more closely with administrators and policymakers seeking to implement these approaches, but in other is it may require social workers taking the lead in articulating the need for approaches of this kind. If these approaches are viewed as an effective adjunct to treatment and rehabilitation, which also prevent recidivism, correctional officials are more likely to be persuaded of their usefulness. In this regard, it is heartening that professional associations such as the National Association of Social Workers are actively advocating for the adoption of re-entry programs.

Social work advocacy designed to reduce the crime and incarceration rates and to address the vast and deep injustice evidenced in the differential rates of incarceration between African Americans and Whites is also urgently needed.

Social workers have recently become interested in the use of restorative justice both within correctional facilities and in community-based programs (van Wormer, 2004), and they are uniquely skilled to work in programs of this kind. In the restorative justice approach, crime is seen as a violation of a relationship and therefore should not be punished for punishment's sake; rather, all efforts must be targeted at healing the relationship and strengthening the bond of community (Braithwaite, 1999; Zehr, 1990). The process of restorative justice requires all parties to voluntarily participate in face-to-face encounters, where truth-telling enables the criminal to accept personal responsibility and the behavioral components of the crime. Victims and others then need to participate in deciding the appropriate reparations for the crime (Llewellyn & Howse, 1998). Restorative justice shows promising results in reducing rates of recidivism, even though the main goal of restorative justice is healing relationships rather than preventing future crime. For example, in a meta-analysis of studies (Latimer, Dowden, & Muise, 2005), it was found that restorative justice reduced the likelihood of recidivism for prisoners who enrolled in restorative justice interventions more than prisoners who merely received traditional prison-to-parole programs.

It is important again to stress that the use of these investment strategies within correctional facilities are most likely to be effective if directly linked to community-based services provided to prisoners after they are released. The provision of adequate community supports, job placement, access to housing, and the reunification of prisoners with their families are essential ingredients of an effective reentry approach. More emphasis should also be placed on interventions that prevent people—especially young people—from committing crime in the first place. Social workers have a critical role to play in the provision of preventive and community-based services of this kind and in linking services behind bars with community interventions.

REFERENCES

Anthony, J., Warner, L., & Kessler, R. (1994). Comparative epidemiology of dependence on tobacco, alcohol, controlled substances, and inhalants: Basic findings from the National Comorbidity Survey. *Experimental and Clinical Psychopharmacology*, 2: 244–268.

Becker, G. (1964). *Human capital*. New York: Columbia University Press.

Bernstein, L. & Houston, E. (2000). *Crime and work: What can we learn from the low-wage labor market*. Washington, D.C.: Economic Policy Institute.

Braithwaite, J. (1999). Restorative justice: Assessing optimistic and pessimistic accounts, in M. Tonry (Ed.) *Crime and Justice: A review of research*. Chicago, IL: University of Chicago Press, pp. 1–127.

Bouffard, J. & Bergeron, L. (2006). Reentry works: The implementation and effectiveness of a serious and violent offender reentry initiative *Journal of Offender Rehabilitation*, 44 (2/3): 1–29.

Bushway, S. (2003). *Reentry and prison work programs*. New York: Urban Institute.

Carlen, P. (1988). *Women, crime, and poverty*. United Kingdom: Open University Press.

California Department of Corrections (1997). *Prevention parolee failure program: An Evaluation*. Sacramento, CA.

Center for Enterprise Development 2007. *Individual development accounts*. Washington.D.C.: Author. Retrieved from http://www.cfed.org/focus.m?parentid=31&siteid=374&id=382, March 20, 2009.

Cnaan, R. Draine, J. Frazier B., & Sinha, J. W. (2008). Ex-prisoners' reentry: An emerging frontier and a social work challenge. *Journal of Policy Practice*, 7 (2/3): 178–198.

DeParle, J. (2005). *American Dream: Three women, ten kids, and a nation's drive to end welfare*. New York: Penguin Books.

Ditton, P. (1999). *Mental health and treatment of inmates and probationers*. Washington, D.C.: US Department of Justice, Bureau of Justice Statistics.

Ensminger, M., Anthony, J., & McCord, J. (1997). The inner city and drug use: Initial findings from an epidemiological study. *Drug and Alcohol Dependence*, 48 (3): 175–184.

Farley. O., Smith, L., & Boyle, S. (2009). *Introduction to social work* (11th Ed). Boston: Allyn & Bacon.

Freeman, R. (2003). Can we close the revolving door? Recidivism vs. employment of ex-offenders in the US. *Employment Dimensions of Reentry: Understanding the nexus between prisoner reentry and work*. Urban Institute Reentry Roundtable, May 19–20, 2003.

Gates, G., Flanagan, T., & Stewart, L. (2000). Adult correctional treatment. *Crime and Justice*, 26: 321–426.

Grameen Bank (2008). What is microcredit? Retrieved from http://www.grameen-info.org/index.php?option=com_content&task=view&id=28&Itemid=108, March 20, (2009).

Gumz, E. (2004). American social work, corrections, and restorative justice: An appraisal. *International Journal of Offender Therapy and Comparative Criminology*, 48 (4): 449–460.

Hagan, J. & Palonni, A. (1990). The social reproduction of a criminal class of working class London, circa 1950-80. *American Journal of Sociology*, 96: 265–297.

Hannon, L. & Defina, R. (2005). Violent crime in African American and White neighborhoods: Is poverty's detrimental effect race-specific? *Journal of Poverty*, 9 (3): 49–67.

Harlow, C. (2003). *Education and correctional populations*. Washington, D.C.: Bureau of Justice Statistics.

Harer, M. (1995). *Prison education program and recidivsm: A test of the normalization hypothesis*. Washington, D.C.: Federal Bureau of Prisons.

Heimer, K. & Kruttschnitt, C. (2005). *Gender & crime: Patterns in victimization and offending*. New York: NYU Press.

Holtzer, H., Raphael, S., & Stoll, M. (2002). *Can employers play a more positive role in prisoner reentry? Paper presentation, Urban Institute's Reentry Roundtable*, Washington, D.C., March 20-21, (2002). Retrieved from http://www.urban.org/url.cfm?ID=410803, March 20, 2009.

International Centre for Prison Studies. (2005). *World Prison Brief*. London: King's College.

Langan, P. & Levin, D. (2002). *Recidivism of prisoners released in (1994)*. Washington, DC: US Department of Justice, Bureau of Justice Statistics.

Latimer, J., Dowden, C., & Muise, D. (2005). The effectiveness of restorative justice practices: A meta-analysis *The Prison Journal*, 85 (2): 127–144.

Lennon, T. (2001). *Statistics on social work education: (1999)*. Alexandria, VA: Council on Social Work Education.

Loury, G. (2007). The new untouchables: Crime, punishment, and race in America. *UN Chronicle*, 44 (3): 53–56.

Liang, S., Bellatty, P., & deHaan, B. (2008). Effects of earned time, inmate age, sentence length, and type of crime on recidivism. Paper presented at the annual meeting of the American Society of Criminology, Royal York, Toronto, 2008-12-12. Retrieved from http://www.allacademic.com/meta/p33962_index.html, March 20, 2009.

Llewellyn, M. & Howse, R. (1998). *Restorative justice: A conceptual framework*. Ottawa: Law Commission of Canada.

Linacre, J. M. (1996). The prison literacy problem. *Rasch Measurement Transactions*, 10 (1): 473–474.

Lynch, J. & Sabol, W. (2001). Prisoner reentry in perspective. *Crime Policy Report (v.3)*. Washington, DC: Urban Institute.

Manpower Development Research Corporation (2003). *Building knowledge about successful prisoner reentry strategies*. New York, Author.

Marano, L. (2003). Analysis: Prison education cuts recidivism. UPI: September 10, 2003.

Mauer, M. (2006). *Race to incarcerate*. New York: New Press.

Morales, A. & Sheafor, B. (2002). *The many faces of social workers*. Boston, MA: Allyn & Bacon.

Mosher, C. (2001). Predicting drug arrest rates: Conflict and social disorganization perspectives. *Crime and Delinquency*, 47 (1): 84–104.

National Association of Social Work (2008). *Code of ethics*. Washington, DC: Author.

National Institute on Drug Abuse (2003) *Drug use among racial/ethnic minorities*. Washington, D.C.

Perna, L. (2000). Differences in the decision to attend college among African Americans, Hispanics, and Whites *Journal of Higher Education*, 71 (2): 117–130.

Petersilia, J. (2001). Prisoner reentry: Public safety and reintegration challenges. *The Prison Journal*, 81 (3): 360–375.

Petersilia, J. (1997). Probation in the United States. *Crime and Justice*, 22: 149–200.

Pratt, T. (1998). Race and sentencing: A meta-analysis of conflicting empirical research results. *Journal of Crime Justice*, 26 (6): 513–523.

Przybylski, R. (2008). *What works? Effective recidivism reduction and risk-focused prevention programs*. CO: Division of Criminal Justice.

Rainford, W. (2001). Promoting welfare by enhancing opportunity: The individual enterprise approach to social development. *Social Development Issues*, 3 (1): 51–57.

Rank, M. (2005). *One nation underprivileged: Why American poverty affects us all*. New York: Oxford University Press.

Saleebey, D. (Ed). (1992). *The strengths perspective in social work practice*. New York: Longman.

Saleebey, D. (2000). Power in the people: Strengths and hope. *Advances in Social Work*, 1: 127–136.

Seiter, R. & Kadela, K. (2003). Prisoner reentry: What works, what does not, and what is promising. *Crime & Delinquency*, 49 (3): 360–388.

Schlesinger, T. (2008). Criminal processing, in R. Schaefer (Ed.) *Encyclopedia of Race, Ethnicity, and Society*. Thousand Oaks, CA: Sage Publications, pp. 341–344.

Schlesinger, T. (2005). Racial and ethnic disparities in pretrial criminal processing. *Justice Quarter*, 22: 170–192.

Sherraden, M. (1991). *Assets and the poor: A New American welfare policy*. New York: M.E. Sharpe.

Steffensmeier, D. & Demuth, S. (2000). Ethnicity and sentencing outcome in US Federal Courts: Who is punished more harshly? *American Sociological Review*, 65: 705–729.

Steurer, S., Smith, L., & Tracy, A. (2003). *The three state recidivism study*. Maryland Department of Public Safety and Correctional Services. Retrieved from http://www.dpscs.state.md.us/doc/pdfsa/three-state-recidivism-study-summary.pdf, March 22, 2005.

Studt, E. (1959). *Education for social workers in the correctional field*. New York: CSWE.

Swain, C. (2002). *The new White nationalism in America*. New York: Cambridge University Press.

Taxman, F. (1998). Reducing recidivism through a seamless system of care. *Office of National Drug Control Policy, Treatment, and Criminal Justice System Conference*, Feb. 20, (1998). Retrieved from http://www.whitehousedrugpolicy.gov/treat/consensus/consensus.htm, March 22, (2009).

Travis, J. & Petersilia, J. (2001). Reentry reconsidered: A new look at an old question. *Crime & Delinquency*, 47 (3): 291–313.

Urban Institute (2002) *Beyond the prison gates. The state of parole in America*. New York, Urban Institute.

US Bureau of the Census (2008). *2005–2007 American community survey 3-Year Estimates*. Washington, DC: Author.

US Department of Justice (2008a). *State prison expenditures, (2007)*. Washington, D.C.

US Department of Justice (2008b). *Probation and parole in the United States, (2007)*. Washington, D.C.

US Department of Justice (2008c). *Crime in the United States, (2007)*. Washington, D.C.

US Department of Justice (2008d). *Prison statistics, (2007)*. Washington, D.C.

US Department of Justice (2007). *Criminal offender statistics*. Washington, D.C.

US Department of Justice (2006). *Correctional populations in the United States, Annual*. Washington, D.C.

US Department of Justice (2004a). *State prison expenditures, (2004)*. Washington, D.C.

US Department of Justice (2004b). *Learn about reentry*. Washington, D.C.

US Department of Justice (2004c). *Drug use and crime*. Washington, D.C.

US Department of Justice (2000). *Correctional populations in the United States*. Washington, D.C.

van Wormer, K. (2004). *Confronting oppression, restoring justice: From policy analysis to social action*. Alexandria, VA: CSWE Press.

Wilson, W. (1996). *When work disappears: The World of the New Urban Poor*. NY: Alfred A. Knopf.

Zehr, H. (1990). *Changing lenses: A new focus for crime and justice*. PA: Herald Press.

8

Social Development, Social Enterprise, and Homeless Youth

KRISTIN FERGUSON

They are a barometer for social progress in urban America and abroad as well as a conspicuous sign that social and economic development often do not progress in harmonious strides. They are the 2 million homeless children and youths in the United States and the tens of millions on the streets of the developing world (Burt, 2007; UNICEF, 2005). Homeless, street-involved youths are an at-risk population who often use survival behaviors to meet their basic needs. Compounding their high-risk behaviors, these youths also have histories of depression, trauma, self-harm, substance abuse, and physical and sexual abuse (Cauce et al., 2000).

Traditional service delivery for homeless youths consists of the outreach model—both mobile and fixed-site services (Kipke et al., 1997; Morse et al., 1996) as well as short- and long-term shelter services. Although traditional services aim to mitigate the health, mental health, and social problems of homeless youths, this approach fails to replace their street-survival behaviors with other legal, income-generating activities. Rather than changing the youths' unhealthy behaviors, the traditional approach focuses on providing basic services and can, in effect, sustain the youths' deviant behaviors on the streets. Because of its focus on correcting the youths' deficits and on meeting their basic needs, traditional service provision for these youths reflects a remedial approach to social work (Midgley, 1995).

In the case of homeless youths, successful strategies to move them from the informal to the formal economy require more than moving them into low-paying positions, such as the service sector and construction industries. Formal labor-market participation by homeless youths is often hindered by the challenges inherent in living on the streets, including the lack of a permanent address, difficulty maintaining personal hygiene, and untreated mental health issues (Cauce et al., 2000; Gaetz & O'Grady, 2002). Given many homeless youths' street-survival behaviors, successful strategies must aim to replace these "street" skills with marketable job skills and offer supportive employment opportunities where they can hone their skills and earn comparable income that substitutes their street-based earnings (Kipke et al., 1997; Thompson, Safyer, &Pollio, 2001). Finally, given the epidemiological data indicating the prevalence of mental illness among this population, successful interventions must also identify and address the youths' clinical and substance-abuse issues (Rotheram-Borus & Milburn, 2004; Russell, 1998).

Drawing on social development principles, social investment strategies (including social enterprises, vocational cooperatives, affirmative businesses and peer lending) are proposed as an alternative approach. Such interventions, when integrated with clinical services, are successful in influencing positive mental health, behavioral, functional, and service outcomes among street youths. This chapter compares existing social investment strategies for homeless youths and suggests that through these approaches, street youths can acquire vocational and business skills, mentorship, clinical treatment, and linkages to services to facilitate their economic and social self-sufficiency.

The Nature and Scope of Youth Homelessness

This chapter adopts the United Nations' definition of street youths as: "any boy or girl. . . for whom the street (in the widest sense of the word, including unoccupied dwellings, wasteland, etc.) has become his or her habitual abode and/or source of livelihood, and who is inadequately protected, supervised, or directed by responsible adults" (Lusk, 1992, p. 294). A similar classification by the United Nations Infant and Children's Emergency Fund (UNICEF) consists of youths *on* the streets and *of* the streets. Youths *on* the streets are those who earn their living in the streets but maintain some family ties. Youths *of* the streets are those who are completely on their own and frequently live with other street youths (Ennew, 1994). This chapter utilizes the term street-involved youths, which combines both concepts, for it recognizes that the categories are not discrete, fixed, or homogeneous (Panter-Brick, 2002).

One of the most pressing global challenges in social development is the increasing number of children and youths living and working on the streets of urban centers across the Global North and South. UNICEF estimates that there are over 100 million children who live and work on the city streets in the developing world to survive (UNICEF, 2005). The International Labour Organization (ILO) estimates that there are 218 million child laborers worldwide, with 126 million working in hazardous conditions (Hagemann et al., 2006). Street children who live and work in urban centers constitute one of the most visible groups of child laborers, who participate in the informal street economy by selling commercial items, washing car windshields at intersections, shining shoes, collecting recyclable and other items from garbage sites, and begging. Some child street workers may also earn a living through theft, prostitution, drug trafficking or other illicit activities. Often having little or no protection, these children are frequently exposed to exploitative employment, illegal substances, urban crime, and abuse by authorities. They perform unskilled and labor-intensive tasks in the streets for long hours while receiving minimal pay, all of which can consequently affect their health, safety, and psychosocial and moral development. Given this negative effect, child street work constitutes one of the worst forms of child labor (ILO, 1999).

In the United States, the Urban Institute estimates that over 2 million children and youths experience homelessness in a given year (Burt, 2007). Among homeless children, at least 5,000 die from illnesses, suicide, and assault each year (National Runaway Switchboard, 2008). One quarter of homeless children experience homelessness more than once in their lives, suggesting a recurrent pattern among minors. On average, children are on the streets for 10 months at each episode of homelessness (USDHHS, 2001).

Myriad individual, familial, and structural factors precipitate the movement of youths into the streets to meet their needs. Individual risk factors include influences such as school difficulties and dropout, unwanted pregnancies, gang involvement, and alcohol and substance abuse (Greene, Ennett, & Ringwalt, 1997; Halcon & Lifson, 2004; Kipke et al., 1995). Problems in the youths' families of origin also influence homelessness, as youths on the streets are highly likely to come from dysfunctional and/or abusive families, characterized by familial conflict and parental abuse and neglect. Prior studies reveal that 50% to 83% of these youths have experienced physical and/or sexual abuse, neglect, and parental rejection (Cauce et al., 2000; Molnar et al., 1998; Ryan et al., 2000; Thrane et al., 2006; Tyler, Cauce, & Whitbeck, 2004). Parental substance abuse is also frequently cited among the reasons youths leave home (Ryan et al., 2000; Tyler et al., 2004). Both parental violence and substance abuse characteristic among these families often lead to multiple contacts with the social service system (Ryan et al., 2000). Additional family factors, such as poverty, residential instability, and homelessness are also implicated in the reasons youths run away (Halcon & Lifson, 2004).

Structural influences of youth homelessness include economic crises, unemployment, and social and labor exclusion of marginal groups (Basu, 1999; ILO, 2002; UNICEF, 2005). Lack of affordable housing is another major issue associated with homelessness in many urban centers. The gap between the number of affordable housing units and demand in many major cities, such as Los Angeles, is currently the largest on record (Burns et al., 2003). This crisis has had a particularly severe effect on poor families with children, fueling the growth in the numbers of homeless women and children (Dennison et al., 2001).

Previous studies have revealed that street-involved youths are a heterogeneous group encompassing multiple subgroups. As evidenced, youth homelessness can be triggered by both short- and long-term crises. Thus, youths on the streets comprise those who have substantial street histories as well as those who are temporarily homeless (Halcon & Lifson, 2004). They may include *runaway-homeless youths* who have left home for one or more nights, without notifying their parents or guardians; *throwaway youths* who have left home because their parents have asked them to leave or have locked them out; or *independent youths* who do not have a home to which they can return. Youths who live on the streets may also be part of biological *homeless families* or fictive *street families* (Denfeld, 2007). *Undocumented, unaccompanied youths*, whose families often reside in the youths' country of origin, are also comprised in the homeless youth population. Finally, *emancipated foster youths*, who have aged-out of foster care, are disproportionately represented among homeless youths in many cities. Across the United States, the National Alliance to End Homelessness (NAEH, 2007) estimates that each year, 20,000 to 25,000 youths ages 18 years and older transition out of the foster care system. Many of these youths end up homeless as a result of a lack of family and social support. As many as one-fourth of former foster youths nationwide report that they were homeless within 2.5 to 4 years of exiting the foster care system (NAEH, 2007). These figures are even higher in some urban centers. In Los Angeles and Alameda counties, for example, of the 1500 youths who exit the foster care system each year, an estimated 50% are homeless within 6 months (Covenant House California, 2008).

Homeless, street-involved youths are commonly involved in high-risk survival behaviors to meet their basic needs (Greene et al., 1997; Halcon & Lifson, 2004; Kipke et al., 1997). These behaviors may include prostitution or survival sex (which involves participating in sexual acts in exchange for money, food, lodging, clothing, or drugs), pimping, pornography, panhandling, theft, selling stolen goods, mugging, dealing drugs, or conning others for goods. In an epidemiological study of 752 homeless youths and their subsistence and service-use patterns, Kipke et al. (1997) explored the multiple ways in which homeless youths financially support themselves. Among the most common means of subsistence were panhandling (73%) followed by survival sex/prostitution (46%), some form of formal employment (34%), dealing drugs (32%), and stealing (29%).

Compounding these high-risk behaviors, street-involved youths also have histories of depression, low self-esteem, trauma, self-harm, substance abuse, and physical and sexual abuse (Cauce et al., 2000). In a study among street youths in Hollywood ages 13 to 17 years, 26% met the Diagnostic and Statistical Manual of Mental Disorders criteria for major depression compared to 4% to 6% of community and school samples of adolescents (Russell, 1998). Major depression, post-traumatic stress disorder, and conduct disorder are found to be three times higher in runaway youths than in youths who have not left home (Robertson & Toro, 1998).

Additionally, of homeless youths in Los Angeles who have been on the streets for 6 months or more, 35% have attempted suicide (Rotheram-Borus & Milburn, 2004). Their mental health issues are often exacerbated by substance abuse and high-risk sexual behaviors. Of youths on the streets for 6 months or more, 72% reported using drugs as a coping mechanism (Rotheram-Borus & Milburn, 2004). In an earlier study, 36% of homeless youths reported having injected drugs at some point in their lives. Of these youth, 58% had injected within the past 30 days—21%

of whom reported having shared needles (Kipke et al., 1995). In a national study, 57% of homeless youths reported being high during their last sexual encounter with someone other than their main partner, whereas 25% reported being high during the last sexual encounter with a main partner (Children's Defense Fund, 2000).

Homeless youths' high-risk subsistence behaviors also make them particularly susceptible to various health problems. Common physical illnesses among this population include respiratory and skin infections, gastrointestinal problems, and malnutrition. Youths on the streets are also disproportionately affected by sexually transmitted diseases and HIV/AIDS (Bailey, Camlin, & Ennett, 1998; Epstein, 1996; Halcon & Lifson, 2004).

Socially, homeless youths are often unemployed, have limited formal job skills, and have low literacy and educational levels (Epstein, 1996). Patterns of intermittent and persistent homelessness among these youths are precipitated by their limited educational and employment skills, which can ultimately lead to their social exclusion. Several studies document that more than one-third of homeless youths have dropped out of school, do not attend school regularly or fail to earn a high-school diploma by age 18 years (Burt & Aron, 2001; Thompson, Pollio & Constantine, 2002; Thompson et al., 2001). Over half (53%) of homeless adults report having deserted compulsory education for an indefinite period of time during their lives (Burt & Aron, 2001).

Despite the myriad health and mental health issues street-involved youths confront, considerable evidence indicates their limited service utilization. Often treatment for homeless youths' health and mental health issues is inadequate, or absent altogether, as street youths tend to have limited service engagement outside of frequenting local drop-in centers for food, clothing, and showers (ISHP, 2004). In a study of the service utilization patterns among homeless youths in Los Angeles, De Rosa et al. (1999) found that homeless youths most frequently reported using drop-in centers and shelters (reported by 78% and 40%, respectively). In contrast, these youths reported using other health and mental health services less often: 28% used medical services, 10% sought substance abuse treatment, and 9% used mental health services. Given their limited service use beyond basic needs services, combined with their high-risk street behaviors, these youths are at risk for developing new and exacerbating existing mental health illnesses, as well as for chronic homelessness and social exclusion (Cauce et al., 2000).

Limited service engagement among homeless youths' can be explained in a variety of ways. Their distrust of adults and institutions, transient nature, low self-esteem, and concern for daily survival can all contribute to their disconnection from services (ISHP, 2004; Raleigh-DuRoff, 2004). High levels of stressors associated with living on the streets can also limit their engagement, particularly in long-term services (Unger et al., 1998). Low self-esteem is related to these youths' service disengagement as well. Smart and Ogborne (1994) found that homeless youths were more likely than housed youths to display low self-esteem; only 50% of homeless youths reported feeling good about themselves compared with 66% of the

housed youths. De Rosa et al. (1999) identified additional barriers to appropriate and consistent use of services among homeless youths, including their perceptions of restrictiveness of agency rules, concerns about confidentiality and mandated reporting, lack of insurance, and limited transportation.

Social Services and Social Work with Homeless Youth

Throughout the early 20th century, the needs of homeless and street-involved youths were largely addressed locally through child welfare agencies and juvenile justice courts (Fernandes, 2007). Then in the 1960s, child welfare responses to youth homelessness experienced a turning point when states began to treat youths involved in "status offenses" separately from youths who were abused/neglected or juvenile delinquents. These status offenses included truancy, curfew violations, and running away from home. Child victims of abuse and neglect were largely treated within the child welfare system, whereas child and youth perpetrators of crimes were referred to the juvenile justice system. Neither system, however, was appropriately designed to meet the needs of status-offending youths. As a result, during the Johnson Administration, lawmakers approved the deinstitutionalization of status offenders from more restrictive correctional and detention facilities on the grounds that such offenses did not warrant the restrictive treatment within the juvenile justice system. In response to the return of low-risk youths to local communities, grassroots and nongovernmental organizations began developing services to meet the needs of homeless, runaway, and transient youths. Both runaway shelters and hotlines emerged during this period as local responses to care for the safety and to address the needs of this population (Staller, 1997).

In 1970, the federal response to youth homelessness shifted toward a more rehabilitative model for delinquent youths, including status offenders, such as runaway youths. This shift was largely motivated by various sociological theories that emerged in the mid-20th century that sought to explain why youths participated in deviant behaviors, both individually and collectively (Fernandes, 2007). The Runaway Youth Act was established in 1974 as Title III of the Juvenile Justice and Delinquency Prevention Act (P.L. 93-415) to assist runaways who were not served by the juvenile justice and child welfare systems. The Act authorized funding for local runaway youth shelters and for a crisis hotline in Chicago, which eventually became the National Runaway Switchboard (Staller, 1997). In 1977, Congress expanded the Act to include homeless youths through the Runaway and Homeless Youth Act (P.L.93-415). The legislation also established services for homeless minors and their families through the Basic Center Program. It has subsequently been reauthorized on three occasions. In 1988, a provision was added to the Runaway and Homeless Youth Act to create the Transitional Living Program (P.L. 100-690). Then in 1999, the administration and funding for both the Basic Center and Transitional Living Programs were combined under the Consolidated Runaway and Homeless Youth Program (P.L. 106-71) (Fernandes, 2007).

The third and most recent reauthorization, titled the Runaway, Homeless, and Missing Children Protection Act, occurred in 2003 (P.L. 108-96). The Act authorizes federal funding for three programs—the Street Outreach Program, the Basic Center Program and the Transitional Living Program—each of which is administered by the Department of Health and Human Services, through the Family and Youth Services Bureau (Fernandes, 2007; Staller, 1997). The Street Outreach Program offers education, treatment, counseling, and referrals to runaway, homeless, and street youths who have experienced—or are at risk of experiencing—sexual abuse and exploitation. These services can be provided in both nontraditional settings, such as the streets and other public spaces where street youths congregate, as well as in agencies, including drop-in and resource centers. The role of the outreach worker in both mobile and fixed-site services is to connect youths with services and resources, provide counseling, and foster an open and trusting relationship with them (Kipke et al., 1997; Morse et al., 1996). The Basic Center Program provides temporary shelter, mental health counseling, and after-care services to runaway and homeless minors and their families. The Transitional Living Program focuses on the longer-term needs of youths ages 16 to 21 years. Youths receiving transitional living services are offered longer-term housing with supportive services, such as mental health counseling, educational/vocational training, and health care (Fernandes, 2007). Today, the Runaway and Homeless Youth Act continues to be the primary federal legislation that aims to eradicate youth homelessness through funding crisis-hotline services, emergency shelters, family reunification, street-based outreach, basic center services, and transitional housing.

One criticism of the traditional approach to serving homeless youths through street outreach, basic centers, and transitional living is that given the array of street- and agency-based services available, many youths are able to meet their basic needs while continuing to live in the streets and to maintain their high-risk survival behaviors. Although the traditional street outreach model aims to mitigate the health, mental, and social problems of homeless youths, this approach fails to address the lure of lucrative profits in the streets for many of these youths. Focusing on meeting street youths' basic needs by alleviating hunger, addiction, and illness, the traditional outreach model does not offer youths an alternative to replace their profitable street survival activities with other legal, income-generating activities. Rather than changing the youths' deviant behaviors, outreach focuses on providing basic services and can, in effect, sustain the livelihoods and behaviors of youths on the streets. Given traditional outreach's focus on remediating faults or deficits in the youths and on meeting their basic needs, this model is characteristic of the remedial or maintenance–consumption approach to social work (Midgley, 1995).

Conversely, homeless youth drop-in centers and shelters, such as basic center programs, frequently offer educational and job skills training programs within their installations. However, given street-involved youths' lack of engagement with agency-based services, many are unlikely to benefit from these services. Other traditional job training programs, such as Job Corps, focus exclusively on job skills training but do not have a mental health component. These programs thus fail to address many of the health and mental health issues that constitute barriers to homeless youths' competitive employment. Similarly, programs for older youths, such as transitional living programs, are documented to have a positive impact on homeless clients' mental health status, wages, savings, housing status, and employment. However, often these programs impose entry restrictions, such as requiring that clients do not have any mental health or substance abuse problems that would be severe enough to preclude them from maintaining full-time employment (Murray et al., 1997; Rashid, 2004). As such, many of the existing vocational programs are tailored to the most highly functioning and engaged homeless youths with the least severe mental health and substance abuse problems.

As noted earlier, the literature reveals that service engagement among homeless youths is limited. Nonetheless, it is also evident that vocational interventions for homeless youths have a documented impact on their mental health status, involvement in the formal economy, and other prosocial behaviors, such as achieving employment and housing stability. Considering the difficulties in engaging and retaining street-involved youths in services—particularly the most high-risk youths—it is vital that interventions for this population go beyond existing outreach and job training efforts. To reach the broader population of street-involved youths who are least involved in services, who have the most pressing mental health needs, and who participate in the most high-risk behaviors, interventions are needed that provide them with marketable job skills, address their mental health issues, *and* successfully engage and retain them in services.

The Social Enterprise Approach

Social development, which seeks to harmonize social and economic processes for vulnerable populations, is an alternative to conventional service provision for homeless youths. Social development consists of a planned process of human and social investment that aims to promote individual well-being in conjunction with the process of economic development (Midgley, 1995). Social investment strategies derived from the social development approach seek to enhance the learning and earning capacities of individuals through strengthening human capital, building interpersonal skills, facilitating access to financial capital, and enhancing social networks. The underlying philosophy is that one's economic well-being influences all dimensions of personal well-being. Through employment, individuals benefit from time structure, social contact, social context, and social identity, all of which affect people's health and mental health status (Harnois & Gabriel, 2000). In catering to socially and economically disenfranchised populations, social investment strategies expand on remedial services by incorporating marginalized individuals into the formal economy (Elliott & Mayadas, 1999; Midgley, 1995).

As one type of social investment strategy, *social enterprises* can refer to a nonprofit organization, a socially minded business, or a revenue-generating venture established to create positive social impact in the context of a financial bottom line

(Dees, 1998). Common social enterprises used with vulnerable populations include vocational cooperatives, affirmative businesses or social firms, micro-enterprises, and peer-lending institutions. Drawing on social development values such as empowerment, equality, social justice, and asset development, these socially oriented and income-generating activities aim to alleviate poverty and disadvantage as well as increase economic opportunities (Midgley & Livermore, 2004). See also chapter 4 for additional discussion of social enterprise.

Social enterprises have assisted disenfranchised and low-wealth people around the world, including gang-affiliated youths, unemployed women, homeless adults, and recovering addicts, in their efforts to achieve economic and social self-sufficiency (Counts, 1996; Midgley & Livermore, 2004; Wood & Wetzel, 2004). Specifically, vocational cooperatives have been used successfully with clients with special needs, such as homeless youths, who learn the value of reciprocal support and teamwork with peers while acquiring technical skills to facilitate their entry into competitive employment. The well-known Grameen Bank cooperatives and their global replications have been used throughout the world with groups of poor women and men to increase their household income and participate in the formal economy (Yunus, 2003).

Using social enterprises as a poverty-reduction strategy is not without criticism, as the literature offers mixed results on their effectiveness. Several researchers contend that micro-enterprises have had a limited impact on alleviating poverty (Schreiner, 1999) and can actually perpetuate poverty by offering low-paying jobs and maintaining existing power structures (Sanders, 2004). This is the case particularly for women, who often work in small-scale and home-based businesses that operate on the periphery of the formal economy in occupations such as childcare, tailoring, and food preparation. Research comparing micro-enterprise assistance programs to self-employment and wage labor for low-income women suggest that micro-enterprise participation does not appear to assist low-income women in moving out of poverty any better than involvement in other forms of employment (Sanders, 2004). Other authors highlight the importance of microenterprise and microfinance in the alleviation of global poverty but call for their inclusion in a more comprehensive social development strategy that includes input from individuals, communities, markets, and governments (Midgley, 2008).

The literature offers multiple examples of using evidence-based, supported employment interventions that are consistent with the social development framework with persons with mental illness. One key feature of programs for persons with mental illness with demonstrated efficacy in obtaining and maintaining employment is the integration of clinical and vocational services (Cook, 2006; Cook et al., 2005). Considerable evidence indicates that clients who participate in vocational rehabilitation programs with integrated and coordinated clinical services report improvements in relationships, self-esteem, hope, and life satisfaction, in addition to gains in employability, work functioning, work hours, and income (Bond et al., 2001; Cook et al., 2005; Drake et al., 1999; Salyers et al., 2004). Findings also reveal that clients who receive greater amounts of employment-specific vocational services and who remain for longer durations in vocational programs achieve significantly better outcomes than those who receive fewer vocational services for shorter durations (Cook, 2006). Additionally, increased amounts of vocational services have been found to have a positive impact on employment outcomes, whereas greater amounts of clinical services are associated with poorer employment outcomes (Cook, 2006). These findings suggest that enhancing the amount of vocational services to clients with mental illness to complement or exceed their existing levels of clinical services may ultimately benefit them in obtaining and maintaining competitive employment.

One particular model of supported employment that provides job opportunities and clinical services for people with psychiatric and physical disabilities is the affirmative business, or social firm (Krupa, LaGarde, & Carmichael, 2003; Warner & Mandiberg, 2006). Affirmative businesses are created with the dual mission of employing individuals with disabilities and providing a product or service needed by society. They are distinct from sheltered workshops in that affirmative businesses operate according to a defined set of principles. Namely, they hire over one-third of employees with disabilities or labor-market disadvantages; they pay a fair market wage to employees; and they operate without subsidies (Krupa et al., 2003; Warner & Mandiberg, 2006). Collectively, these businesses offer both transitional and permanent competitive employment to people with disabilities in a supportive, empowering, and community-based setting. Findings from several studies with adults suggest that affirmative businesses facilitate access to competitive employment for clients experiencing homelessness and/or mental illness. These clients benefit from teamwork with peers, while acquiring the vocational skills and clinical services needed to obtain and keep a job (Krupa et al., 2003; Shaheen & Rio, 2007; Warner & Mandiberg, 2006).

Although these studies suggest that similar strategies can be used with homeless, street-involved youth, there has been limited research to date that examines social enterprise employment models with homeless youths with mental illness. However, research with youths and young adults with severe mental illness who are not homeless suggests that this population faces multiple illness-related obstacles, stigma, and poor service coordination, all of which can result in poor rates of engagement and retention in competitive employment (Cook et al., 1997). Findings from studies evaluating model demonstration transition programs for youths with emotional and behavioral disorders who are not homeless have revealed that unemployment rates for this population can be as high as 46% (Carter & Wehby, 2003). In the case of homeless youths with mental illness, these youths not only face the aforementioned employment barriers but also the challenges inherent in living on the streets, including a lack of stable housing, difficulty maintaining personal hygiene, food insecurity, use of street-survival behaviors, and frequent criminal records (Cauce et al., 2000; Gaetz & O'Grady, 2002).

Hence, successful strategies to move youths off the streets require more than moving them into low-paying positions, as their participation in competitive employment is often hindered by the dual challenges of their mental illness and homelessness status. Given their frequent use of high-risk—and often lucrative—survival strategies, successful efforts must also aim to replace their street-survival skills with marketable job skills, provide comparable income that substitutes their street earnings, and offer them a supportive environment in which they can apply their employment skills (Kipke et al., 1997; Thompson et al., 2001). Finally, given the epidemiological data indicating the presence of mental illness and high-risk behaviors among these youths, successful interventions must also identify, assess, and treat their clinical and substance-abuse issues (Rotheram-Borus & Milburn, 2004; Russell, 1998).

The Social Enterprise Intervention Model for Homeless, Street-Involved Youths

Because of the limitations of traditional service-delivery methods with homeless youths, the author has designed the *Social Enterprise Intervention* (SEI) as an alternative social investment approach to address youth homelessness (Ferguson, 2007). A logic model of the SEI is depicted in Figure 8–1.

The Social Enterprise Intervention model draws on principles of social development and seeks to impact street youths' mental health, behavioral, functional, and service outcomes. It serves as a portal into the formal economy by training the youths in market-based skills and facilitating their involvement in an affirmative business. Similarly, it also functions as a portal to mental health services for these youths by providing them with clinical and social services for the treatment of existing conditions or for the amelioration of factors that place them at risk for physical and mental illnesses. Table 8–1 details the stages, timeframes, characteristics, and objectives of the Social Enterprise Intervention model.

In the first stage, *Vocational Skill Acquisition*, the youths participate in a 4-month course in the vocational skill that is determined most appropriate by the host agency staff and clients as well as by a local market analysis. In this course, the youths learn the technical skills necessary to participate in an affirmative business. Following the vocational course, the youths enter the 4-month *Small Business Skill Acquisition* stage, during which they learn the skills needed to run the business, such as accounting, budgeting, marketing, and management. Finally, after the conclusion of both courses, the youths enter the third stage, *Affirmative Business Formation and Distribution*. Over 12 months, the youths establish an affirmative business among their peers in a supportive, empowering, and community-based setting in the host agency, within which they develop and market their target product(s). The Social Enterprise Intervention instructor continues to provide guidance to the youths during this stage. The youths design a website to showcase and sell their products. They create an online store, participate in local flea markets, and work with local venders for increased public exposure and profit.

The mental health component of the model is woven throughout its stages over 20 months. The Social Enterprise Intervention clinical social worker tracks all participating youths by scheduling weekly meetings with them to identify, assess,

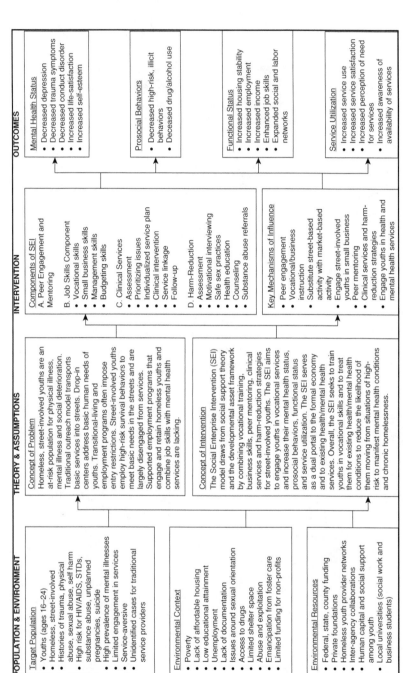

Fig. 8–1 Social Enterprise Intervention Logic Model.

Table 8–1 Stages, Timeframes, Characteristics, and Objectives of the Social Enterprise Intervention

Stage	Time	Characteristics	Objectives
I. Vocational Skill Acquisition	4 months	Vocational skill classes are taught by a qualified instructor to a small group of street-involved youths.	1. Youths learn vocational skills needed to form business with peers. 2. Youths develop rapport and trust among peers.
II. Small Business Skill Acquisition	4 months	Youths participate in a seminar on small-business skills, including accounting, budgeting, marketing, and management. Graduate business students from local university assist youths in conducting a feasibility analysis of the business and in exploring product marketability.	1. Youths learn business skills. 2. Youths develop business plan. 3. Youths identify local market for target product(s).
III. Affirmative Business Formation and Distribution	12 months	An affirmative business is established in the host agency for youths to develop and market their target product(s). Youths design website to showcase and sell their product(s). Youths locate venues/clients to sell product(s). Social Enterprise Intervention instructor provides business oversight.	1. Youths have increased opportunities for applying business skills. 2. Affirmative business works towards self-sufficiency with sales from target product(s).
IV. Clinical Services (ongoing throughout Stages I–III)	20 months	Youths meet weekly with Social Enterprise Intervention clinical social worker to identify, assess, prioritize and treat target areas of need. Social worker uses motivational interviewing, cognitive behavioral therapy, and harm-reduction strategies, among other interventions determined from baseline assessment of youths.	1. Social worker and youths identify clinical needs and goals. 2. Social worker assesses and treats youths' mental health conditions. 3. Social worker tracks youths' progress.

prioritize, and treat their target areas of need. The social worker tailors the intensity and focus of the clinical services to the severity of the youths' presenting conditions and needs. Consistent with research on supported employment programs that integrate vocational and clinical services, it is anticipated that the frequency of clinical services will decrease over the duration of the intervention (Cook, 2006).

Review of the literature on homeless and street-involved youths suggests that in addition to participating in risky behaviors, this population is likely to experience depression, anxiety, post-traumatic stress disorder, and substance abuse, among other mental illnesses. For youths with depression or bipolar or anxiety disorders, the clinical social worker uses cognitive behavioral therapy, coupled with referrals to collaborating psychiatrists for medication when requested by the youths. For youths with histories or symptoms of trauma, the social worker provides individual and group trauma intervention services, such as cognitive behavioral therapy, support groups, relaxation techniques, and referrals for medication. To address the youths' high-risk behaviors, the social worker uses motivational interviewing to identify risky behaviors and to help the youths move toward change. Consistent with the values of motivational interviewing, the social worker and youths work in a partner-like relationship in which the social worker elicits the youths' own values, goals, and motivation for change (Miller & Rollnick, 2002). Because motivational interviewing can be utilized with youths who have varying levels of readiness to change, it is considered an appropriate technique for homeless youths with differing degrees of street involvement (Barnett, Monti, & Wood, 2001). Various individual and group-based harm-reduction strategies, including safe sex practices, health education, sexually transmitted disease prevention, HIV counseling and testing, and substance abuse referrals, can also be used by the social worker to reduce the youths' harmful, high-risk behaviors through small achievable steps (Denning, 2001). Evidence suggests that continuous access to high-quality, integrated substance abuse and mental health treatment helps people recover (Drake et al., 2004).

The Social Enterprise Intervention model is designed as an asset-based model of youth development, which builds on prior work on internal developmental assets and thriving in youths (Benson, 1999, 2003). Internal assets are grouped in four categories: commitment to learning, social competencies, positive values, and positive identity. The Social Enterprise Intervention components collectively aim to strengthen the youths' internal assets to enhance positive outcomes and protect them against high-risk behavior.

The vocational and business courses seek to promote the youths' *commitment to learning* by offering them vocational and business training that builds on their entrepreneurial skills and strengths, is tailored to their previous experience, and promotes active and hands-on learning. Social Enterprise Intervention courses are also designed to promote *social competencies* in the youths—particularly planning and decision making—by incorporating them in the decision-making aspects. One way to build social competencies is to invite the youths to establish class rules, consequences for rule-breaking, and incentive structures for compliance. The youths can also work with the instructor to formalize the class syllabi, depending on their identified areas of interest and direction of the affirmative business. There is evidence that client involvement in planning services can increase their satisfaction with services, which may have implications for both client retention and outcomes (James & Meezan, 2002).

Further, through the Social Enterprise Intervention mental health component, the social worker partners with the youths to develop and exercise *positive values*, particularly those of responsibility and restraint. The social worker and youths work together on identifying and prioritizing their areas of need and taking personal responsibility for their actions. Similarly, by learning to use various harm-reduction strategies, the youths are able to practice the positive value of restraint, particularly with their high-risk behaviors.

Finally, the Social Enterprise Intervention model is designed to promote *positive identity* in the youths by affirming their capacity for self-direction in the worker–client relationship, thus strengthening the youths' personal power. Through participation in the affirmative business, the youths are able to identify and develop their areas of vocational expertise, thus enhancing their sense of purpose. Collectively, these different components are consistent with the social development framework as well as with the social work value base in their aim to strengthen clients' assets, empower them to participate in the formal economy, and promote social justice and equality (Midgley & Livermore, 2004).

Case Examples of Social Enterprise Interventions

In the extant literature, several additional examples exist of using micro-enterprises and other social enterprise interventions with street-involved youths to develop niche markets for particular products or as portals to the formal economy, where these youths can learn and hone business and job skills. The following host social service agencies in the developing and developed world have designed innovative interventions using social enterprises to address youth homelessness. The dual focus on employment and mental health support of the following examples also mirrors the Social Enterprise Intervention model and is consistent with the social development approach.

Mexico currently uses a model of *triangular solidarity*, which brings together different sectors, including nongovernmental organizations, public institutions, and corporations to address the street youth phenomenon. In this model, nonprofit organizations, which include *Casa Alianza*, assist homeless youths in exiting the street milieu and receiving the necessary health, mental health, and social services to lead self-sufficient lives off of the streets. The public sector, which is primarily the Ministry of Education, then provides these youths with vocational training and certification programs to teach them trade skills and increase their employability. Finally, local and national corporations agree to hire youths who have completed the training program (Covenant House, 2001). The Mexican model of triangular solidarity seeks to support street-involved youths with mental health services and equip them with market-based vocational skills to facilitate their entry into the formal economy.

In the United States, social enterprises such as vocational cooperatives and consumer-run businesses provide at-risk, gang-involved, and homeless youths with opportunities to become self-sufficient by learning and applying labor skills in the formal economy and by receiving the mental health support needed to reintegrate into society. *Homeboy Industries* is a nonprofit organization in Los Angeles that assists at-risk and former gang youths in developing social and vocational skills to facilitate their re-entry into society and the formal economy. By combining counseling, case management, education, vocational training, and job placement, former gang youths become contributing members in their families and communities and in society at large (Homeboy Industries, 2005).

Ashbury Images in San Francisco is another social enterprise that specifically targets individuals in recovery from homelessness and substance abuse for employment. Working in coordination with its nonprofit parent organization, *New Door Ventures*, vocational training in embroidery, silk-screening, and restaurant operation, together with mental health workshops in self-esteem, are offered to individuals in recovery. Graduates are currently employed in a variety of industries, including multimedia, retail, law enforcement, and youth counseling (Ashbury Images, 2008).

The *Reciprocity Foundation* in New York is a social enterprise that facilitates the permanent exit of homeless and high-risk youths from the street milieu and social service system by assisting them in starting sustainable careers in fashion, graphic design, and marketing within the formal economy. Linking the creative economy with social responsibility, industry professionals teach the youths marketable job skills and mentor them in becoming leaders of their own socially responsible enterprises. Staff employ a sustainable approach with the youths by offering them services in both professional development, such as technical training, and personal well-being, such as health and mental health services (Reciprocity Foundation, 2007).

Social Work and the Social Enterprise Approach

Collectively, social enterprise interventions aim to equip homeless, street-involved youths with the necessary vocational training, business skills, and mental health support to facilitate their involvement in income-generating activities as a replacement for their street behaviors. These alternatives to traditional services for street youths draw on principles of social development and are supported by research demonstrating their success in promoting economic and social self-sufficiency among vulnerable populations. Although useful in helping street youths transition out of the informal economy and into competitive employment, these interventions remain largely outside of social work literature, education, and professional practice with these youths.

Gray, Healy, and Crofts (2003) made a major theoretical contribution to social work by operationalizing the values that undergird business and social enterprises and by delineating the roles that each play in using social enterprises to pursue social justice—an ethical cornerstone of the social work profession. Social enterprises capitalize on private sector expertise, resources, and profit and apply these assets to solve social problems through the transfer of resources and opportunities to vulnerable populations. Of interest to the social work profession are the social and economic benefits garnered by disadvantaged populations and society at large from the profits accrued by the social enterprise. Through increased involvement in social enterprises, social workers can play a key role in asking the question "Who benefits?" and in ensuring that our profession's target populations are comprised among the beneficiaries of social-enterprise ventures.

In addition to their relevance to social justice, social enterprise interventions with street-involved youths are also consistent with other professional ethics and values. For example, social enterprise programs recognize the inherent resiliency and entrepreneurial qualities of homeless youths and provide them with income-generating opportunities to apply and hone these skills. Conversely, traditional service models aim to mitigate the youths' health, mental, and social problems within the street environment, in drop-in centers, and in shelters. By providing basic services to these youths in the absence of employment skills and placement, the traditional approach can in effect sustain the youths' livelihoods and survival behaviors on the streets. Additionally, because homeless youths frequently use survival behaviors as a primary means of economic subsistence on the streets, the traditional service approach is limited in that it fails to replace these activities. In contrast, social enterprises enhance homeless youths' personal agency by equipping them with vocational and business skills to facilitate their involvement in the formal economy.

Given the social enterprise approach's consistency with social work's professional value base, yet relatively new status within the profession, social work practitioners and researchers play a vital role in integrating this approach more centrally into the existing system of care for homeless youths. Social work practitioners, who draw from a person-in-environment framework, are ideally positioned to contribute to the evolvement of social enterprise practice with homeless youths within agencies and communities. Social enterprise programs capitalize on the youths' existing strengths and skills and channel them into an income-generating activity within the formal economy. Affirmative businesses provide an on-site setting within a host social service agency in which the youths receive vocational training and clinical services and, at the same time, have the opportunity to practice and hone their skills. At the agency level, in an era of increasing unemployment and limited federal and private funding for nonprofit agencies, businesses that are run within nonprofits create not only sources of employment for clients but also alternate funding streams for the host agency. In the community milieu, established social enterprises create job opportunities for local residents as well as needed products and services for the community. In both the agency and community realms, social workers can facilitate the use of social enterprises with homeless youths by building partnerships with private businesses, alleviating the social disadvantage of clients and communities, and monitoring and ensuring that all social enterprise gains and profits ultimately benefit the clients and communities involved.

Social work researchers also play an important role in designing, testing, and evaluating the effectiveness of social enterprise interventions with homeless youths. To more clearly understand the impact of the social enterprise approach on street youths' mental health, social, and economic well-being, future qualitative and quantitative research is needed to identify and evaluate existing social enterprise interventions with homeless youths. Additional qualitative research will help to further conceptualize and operationalize outcome measures for this population. Adopting an inclusive approach that incorporates youth clients, service providers, researchers, and policymakers in defining outcomes for homeless youths will also further enhance the validity of these concepts. Similarly, an inclusive approach will provide much-needed examples to the field regarding how to incorporate the practice community into service design and evaluation. Randomized controlled trials would also increase our understanding of the efficacy and effectiveness of social enterprise interventions with homeless youths. Such large-scale studies would allow comparisons of mental health, behavioral, functional, and service-related outcomes among homeless youths in social enterprise programs, those in traditional vocational training programs, and those in usual care.

In an age of evidence-based practice, partnerships between researchers and practitioners are crucial for integrating scientific evidence with both clinical expertise and client values and, ultimately, advancing the social work profession (Gambrill, 1999). The social enterprise models described in this chapter can serve as a guide for social work practitioners and researchers in implementing and evaluating social enterprise interventions to assist homeless youths in transitioning to the formal economy and addressing the mental health issues that often preclude them from full economic participation.

REFERENCES

Ashbury Images. (2008). *Rebuilding lives*. Available from http://www.ashburyimages.org (Accessed March 26, 2008).

Bailey, S. L., Camlin, C. S., & Ennett, S. T. (1998). Substance use and risky sexual behavior among homeless and runaway youth. *Journal of Adolescent Health*, 23(6): 378–388.

Barnett, N. P., Monti, P. M., & Wood, M. D. (2001). Motivational interviewing for alcohol-involved adolescents in the emergency room. In E. F. Wagner & H. B. Waldron (Eds.), *Innovations in adolescent substance abuse interventions*. New York: Pergamon, pp. 143–168.

Basu, K. (1999). Child labor: Cause, consequence, and cure with remarks on international labor standards. *Journal of Economic Literature*, 37(3): 1083–1119.

Benson, P. L. (1999). *A fragile foundation: The state of developmental assets among American youth*. Minneapolis, MN: Search Institute.

Benson, P. L. (2003). Developmental assets and asset-building community: Conceptual and empirical foundations. In R. Lerner & P. L. Benson (Eds.), *Developmental assets and asset-building communities: Implications for research, policy and practice*. New York: Kluwer Academic/Plenum Publishers, pp. 19–43.

Bond, G. R., Becker, D. R., Drake, R. E., et al. (2001). Implementing supported employment as an evidence-based practice. *Psychiatric Services*, 52(3): 313–322.

Burns, P., Drayse, M., Flaming, D., & Haydamack, B. (2003). *Prisoners of hope: Welfare to work in Los Angeles.* Los Angeles, CA: Economic Roundtable.

Burt, M. R. (2007, June). *Understanding homeless youth: Numbers, characteristics, multisystem involvement, and intervention options.* Testimony Submitted before the U.S. House Committee on Ways and Means Subcommittee on Income Security and Family Support. Urban Institute. Available at http://www.urban.org/ UploadedPDF/901087_Burt_Homeless.pdf (Accessed March 30, 2008).

Burt, M. R., & Aron, L. Y. (2001). *Helping America's homeless.* Washington, DC: Urban Institute Press.

Carter, E. W., & Wehby, J. H. (2003). Job performance of transition-age youth with emotional and behavioral disorders. *Exceptional Children,* 69(4): 449–465.

Cauce, A. M., Paradise, M., Ginzler, J. A., et al. (2000). The characteristics and mental health of homeless adolescents: Age and gender differences. *Journal of Emotional and Behavioral Disorders,* 8: 230–239.

Children's Defense Fund. (2000). *Domestic violence and its impact on children.* Washington, DC: Author.

Cook, J. A. (2006). Employment barriers for persons with psychiatric disabilities: Update of a report for the president's commission. *Psychiatric Services,* 57(10): 1391–1405.

Cook, J. A., Leff, S., Blyler, C. R., et al. (2005). Results of a multisite randomized trial of supported employment interventions for individuals with severe mental illness. *Archives of General Psychiatry,* 62(5): 505–512.

Cook, J. A., Solomon, M. L., & Mock, L. O. (1997). What happens after the first job: Vocational transitioning among severely emotionally disturbed and behaviorally disordered adolescents. In S. Braaten, R. Rutherford, T. Reilly, & S. D. DiGamgi (Eds.). *Programming for adolescents with behavioral disorders.* Reston, VA: Council for Exceptional Children, pp. 71–93.

Counts, A. (1996). *Give us credit.* New York: Times Books.

Covenant House. (2001). *World economic forum in Mexico to include a voice for street children.* Available at http://www.casa-alianza.org (Accessed March 4, 2008).

Covenant House California. (2008). *Statistics.* Available at http://www.covenanthouseca.org (Accessed April 25, 2008).

Dees, J. G. (1998). Enterprising nonprofits. *Harvard Bus Rev,* Jan.-Feb: 55–67.

Denfeld, R. (2007). *All God's children: Inside the dark and violent world of street families.* New York: Public Affairs.

Denning, P. (2001). Strategies for implementation of harm reduction in treatment settings. *Journal of Psychoactive Drugs,* 33(1): 23–26.

Dennison, B., Mantley, R., Mendizabal, A., & White, P. (2001). *Downtown women's needs assessment.* Los Angeles, CA: Downtown Women's Coalition.

De Rosa, C. J., Montgomery, S. B., Kipke, M. D., Iverson, E., Ma, J. L., & Unger, J. B. (1999). Service utilization among homeless and runaway youth in Los Angeles, California: Rates and reasons. *Journal of Adolescent Health,* 24(6): 449–458.

Drake, R. E., McHugo, G. J., Bebout, R. R., et al. (1999). A randomized clinical trial of supported employment for inner-city patients with severe mental disozrders. *Archives of General Psychiatry,* 56(7): 627–633.

Drake, R. E., Mueser, K. T., Brunette, M. F., & McHugo, G. J. (2004). A review of treatments for people with severe mental illnesses and co-occurring substance use disorders. *Psychiatric Rehabilitation Journal,* 27(4): 360–374.

Elliott, D. & Mayadas, N. (1999). Infusing global perspectives into social work practice. In C. S. Ramanathan & R. J. Link (Eds.). *All our futures. Principles and resources for social work practice in a global era.* Belmont, CA: Wadsworth Publishing Company, pp. 52–68.

Ennew, J. (1994). *Street and working children: A guide to planning.* London: Save the Children.

Esptein, I. (1996). Educating street children: Some cross-cultural perspectives. *Comparative Education*, 32(3): 289–302.

Ferguson, K. (2007). Implementing a social enterprise intervention with homeless, street-living youth in Los Angeles. *Social Work*, 52(2): 103–112.

Fernandes, A. L. (2007). *Runaway and homeless youth: Demographics, programs, and emerging issues.* CRS Report for Congress. Order code RL33785. Washington, DC: Congressional Research Service.

Gaetz, S., & O'Grady, B. (2002). Making money: Exploring the economy of young homeless workers. *Work, Employment & Society*, 16(3): 433–456.

Gambrill, E. (1999). Evidence-based practice: An alternative to authority-based practice. *Families in Society: The Journal of Contemporary Human Services*, 80(4): 341–350.

Gray, M., Healy, K., & Crofts, P. (2003). Social enterprise: Is it the business of social work? *Australian Social Work*, 56(2): 141–154.

Greene, J. M., Ennett, S. T., & Ringwalt, C. L. (1997). Substance use among runaway and homeless youth in three national samples. *American Journal of Public Health*, 87(2): 229–235.

Hagemann, F., Diallo, Y., Etienne, A., & Mehran, F. (2006). *Global child labour trends 2000 to 2004.* Geneva: International Labour Office.

Halcon, L. L., & Lifson, A. R. (2004). Prevalence and predictors of sexual risks among homeless youth. *Journal of Youth and Adolescence*, 33(1): 71–80.

Harnois, G., & Gabriel, P. (2000). *Mental health and work: Impact, issues and good practices.* World Health Organization and International Labor Organization. Geneva: World Health Organization.

Homeboy Industries. (2005). *Welcome to Homeboy Industries.* Available at http://www.homeboy-industries.org/index.php (Accessed March 26, 2008). ILO – See International Labour Organization.

Institute for the Study of Homelessness and Poverty (ISHP). (2004). *Homelessness in Los Angeles. Just the facts.* Los Angeles, CA: Author.

International Labour Office. (2002). *A future without child labour: Global report under the follow-up to the ILO Declaration on Fundamental Principles and Rights at Work.* Geneva: International Labour Organization.

International Labour Organization. (1999). *C182 Worst Form of Child Labour Convention, 1999* (Article 3). Available at http://www.ilo.org ISHP – See Institute for the Study of Homelessness and Poverty (Accessed April 23, 2008).

James, S., & Meezan, W. (2002). Refining the evaluation of treatment foster care. *Families in Society*, 83(3): 233–244.

Kipke, M. D., O'Connor, S., Palmer, R. F., & MacKenzie, R. G. (1995). Street youth in Los Angeles: Profile of a group at high risk for HIV. *Archives of Pediatric Adolescent Medicine*, 149(5): 513–519.

Kipke, M. D., Unger, J. B., O'Connor, S., Palmer, R. F., & LaFrance, S. R. (1997). Street youth, their peer group affiliation and differences according to residential status, subsistence patterns, and use of services. *Adolescence*, 32(127): 655–669.

Krupa, T., LaGarde, M., & Carmichael, K. (2003). Transforming sheltered workshops into affirmative businesses: An outcome evaluation. *Psychiatric Rehabilitation Journal,* 26(4): 359–367.

Lusk, M. W. (1992). Street children of Rio de Janeiro. *International Social Work,* 35(3): 293–305.

Midgley, J. (1995). *Social development. The developmental perspective in social welfare.* Thousand Oaks, CA: SAGE Publications.

Midgley, J. (2008). Microenterprise, global poverty and social development. *International Social Work, Work,* 51(4): 467–479.

Midgley, J., & Livermore, M. (2004). Social development: Lessons from the global south. In M. C. Hokenstad, & J. Midgley (Eds.). *Lessons from abroad: Adapting international social welfare innovations.* Washington, DC: NASW Press, pp. 117–135.

Miller, W. R., & Rollnick, S. (2002). *Motivational interviewing: Preparing people to change addictive behavior (2*nd *Edition).* New York: Guilford Press.

Molnar, B. E., Shade, S. B., Kral, A. H., Booth, R. E., & Watters, J. K. (1998). Suicidal behavior and sexual/physical abuse among street youth. *Child Abuse & Neglect,* 22(3): 213–222.

Morse, G. A., Calsyn, R. J., Miller, J., Rosenberg, P., Gilliland, J., & West, L. (1996). Outreach to homeless mentally ill people: Conceptual and clinical considerations. *Community Mental Health Journal,* 32(3): 261–274.

Murray, R., Baier, M., North, C., Lato, M., & Eskew, C. (1997). One-year status of homeless mentally ill clients who completed a transitional residential program. *Community Mental Health Journal,* 33(1): 43–50.

NAEH – See National Alliance to End Homelessness.

National Alliance to End Homelessness. (2007, June). Fact checker: Accurate statistics on homelessness. *Youth homelessness.* Available at http://www.naeh.org/section/data/factsheets (Accessed April 25, 2008).

National Runaway Switchboard. (2008). *NRS call statistics.* Available at http://www.1800runaway.org/news_events/call_stats.html (Accessed April 14, 2008).

Panter-Brick, C. (2002). Street children, human rights and public health: A critique and future directions. *Annual Review of Anthropology,* 31: 147–171.

Raleigh-DuRoff, C. (2004). Factors that influence adolescents to leave or stay living on the street. *Child and Adolescent Social Work Journal,* 21(6): 561–571.

Rashid, S. (2004). Evaluating a transitional living program for homeless, former foster care youth. *Research on Social Work Practice,* 14(4): 240–248.

Reciprocity Foundation. (2007). *Reciprocity Foundation: Designing a better future.* Available at http://www.reciprocityfoundation.org/aboutus.php (Accessed March 26, 2008).

Robertson, M., & Toro, P. (1998). Homeless youth: Research, intervention, and policy. In L. B. Fosberg, & D. L. Dennis (Eds.). *Practical lessons: The 1998 symposium on homelessness research.* Washington, DC: U.S. Department of Health and Human Services, pp. 3.1–3.32.

Rotheram-Borus, M. J., & Milburn, N. (2004). *Project I: Pathways into homelessness.* UCLA Center for Community Health. Los Angles, CA: University of California Los Angeles.

Russell, L. A. (1998). *Child maltreatment and psychological distress among urban homeless youth.* New York: Garland Publishing.

Ryan, K. D., Kilmer, R. P., Cauce, A. M., Watanabe, H., & Hoyt, D. R. (2000). Psychological consequences of child maltreatment in homeless adolescents: Untangling the unique effects of maltreatment and family environment. *Child Abuse & Neglect*, 24(3): 333–352.

Salyers, M. P., Becker, D. R., Drake, R. E., Torrey, W. C., & Wyzik, P. F. (2004). A ten-year follow-up of a supported employment program. *Psychiatr Serv*, 55(3): 302–308.

Sanders, C. (2004). Employment options for low-income women: Microenterprise versus the labor market. *Social Work Research*, 28(2): 83–92.

Schreiner, M. (1999). Self-employment, micro-enterprise and the poorest Americans. *Social Service Review*, 73(4): 496–523.

Shaheen, G., & Rio, J. (2007). Recognizing work as a priority in preventing or ending homelessness. *Journal of Primary Prevention*, 28(3-4): 341–358.

Smart, R. G., & Ogborne, A. C. (1994). Street youth in substance abuse treatment: Characteristics and treatment compliance. *Adolescence*, 29(115): 733–745.

Staller, K. M. (1997). Homeless and runaway youth. In G. P. Mallon and P. McCartt Hess (Eds.). *Child welfare for the twenty-first century: A handbook of practices, policies, and programs*. New York: Columbia University Press, pp. 228–245.

Thrane, L. E., Hoyt, D. R., Whitbeck, L. B., & Yoder, K. A. (2006). Impact of family abuse on running away, deviance, and street victimization among homeless rural and urban youth. *Child Abuse Neglect*, 30(10): 1117–1128.

Thompson, S. J., Pollio, D. E., Constantine, J., & Von Nebbitt, D. R. (2002). Short-term outcomes for youth receiving runaway and homeless shelter services. *Research on Social Work Practice*, 12(5): 589–603.

Thompson, S. J., Safyer, A. W., & Pollio, D. E. (2001). Differences and predictors of family reunification among subgroups of runaway youths using shelter services. *Social Work Research*, 25(3): 163–172.

Tyler, K. A., Cauce, A. M., & Whitbeck L. B. (2004). Family risk factors and prevalence of dissociative symptoms among homeless and runaway youth. *Child Abuse Neglect*, 28(3): 355–366.

UNICEF – See United Nations Infant and Children's Emergency Fund.

United Nations Infant and Children's Emergency Fund UNICEF. (2005). *State of the world's children: Childhood under threat*. Available at http://www.unicef.org/sowc05/english/index.html (Accessed March 17, 2008).

Unger, J. B., Kipke, M. D., Simon, T. R., Johnson, C. J., Montgomery, S. B., & Iverson, E. (1998). Stress, coping, and social support among homeless youth. *Journal of Adolescent Research*, 13(2): 134–157.

USDHHS – See United States Department of Health and Human Services.

United States Department of Health and Human Services [USDHHS]. (2001). *No place to call home*. Bureau of Primary Health Care. Washington, DC: Author.

Warner, R., & Mandiberg, J. (2006). An update on affirmative businesses or social firms for people with mental illness. *Psychiatric Services*, 57(10): 1488–1492.

Wood Wetzel, J. (2004). Mental health lessons from abroad. In M. C. Hokenstad, & J. Midgley (Eds.). *Lessons from abroad: Adapting international social welfare innovations*. Washington, DC: NASW Press, pp. 93–116.

Yunus, M. (2003). *Banker to the poor: Micro-lending and the battle against world poverty*. New York: Public Affairs, Perseus Books Group.

9

Community Practice and Developmental Social Work

JAMES MIDGLEY

Developmental social work is closely associated with community social work practice. As shown in the Chapter 1, developmental social work emerged out of community development activities in the Global South in the 1950s, and today developmental social work relies extensively on community-based interventions. However, there are significant differences between conventional community practice and the developmental approach. Whereas the former emphasizes local community capacity building, social services planning, or social activism, developmental community work stresses the use of economic and social investments that meet the material needs of poor communities. This is particularly relevant to the developing countries, where widespread poverty and deprivation requires immediate action.

Although the importance of economic development is now recognized by community practitioners in the Western countries, social workers have not been extensively involved in promoting community-based economic development projects that raise living standards in deprived areas. Often they assume that mobilizing poor people, strengthening local networks, and promoting participation will empower the poor to meet their own material needs. But, as argued in Chapter 1, tangible investments that have a direct impact on living standards are required if the problems of poverty and deprivation are to be addressed. This does not mean that developmental community work rejects the need for organizing activities that promote community participation. Nor does it reject the importance of activism. Although community action is an invaluable tool for mobilizing local support and for securing much-needed resources, it should augment developmental interventions.

This issue is discussed in more depth in this chapter. It begins with a brief overview of the nature and history of community social work in the Western countries and shows how economic activities have been neglected. It contends that community-based economic development projects and programs contribute positively to poverty alleviation. This argument is illustrated by examining the role of community development in the Global South and local economic development innovations in the United States. Both demonstrate the need for a greater focus on economic projects that meet the material needs of poor communities. The chapter concludes by discussing some of the ways community social work practice can contribute to this task.

Community Social Work Practice

Although the nature of community social work has been debated for more than a century, there are sharp disagreements about what it involves. Even terminologies are not standardized, and therefore community social work is known by different names. These include community organization, community development, community action, community building, indirect practice, and macro-practice. Community organization is generally favored, but the term community practice has been popularized in recent years. It has also proved difficult to incorporate the diverse activities undertaken by community social workers over the years into a coherent, single definition. For example, the neighborhood building activities of the settlements were very different from those of the Charity Organization Society. In turn, they had little in common with the political lobbying of some settlement leaders. Consequently, early attempts to define community organization were based exclusively on one of these approaches while the others were ignored. This practice continued as the field subsequently developed. However, by the 1950s, community organization was generally associated with social services agency coordination and planning. Although community building and social activism were well-established, they were not accorded the same status as social services planning in social work.

Some scholars eventually recognized that the disparate activities undertaken by community social workers could be viewed as different applications of common principles and practice skills. This idea gave rise numerous typologies of community practice. One of the first was proposed by Ross (1955), who identified three forms of community practice that he labeled the planning, process, and reform orientations. Ross associated the planning orientation with welfare agency coordination and the process orientation with the local neighborhood capacity enhancement approach. Ross did not regard community activism as a legitimate form of community social work but believed that the profession's social reform activities should be viewed as an appropriate social work activity. Subsequently, Rothman (1968) published a widely cited typology that also recognized three types of community social work practice—namely, locality development, social planning, and social action. He linked the locality development approach with neighborhood community building, the social planning approach with social services coordination and fundraising, and the social action approach with efforts to mobilize local people to demand improved social conditions. Rothman's model has subsequently been extended to account for other community practice approaches such as feminist organizing, which were generally ignored in the literature (Hyde, 1986). Indeed, community social work has historically been dominated by men who have not paid much attention to women's organizing efforts. These developments expanded the original typologies. In 1985, Taylor and Roberts added two more categories to Rothman's original three, and in 1995, Weil and Gamble extended the model to eight. In 2004, Smock reduced the number to four.

On the other hand, some scholars believe that many of the activities depicted in these typologies do not form a part of community social work. In his comprehensive history of community organizing, Fisher (1994) differentiates what he calls the social work approach from the neighborhood maintenance and political activist approaches. For Fisher, community social work is confined to neighborhood building and social services planning by community agencies such as the United Way. Social activism and the activities of the neighborhood associations found in many middle-class communities do not, he believes, comprise community social work practice. Although many will disagree with Fisher's typology, he shows that many forms of community organization are not undertaken by social workers. This point is particularly relevant to this chapter. Despite the claim that community economic development is a form of social work practice, it will be shown that social workers have only been marginally involved in the field.

The following offers a brief overview of the activities associated with community social work practice over the years. These activities are neighborhood building, social services planning, and social activism. They have been formulated into coherent conceptual definitions that have informed the field's rich body of literature. Despite disagreements about the scope of community social work, many would agree that they comprise the core practice commitments of community social work. As will become apparent, these approaches are rooted in the profession's historical evolution.

Neighborhood Participation and Community Building

Community practice emerged as a distinctive field of social work in the late 19th century when the idea that professionally trained workers were needed to deal with the problems facing poor families gained widespread support. Whereas the charities believed that these problems should be addressed through individualized casework, the settlements responded by establishing residential facilities in poor neighborhoods where middle-class students from the universities lived or "settled." Supervised by paid staff, they sought to inspire the poor to improve their lives. Literacy classes, organized sports, recreational activities, and visits to museums were some of the mechanism by which they hoped this goal would be achieved. In addition, the settlements engaged in neighborhood improvement and the municipal authorities were often lobbied to provide street lighting, remove garbage, and build playgrounds. Some of settlement leaders also worked closely with the trades unions and progressive politicians and actively campaigned for wider social reforms. Jane Addams' association with President Roosevelt and other progressive politicians has been widely documented.

The work of the settlements was augmented by the emergence of the community centers movement, which provided after-class activities at local schools in many poor communities (Fisher, 1990). The movement's leaders believed that the centers would fill the void created by corrupt and indifferent politicians, inculcate a strong sense of civic responsibility, and foster democratic participation. Participation would be promoted through educational, recreational, and cultural activities, including reading circles, amateur concerts and plays, debating societies, gymnastic and athletic events, and discussion groups. Like the settlements, the centers employed trained workers who mobilized local participation and organized events. In the early 20th century, thousands of community centers had been established all over the United States, and a national association to represent their interests had also been formed. By this time, the settlements had also expanded significantly. Fisher (1994) reports that only six settlements (including the famed Hull House) had established by 1891, but that more than 200 were in operation by the end of the century. By 1911, this number doubled to about 400.

The settlements, community centers, and similar local initiatives laid the foundations for neighborhood organizing. They pioneered the idea that social work services should be located within poor communities and that local people should be actively involved in addressing community needs. Their group activities were designed to socialize and educate, foster local participation, strengthen community bonds, and promote what subsequently became known as community building. However, relatively small numbers of local people participated in settlement activities. Although Hull House was located within an area containing more than 70,000 people, only about 2,000 visited on a regular basis (Fisher, 1994). Nor did the settlements always forge strong links with local churches or with immigrant clubs and associations; in many cases, they were outposts of middle class benevolence providing limited services to some local people. Although the settlement's social action and reform activities are emphasized in the literature, many were politically cautious and conservative. Many also augmented their efforts to paternalistically "socialize" the poor by seeking to "Americanize" the millions of immigrants who came to the United States (Karger, 1987). However, people of color were generally excluded. Many of the settlements reflected the institutionalized racism of the time, and although separate settlements for African Americans were established, most settlements were created exclusively for White neighborhoods.

Nevertheless, the settlements made a vital and longlasting contribution. Although many have now disappeared, their approach is perpetuated in the thousands of local community centers that operate today (Yan, Lauer, & Sin, 2009). Their contribution is also recognized in the community practice literature. Indeed, their activities inspired the first scholarly accounts of community organizing.

One of the earliest books on the subject by Hart (1920) drew on the work of the settlements to stress the importance of promoting participation in civic life. Neighborhood activities, he believed, would build democracy at the local level and bring other positive social benefits. This idea was reinforced by Lindeman's (1921) highly influential book, which articulated 10 steps in the community organizing process. Lindeman emphasized the role of local leadership in identifying community needs and mobilizing support through community meetings. Although he believed that formal community associations played a key role in meeting local needs, people's participation was essential if community problems were to be solved.

These ideas have since been restated in many publications stressing the importance of neighborhood community building in community social work. Most typologies recognize this approach. For example, Rothman (1968) identifies locality development with community building, primarily within small geographic communities, and like Ross, believes that locality development is concerned with process rather than task goals. In locality development, building strong community networks, fostering democratic decision making, and maximizing local participation is prioritized over social services provision and the material and other substantive needs of local communities. As Naperstek and Dooey note, ". . . community building is not about simply giving money or services to poor people" (1997, p. 79). By focusing on process goals, communities can be helped to develop their own responses to these problems. Kretzman and McKnight (1993) subsequently developed this idea by arguing that solutions to local problems can be found by community members themselves provided that they are helped to identify and utilize the assets they possess.

In the 1960s, these activities became known as community development. This reflected a greater awareness of community development ideas from the Global South and the influence of the community revitalization initiatives of the Johnson administration's War on Poverty. However, unlike these innovations, which were directly associated with economic projects, the term *community development* connoted local capacity enhancement activities, network building, increasing the participation of local people, and identifying leaders who could collaborate with social workers to "develop" the capacities of communities to address local problems. By the 1990s, the terms *community capacity enhancement, community building,* and *asset building* became more popular, but as Chaskin and his colleagues (2001) reveal, these terms generally refer to the same activities that characterized earlier neighborhood building. However, the notions of strengths and empowerment now pervade the literature. It is difficult, if not impossible, nowadays to find a text on community organizing that does not emphasize the need for community empowerment. This idea also affects the role of the community organizer, who is viewed as an enabler who identifies local leaders, helps them to form local associations, and builds effective networks. Community social workers do not adopt a directive posture, prescribe solution, or provide social services but facilitate the capacity enhancement process. Indeed, Kretzman and McKnight (1993) believe that they should limit their involvement to educating local people about their innate strengths and assets.

Social Services Organization and Planning

Community social service planning is arguably the most prominent form of community social work. It has dominated the field's literature for many years and is universally taught at schools of social work. Unlike the neighborhood building approach, it has a wider geographical scope and is often concerned with citywide social services planning. It makes use of rational decision-making tools to address substantive community problems and it is primarily concerned with task goals. It requires that practitioners have technical skills in needs assessment, research, policy formulation, program implementation, and evaluation.

Community social services planning is rooted in the activities of the Charity Organization Society, which sought to coordinate the services of local welfare organizations to prevent duplication and abuse. Although the Society is best known for promoting individualized social casework, its social services planning role was equally important. In fact, some of the organization's founders, such as Charles Loch and Humphrey Gurteen, placed more emphasis on local social services planning than on the use of trained caseworkers. However, the Society had difficulty in securing the cooperation of the other charities whose leaders often resented its heavy-handed approach. As similar social services coordinating organizations such as Councils of Social Agencies emerged in different American cities, the Society's monopolistic control over community planning activities declined. Although many of these organizations adopted the Society's methods, they relied on the voluntary participation of member agencies and were less directive and more collaborative. Generally, they had citywide scope, although in larger metropolitan areas, several coordinating and planning agencies serving different parts of the city emerged. Examples of early citywide social services planning agencies include the Pittsburgh Council of Associated Charities, which was founded in 1908, and the Cleveland Federation of Charities and Philanthropies, which was established in 1913.

Some community planning agencies subsequently engaged in joint fundraising and cooperative lobbying. Collaborative or federated fundraising became popular after World War I when the first Community Chests were established. These had emerged during the War to raise funds for wounded servicemen and other war-related charities but continued their activities after the War and proved to be a more secure source of income than the idiosyncratic generosity of individual donors. In particular, the Chests organized annual fundraising drives that were highly successful. However, in some cities, Community Chests functioned independently of the Councils of Social Agencies, giving rise to unhelpful competition. This problem was eventually solved in the 1950s with the amalgamation of the Chests and agencies and the emergence in 1970 of the United Way, which now serves as a focal point for fundraising and community social services planning in many American cities.

Although some of the earliest publications on community organizing in the United States were based on the settlement's neighborhood building approach, others were inspired by the Charity Organization Society to define community social work as the planning and coordination of local welfare organizations. These publications were largely concerned with managerial and planning methods, and by the late 1920s, a technical approach dominated the field. This is exemplified in McClenehan's (1922) emphasis on the managerial dimensions of community organization and Pettit's (1928) case studies of successful community social services planning. On the other hand, scholars such as Lindeman recognized the wider implications of these activities, suggesting that they would foster democratic participation, promote civic virtue, and reduce social conflict. This was true also of Steiner (1925), who thought that federated associations were preferable to neighborhood activities. Although local organizations were able to deal with single issues, he believed that the "amalgamation" of neighborhood efforts was likely to be a more effective way of addressing community needs.

The social services planning approach was reinforced with the publication of the much cited report by Robert Lane for the National Conference on Social Work in 1939. The report definitively conceptualized community social work in organizational and planning terms and shaped the field for many years to come. It also shaped community social work training at schools of social work, many of which had, by that time, introduced community organization courses. At some schools, community organization was a major professional activity, but at others, community organization teaching was limited to only one course or was otherwise combined with courses in social services administration and management. Nevertheless, by the 1950s, the social services coordination and planning approach was well-established. This was facilitated by the publication of new textbooks by Dunham, (1959), Harper (Harper & Dunham, 1959) and Ross (1955), which helped consolidate social services planning as a core community practice activity. By 1959, when the Council of Social Work Education (CSWE) commissioned a major study of the curricular offerings of schools of social work, community social services planning was given high priority and was regarded by many faculty as the primary form of community practice (Weil, 1996).

In the 1960s, community social services planning was further strengthened by the adoption of advanced budgeting and organizational techniques. These sought to maximize the efficiency of social services agencies and enhance service delivery. Numerous publications that specifically introduced planning ideas into community social services organization subsequently appeared (Perman & Gurin, 1972; Laufer, 1978; Gilbert & Specht; 1977). These publications reinforced the technicism which dominated community organization at the time and reiterated the need for highly trained profession staff who could implement planning technologies. These developments were also compatible with social work's professional and "expert" approach. However, it was soon challenged by the emergence of a new radicalism in community organization. This was fostered the Civil Rights Movement, the War on Poverty, the Radical Student Movement, the Vietnam War, and other events that challenged the status quo. The Civil Rights Movement and the struggle for racial justice was particularly important, and many activists at the time were people of color. These developments injected a new activism into community organization.

Community Activism and Social Action

The social action approach mobilizes poor communities and other oppressed groups to challenge institutionalized power structures and bring about positive social change. Unlike other community practice approaches that are based on consensus organizing, social action relies extensively on conflict and confrontation. This approach is rooted in the activism of settlement leaders such as Jane Addams, Florence Kelly, and Lillian Wald. It also reflects the political activities of the Rank and File movement of the 1930, which campaigned for the unionization of social workers and for closer links with working class movements.

The community action approach became popular among community practitioners after the work of Alinsky (1946, 1971) and the Industrial Areas Foundation became known in social work circles. Although Rothman (1999) notes that Alinky had little time for social workers, his work was widely admired by community social workers. He articulated a confrontational style of community organization and trained local people to embarrass and pressure politicians, bureaucrats, and business owners to respond to demands for community improvements. Alinsky had been inspired by trade union organizers and applied their techniques to mobilize local communities. His early campaigns in Chicago were subsequently replicated in other parts of the country and adopted by other organizations and popular movements.

When the Johnson administration launched the War on Poverty in the 1960s, community activism gained wider support. A primary goal of the War on Poverty was the revitalization of inner-city communities that had become increasingly impoverished as a result of deindustrialization, the out-migration of middle-class Whites to the suburbs (with a concomitant loss in tax revenues), declining employment opportunities, and so-called urban renewal projects that created widespread architectural blight. Among a number of federal initiatives designed to address these problems was the Community Action Program, which required the active participation of local people in community revitalization. Although the creation of local businesses and other economic initiatives was stressed, community action provided an opportunity for local, mostly minority residents to realize their political aspirations. Minority politicians increasingly assumed positions of political power, and for the first time, northern cities elected African American mayors. This development was of huge significance in the struggle for minority political representation and further strengthened efforts to confront racism and discrimination in the United States.

Some community social workers were actively involved in these efforts. This development was augmented by "radical social work," which emerged in Britain in the 1970s (Bailey & Brake, 1975) and by similar developments in the United States (Galper, 1980; Grosser, 1973). Greater use was made of Marxist ideas and social workers were urged to abandon individualized casework, end the profession's alleged collusion in class oppression, and mobilize for social change. Many community organizers now redefined their role, believing that they should join with local people to collaboratively challenge injustice and oppression. The popularization of the writings of Freire (1970, 1973) consolidated the activist approach, but more emphasis was placed on the educational role of community workers who, through a process of dialogical exchange, would *conscientize* local people and help them to understand their position in the oppressive class structure. In this way, the poor would be helped to resist.

Subsequently, activist community organization embraced issues of race and diversity. Inspired by civil rights campaigns, the mobilization of people of color in deprived inner-city areas, increased immigration and the Women's Movement, conventional class-based interpretations of oppression were replaced with feminist and multicultural ideas. These soon infused community practice (Gutierrez & Lewis 1999; Rivera & Erlich, 1992). In addition, community organization became increasingly focused on social movements and functional or interest communities rather than on specific geographic locations. Although place-based organizing was not abandoned, the needs of oppressed groups, including people of color, immigrants, people with disabilities, and lesbian, gay, bisexual, and transgendered people were increasingly recognized. The view that these oppressed groups are best served by social workers who are members of these groups also gained support. Because they themselves had suffered discrimination, they were well-placed to empathize with the oppressed and help them to resist (Bankhead & Erlich, 2005). Although the field was still largely dominated by men, community practitioners were more frequently representative of women and minorities. On the other hand, it gradually became clear that a good deal of community organization was being undertaken by people who did not hold professional social work credentials and that local people themselves were increasingly being hired by community organization agencies to staff community projects.

Despite the popularity of community activism among some social work faculty, most social workers maintained the profession's historic, conservative posture on social and political issues, and community organization continued to focus largely on social services planning. The Reagan administration's advocacy of market liberalism and traditionalism reinforced this tendency. As funds for community projects were retrenched, and as privatization and contracting with commercial and nonprofit providers increased, the collectivist assumptions underlying much community social work were undermined. The exultation of individualism also affected community life, and as Fisher and Karger (1997) note, the values of participation, cooperation, and solidarity were enfeebled. In this climate, individualized clinical and private social work practice became much more popular than community organization. Although many community organization faculty continue to stress the importance of activism and to advocate for the adoption of antiracist and anti-oppressive approaches, much community social work has reverted to social services management, planning, and coordination (Kramer, 1999). In addition, social service planning is now also taught at business schools and the field has increasingly become the purview of professional managers, lawyers, and administrators rather than social workers. The United Way, which is the heir to the Charity Organization Society, now employs relatively few professionally qualified social workers. Similarly, grassroots community activism is currently seldom associated with social work.

The Developmental Approach

As has been noted, the three types of community social work practice discussed previously are not primarily concerned with economic projects or with raising incomes and living standards in poor communities. Although community economic development is viewed by some social workers as a form of community practice, social workers have not been extensively involved in the field, which is dominated by urban planners, economists, and advocates of small business development. Few social workers are employed by the numerous nonprofit organizations that manage community-based economic projects around the world today; in the United States, few work for the Community Development Corporations that are the focus for local economic development. Although it true that some were actively involved in the Johnson administration's War on Poverty, their role was usually confined to community building and social action. Of course, they and other social workers engaged in the War on Poverty were very concerned about the material deprivation of poor inner-city communities but they generally believed that mobilizing poor people would empower them to participate in economic activities and campaign for increased resources.

The idea that community social work contributes indirectly to improving living standards in poor communities by organizing and empowering people is still implicit in much of the community social work literature. But, as was argued at the beginning of this chapter, community social workers need to be directly involved in economic development projects that contribute to poverty alleviation. After all, this was a primary goal of the profession's founders more than a century ago. This argument is illustrated in the following section with reference first to community development in the Global South and second to community economic development in the United States. Both show that developmental community interventions have a positive impact on incomes and standards of living. In the developing world, community development focuses primarily on economic development activities in the rural areas. Community economic development programs in the United States have a similar goal, although here they are largely urban-based. Both examples describe a variety of strategies that have been used to promote local economic development and raise incomes and standards of living. They have obvious relevance for the developmental approach to community practice.

Community Development in the Global South

The term *community development* gained popularity in the 1950s when the governments of many developing countries, supported by the United Nations, established national programs designed to raise the standards of living of the impoverished majority of the population living in the rural areas. As discussed in Chapter 1, economic development in the post-World War II years focused on industrialization and the creation of urban wage employment, which, it was hoped, would draw labor out of the agricultural sector and reduce the incidence of subsistence poverty. Because welfare administrators were criticized for failing to contribute positively to economic development, they initiated rural "mass literacy" programs that they hoped would transcend the conventional remedial services provided by their departments. Literacy training was broadly defined to include a variety of development projects, including the construction of bridges, feeder roads, and irrigation systems; the introduction of modern agricultural techniques; the promotion of the village industries and small enterprises; and the creation of community centers, schools, and clinics.

Although these developments were pioneered in India and West Africa, there were similar innovations in other countries. In India, the rural "construction" programs of Tagore and Gandhi laid the foundations for the Indian government's community development program, which was formally inaugurated in 1952. At that time, the British government actively promoted the creation of national literacy education programs in its colonial territories, and several conferences on rural community development were organized to discuss these ideas. In 1948, it recommended that the term *mass literacy* be replaced with *community development*, and by the mid-1950s, this new term was being internationally adopted. Community development was also embraced by other metropolitan powers, such as the French, who preferred the term *animation rurale* to community development.

The United Nations played a leading role in spreading community development by sending expert advisors to many developing countries, convening international workshops and conferences, and publishing a number of reports on the subject. One of these reports (United Nations, 1955, p. 5) defined community development as "a process designed to create conditions of economic and social progress for the whole community with its active participation and the fullest possible reliance upon the community's initiative." This definition reflected the earlier British approach, which had defined community development as "a movement designed to promote better living for the whole community with the active participation and on the initiative of the community" (United Kingdom, 1954, p. 14). In both cases, improving standards of living through economic interventions was given high priority.

Originally, community development was administered by central or provincial governments and operated as a comprehensive, nationwide program through specialized government departments or ministries of community development. Rural districts or groups of villages were usually identified as basic administrative units, and in some countries such as India and the Philippines, community development programs were closely integrated with local government administration. Community development staff were recruited and trained at local universities or government colleges to administer these programs, and teams of paraprofessionals often were employed to implement a variety of local projects. Generally, funding for projects was allocated by national governments and included in 5-year development plans. However, it was expected that local people would participate actively in community development primarily by providing voluntary labor.

Despite these promising beginnings, many national community development programs soon experienced financial, administrative, and political difficulties. Already by the 1970s, community development programs in many countries were being criticized for their "top-down" approach and for failing to ensure that local people participated in decision making. Ruling elites and their political parties frequently exploited these programs for their own benefit, and funds for local projects were often contingent on the electoral support of local voters. In the 1980s, as many developing countries became heavily indebted and were compelled to seek aid from the International Monetary Fund and the World Bank, budgets for community development programs were slashed. Western donor countries had also become disillusioned with the political manipulation and administrative inefficiency of many national community development programs, and funds for local development projects were increasingly diverted to nongovernmental organizations. Local nongovernmental organizations expanded rapidly as more resources from donors were channeled in their direction. This was accompanied by a rapid increase in grassroots organizations managed by village people themselves—particularly by local women. Today, nongovernmental organizations that either serve women or are comprised primarily of women feature prominently in community development in the Global South. On the other hand, government community development programs still operate but are not as well-funded as before.

Many examples of contemporary community development projects in the Global South can be provided, but typically they combine the economic development activities mentioned earlier with social projects such as adult literacy, preschool education, sanitation, maternal and child health, and other services. They also make use of organization and community building techniques and train local people in community organization, leadership, and project implementation. Some also use the legal system either to protect their interests or secure much needed services. Today, community development in the Global South is increasingly concerned with rights-based development. But these programs usually give higher priority to income generating and related economic projects.

Community development programs range from small local initiatives to large-scale nationwide programs operated either by governmental or nongovernmental organizations. Local community-based programs may have a single purpose, such as improving village water supply, or they may sponsor a variety of projects. Many of these projects are created by local people with the support of external organizations that provide funding, technical assistance, or training. In some cases, they emerge through the indigenous initiative of local people themselves who then seek external resources. One example is the Jansenville Development Forum in South Africa, which is located in a poor rural community in the country's Eastern Province. The Forum was founded in 2000 when local community groups began to coordinate their activities and collaborate to secure external resources. It was able to obtain funding from a major foundation and from the South African government, and by 2007, it had an office with paid staff. Together with its partner organizations, the Forum has helped create a variety of small businesses and a daycare center and has constructed homes, water tanks, and toilets. It has also played an active role in assisting poor elderly people and families with young children obtain government benefits to which they are entitled but did not know how to access (Wilkinson-Maposa, 2008).

Larger regional and national community development programs are often multipurpose in scope. In some cases, they do not focus on local geographical areas but instead mobilize people with similar interests. One example of a "functional" program of this kind is the Self-Employed Women's Association (SEWA) in India, which emerged from collaboration between a textile workers' trade union and self-employed women in the city of Ahmedebad in the early 1970s. At this time, these women turned to the union for assistance and this prompted efforts to help them organize and raise their incomes. They were engaged in a variety of informal sector occupations, including home-based quilt and garment making, *bidi* or cigarette rolling, porterage, and street vending. These efforts were successful, and today SEWA has almost 500,000 members, a savings bank, daycare centers, clinics and schools, and training centers for its workers and staff (Chen, 2008). It also promotes the creation of cooperatives among members engaged in similar economic activities. It has opened branches in six other Indian states and is funded by international donors as well as local foundations and the Indian government. It effectively combines income-generating and social service projects with community activism designed to secure rights and improved working conditions for its members.

An example of a multipurpose, nongovernmental community development program operating at the national level is the Bangladesh Rural Advancement Committee (BRAC). Founded in 1971, BRAC created numerous village level organizations around the country that launched a variety of economic and income-generating projects. Over the years, it has prioritized micro-enterprise activities, particularly among poor women, and as with the better-known Grameen Bank, it is a major advocate of micro-enterprise. It has also supported the creation of infra-structural and education and health projects as well as programs that increase awareness among its members regarding their political and social rights. When BRAC was founded, the majority of its members were men, but today they comprise a relatively small proportion of the membership. One reason for this is the emphasis placed on micro-enterprise, women's education, and maternal and child health services. Today, more than 4.5 million Bangladeshi women are engaged in micro-enterprise activities (Reza & Ahmmed, 2009). Although BRAC is a nongovernmental organization, its national scope and its sizable staff and budget are comparable to many national, governmental community development programs.

Despite resource constraints, the government of Ghana continues to operate a national community development program. As noted earlier, it emerged in the 1940s as a *mass literacy* program operated by the Department of Social Welfare. The country's first president, Kwame Nkruma, actively supported the program, and despite administrative reorganization by subsequent governments, its original focus on economic activities and infrastructural development has been maintained. More recently, however, priority has been given to expanding income generating activities for women (Abloh & Ameyaw, 1997). Among a plethora of these activities are palm oil processing, pottery, bead-making, soap-making, and fish-smoking projects. These augment the program's existing agricultural extension and infra-structural development programs as well as its local and health and educational services. The program has also strengthened its "self-help" village outreach pro-gram, which has mobilized local people for a variety of projects, including the construction of community centers, clinics, local markets, schools, and even post offices. Efforts have also been made to integrate the program with local coopera-tives engaged in cocoa production, which is one of the country's major export enterprises.

Community Economic Development in the United States

As in other countries, cooperative activities have long characterized community living in the United States, particularly in the rural areas. However, with industri-alization and urbanization, community social bonds were weakened, especially in communities with high unemployment, delapidated housing, crime, and other social problems. It was in conditions such as these that the settlements sought to foster people's participation in neighborhood building. But, as noted earlier, neigh-borhood building was not directly concerned with economic projects. Indeed, eco-nomic development only emerged as a major priority in community policy in the 1960s. Although the roots of community economic development in the United States may be traced back to the Progressive Era and the New Deal, O'Connor (1999) has reported that it was at the time of the Johnson administration's War on Poverty that community economic development first emerged as a coherent approach to addressing the material needs of people living in deprived areas.

Although the War on Poverty also encompassed deprived rural areas, poor inner-city communities— particularly those with large minority populations— attracted particular attention. Already by the late-1950s, they were characterized by blight, high rates of unemployment, crime, and other problems. As noted earlier, these were caused by deindustrialization, disinvestment, and the exodus of White middle-class families to the suburbs. Many of these communities had high proportions of people of color; not surprisingly, their problems were often linked to racial stereotypes. These and other factors depressed economic demand and employment opportunities. With declining tax revenues, municipal governments struggled to provide much-needed services. These problems were exacerbated by urban renewal programs that permitted the demolition of older buildings and reduced the availability of affordable housing and space for small commercial enterprises.

In was this context that numerous initiatives designed to address the problem were launched. Among these was the small business stimulus program created in terms of the Area Redevelopment Act of 1961. It was replaced by the War on Poverty programs established in terms of the Economic Opportunity Act of 1964. In addition to the Community Action Program mentioned earlier, the Model Cities Program and the Special Impact Program of 1966 formed the core of these initiatives. The Special Impact Program was particularly important to local economic development because it provided funding for community-based organizations—especially the Community Development Corporations that had been established at about this time.

Community Development Corporations are local, nonprofit organizations that promote economic development, affordable housing, and urban regeneration. Many of these organizations were established by African American community activists who were concerned about the growing problems of inner-city communities. Today, they are managed by boards of directors that include local residents and have been successful in securing federal and local funds for their programs. Some have also attracted funds from commercial investors and some operate on a for-profit basis. Although only about 100 Community Development Corporations were in operation in the 1960s, they expanded rapidly and by the end of the 20th century, no fewer than 2,000 were in existence (Green & Haines, 2008). Most Community Development Corporations are small and rooted in local neighborhoods. Two-thirds serve their immediate or surrounding geographical area. Initially, Community Development Corporations focused on small business development, job training, and similar economic projects, but many have since specialized in the construction of affordable housing and today about 90% are engaged in the provision of housing and related services. In 1974, the Nixon Administration consolidated a number of federal funding streams into the Community Development Block Grants, and Community Development Corporations became the primary recipients of these funds. Since then, more than $100 billion has been disbursed through the block grant system (Green & Haines, 2008). Community Development Corporations have also been supported by private donors such as the Ford Foundation through its Local Initiatives Support Corporation (LISC) which has extensively subsidized affordable housing construction by Community Development Corporations.

Another federal initiative that has contributed to community economic development is the Community Reinvestment Act of 1977. The Act requires banks to provide credit to all sections of the communities in which they operate and to desist from the racist practice of "redlining" by which lending in "high-risk" poor and minority areas was discouraged. Although the statute did not require banks to invest in these communities, its antidiscriminatory provisions have in fact resulted in increased credit in these communities, especially for minority-owned businesses (Grogan & Prosio, 2000). This development is also attributable to the adoption of affirmative action policies.

These initiatives were augmented during the Clinton years by the creation of Empowerment Zones and Enterprise Communities (also known as EZ/ECs), which provide tax and other incentives for businesses investments and employment generation in low-income communities. The Clinton initiative was launched in 1994 when 11 Empowerment Zones and 95 Enterprise Communities were created. The Empowerment Zones received tax incentives and subsidies of up to $100 million each, and the Enterprise Communities were provided with smaller subsidies and incentives. In the Empowerment Zones, businesses may claim tax credits of $3,000 for each employed person living in the zone. Although the EZ/ECs are large-scale initiatives and involve hundreds of business enterprises, their employment generation function has obvious implications for local economic development. In addition to the federal EZ/EC initiative, many states have introduced similar programs (Peters & Fisher, 2002).

The Workforce Reinvestment Act of 1998, which replaced earlier employment training and placement programs, has also contributed to local economic development, particularly through promoting job training and job referral services. The statute consolidated a variety of job training and placement programs into local "one-stop" job and advice centers where all employment related services are now located. Local business leaders were invited to participate in local workforce development initiatives, particularly through the Private Industry Councils created by the legislation. Also relevant is the so-called "welfare reform" legislation of 1996, which sought to reduce the number of social assistance recipients by requiring them to seek and accept employment. This initiative provided for contracting with nonprofit organizations providing job training and placement services and has increased the number of organizations engaged in these activities.

Green and Haines (2008) reported that the Bush administration sought to retrench a number of community economic development programs, but, primarily because of their popularity, there was little Congressional support for this proposal. Instead, a greater element of commercial investment was encouraged, and urban development projects increasingly relied on private investors supported by governmental agencies. In some cases, inner-city urban renewal has resulted in a significant degree of gentrification, particularly around harbors, rivers, and other scenic locations where the construction of restaurants, hotels, boutiques, and upscale housing has produced high investment returns and a growing middle class population. Obviously, these developments have not benefited low-income residents to any great extent. On the other hand, the expansion of Community Development Corporations, the creation of many more nonprofit economic development organizations, and continued political support for community economic development initiatives has improved urban conditions and the quality of life for many poor people. Also, it should be noted that despite gentrification, the majority of people living in inner-city areas have low incomes. The Obama administration's economic stimulus package of 2009, which is designed to improve infrastructure and create new employment opportunities, should also benefit these communities.

Today, community economic development projects are implemented by a plethora of organizations, of which the Community Development Corporations are the most prominent. Other nonprofits offering financial services, job training, small business support, and many similar services have proliferated. Faith-based organizations have also become more involved in local economic development. Local and state governments as well as private investors are also engaged in the field. Many organizations promoting community economic development concentrate on one type of activity. Most Community Development Corporations engage in housing construction, whereas other nonprofits specialize in fields such as job training, computer skills, credit counseling, and micro-enterprise. The extension of financial services to people with low incomes has also expanded and, like micro-enterprise, Individual Development Accounts (IDAs) that match the savings of poor people have become popular. Local nonprofit banks have also expanded. Many nonprofit organizations engaged in economic development are small. At the other end of the spectrum, municipal and commercial agencies are involved in large-scale projects such as constructing shopping centers, markets, and other facilities.

Although it is difficult to assess the cumulative impact of these initiatives, many believe that conditions in inner-city areas have improved as a result of community economic development. An article in the magazine *Business Week* (2003) reporting on a study of a 100 large cities concluded that household incomes in inner-city areas grew by about 20% between 1990 and 2000 and that the poverty rate decreased faster than the decline in the national rate. Although job growth was sluggish, rising by only 1% per year during this period, the proportion of minority-owned businesses had increased. The article recognized that much more needed to be done, but it concluded that economic development programs in inner-city areas had produced positive results. Continued unemployment and high rates of violent crime and drug dealing in many poor, inner-city areas underscore the need for continued economic development and social investments that raise incomes and standards of living. Nevertheless, many poor communities have drawn on local assets and have built social capital to improve their social and economic conditions. Governmental resources, affirmative action, and antiracist policies such as the prohibition of "redlining" have also helped.

Social Work and Developmental Community Practice

It is perhaps understandable that community social work practitioners have paid relatively little attention to economic development. Few social workers have been involved in economic projects; rather, interventions that address the nonmaterial needs of clients have been emphasized. It is also true that social workers have little expertise in the field. Obviously, community social workers are not economists, urban planners, or development experts, and few would argue that they should take responsibility for local economic development programs. On the other hand, many are engaged in activities that can be readily linked to economic development projects. It is also the case that many social workers employed in nonprofit, community-based organizations are tangentially involved with economic development projects. Although they may not recognize their contribution, many provide services that have positive economic effects. For example, social workers who work with unemployed youth or help former welfare recipients secure employment, medical services, and daycare for their children are promoting local economic development.

Community practitioners can enhance their role in local economic development by simply being aware of the economic implications of their work. However, they also need to be knowledgable about community economic development and its approaches and goals. Although community building skills, nonprofit management, and social action are emphasized in community organization courses at many schools of social work today, more information about community economic development policies and procedures should be provided. For example, in the United States, all community practitioners need to know about the operations of Community Development Corporations, community development block grants, the provisions of the Community Reinvestment Act, local workforce development programs, and similar economic development initiatives. It is also important, as Sherraden and Ninacs (1998) note, that they understand economic development terminologies, approaches, policies, and procedures. Because many community social workers are committed to a critical, activist approach and shun market-based economic interventions that they believe condone capitalism, few are familiar with the ethos of economic development. Because economic development is an effective way of addressing the problem of poverty, this attitude needs to be re-examined. In addition, it should be recognized that a greater involvement in economic activities does not require that conventional activities such as community building, mobilization, and advocacy be abandoned.

Conventional community practice skills can certainly be applied to promote local economic development. As shown in Chapter 1, skills in mobilizing local community groups and helping them to identify needs and prioritize interventions can contribute positively to economic development. Also relevant are leadership development, brokering, and problem-solving skills. Social workers can also play a vital role in building networks and trust at the local level, and as several scholars (Midgley & Livermore, 1998; Rubin & Sherraden, 2005; Sherraden & Ninacs, 1998;) have noted, these activities are compatible with the mobilization of social capital at the local level. There is a good deal of evidence to show that communities with high levels of social capital are likely to have higher levels of economic development (Gittell & Thompson, 2001; Krishna, 2002; Putnam, Leonardi, & Nanetti, 1993). By helping to build social capital, social workers can contribute positively to economic development goals.

In addition to building social capital through helping local people to form associations and create stronger social networks, community practitioners should use their skills to focus social capital on economic activities. As Krishna's (2002) study of Indian villages reveals, social capital needs to be purposefully mobilized and directed toward economic projects. Community social workers can contribute to this task by drawing on their existing knowledge and skills. For example, their networking skills can be effectively employed to establish job referral networks by working with churches, clubs, and other associations to make information about job openings more readily available. They can also develop links with employers to establish networks by which job seekers have easier access to available opportunities. Assistance with preparing resumes and coaching clients on interviewing skills can also be provided.

They can also help to mobilize support for local businesses. As people on low incomes increasingly shop at supermarkets and other retail outlets located outside the immediate community, local businesses decline. By helping to create an awareness of its wider economic impact, this problem may be addressed. Networking skills can also be used to organize local small businesses to form business associations and to help local entrepreneurs work together to secure resources. Because many are small and family-owned, providing information and support can strengthen their activities. Also, by working with local associations, businesses, and community leaders, they can facilitate the preparation of local economic development plans and marketing strategies. Obviously, closer collaboration with economic development planners and governmental agencies is also needed.

Advocacy and brokering skills also play an important role in promoting economic development. By organizing local people to campaign for improved facilities and resources, community practitioners can help to secure investment funds from governmental agencies, foundations, and even commercial investors. Because external investments play a major role in local economic development, social workers should help to broker links with municipal governments and with politicians who may have access to these resources. They can also work with banks and other financial institutions to secure funds in terms of the Community Reinvestment Act and help to create local savings and credit associations. Predatory lending is not only morally reprehensible but a major contributor to economic stagnation many poor communities (Karger, 2005; Immergluck, 2004). Community practitioners can help to create alternative sources of credit and collaborate with other activists as well as nonprofit savings and loans associations to extend credit facilities to the community (Birkenmaier & Tyuse, 2005).

Community practitioners can also help local people to negotiate effectively with external agencies and assist them to identify potential pitfalls and problems that may have an adverse affect on local economic development. Community action techniques that confront those who are exploiting the community or failing to support local initiatives can also be used. People living in poor communities are exposed to racism, discrimination, and exploitation, and by educating local people about these problems, community practitioners make a positive contribution to empowering and supporting their efforts to address them. By engaging in *conscientization*, exploitative and oppressive power structures may be challenged.

In addition to being directly involved in economic projects of this kind, community practitioners can help promote local economic development by supporting the expansion of educational, nutrition, health, and other social services that are not normally regarded as a part of economic development but that are essential for economic progress. The inculcation of human capital through effectively managed local schools is a vital ingredient in economic development. Similarly, access to medical care, maternal and child health services, and family planning all contribute to economic development. Adequate daycare services not only facilitate the employment of parents but generate human capital through preschool education, nutrition, and medical services. Although the economic impact of these programs was not previously recognized, there is little disagreement today that they have a social investment function that contributes positively to development. Community social work practitioners are obviously well-qualified to promote the expansion, coordination, and planning of these services.

Finally, community practitioners can contribute directly to community economic development by supporting local people and associations to establish a variety of economic projects such as cooperative micro-enterprises, savings associations, afterschool homework classes, and adult literacy and daycare centers, to name but a few. A good deal has now been written about micro-enterprise in the social work literature, and although this approach has limitations, it is widely agreed that micro-enterprise development—particularly at the local level—can form an effective component of the wider economic and social development strategy designed to reduce the incidence of poverty (Midgley, 2008). Social workers have also been actively involved in creating matched savings accounts (or IDAs) in many poor communities. In fact, this important innovation was pioneered by Sherraden (1991, 2005), a social work professor. Many IDA project are operated by nonprofit organizations that employ social workers. Job training and job referral programs provided by nonprofit organizations in many low-income communities also involve social workers. These are just some examples of specific initiatives with a direct economic impact on communities in which social work practitioners can be involved. By engaging more actively in developmental activities of this kind, community social workers can make a positive contribution to enhancing the well-being of people living in poor communities throughout the world.

REFERENCES

Abloh, F. & Ameyaw, S. (1997) Ghana. In H. Campfens (Ed.) (1997). *Community Development Around the World: Practice, Theory, Research, Training.* Toronto: University of Toronto Press, pp. 277–327.

Alinsky, S. (1946). *Reveille for Radicals.* Chicago: University of Chicago Press.

Alinsky, S. (1971). *Rules for Radicals.* New York: Random House.

Bailey, M. & Brake. R. (Eds) (1976). *Radical Social Work.* New York: Pantheon.

Bankhead, T. & Erlich, J. L. (2005). Diverse Populations and Community Practice. In M. Weil (Ed.). *The Handbook of Community Practice*. Thousand Oaks, CA: Sage Publications, pp. 59–83.

Birkenmaier J. & Tyuse, S. W. (2005). Affordable Financial Services and Credit for the Poor: The Foundation of Asset Building. *Journal of Community Practice*, 13 (1): 69–78.

Business Week, An Inner-city Renaissance. October 27, 2003, pp. 64–68.

Chaskin, R., Brown, P., Venkatesh, S., & Vidal, A. (2001). *Building Community Capacity*. Hawthorne, NY: Aldine de Gruyter.

Chen, M. (2008). A Spreading Banyan Tree: The Employed Women's Association, India. In A. Mathie & G. Cunningham (Eds.). *From Clients to Citizens: Communities Changing the Course of their Own Development*. Rugby, Warwickshire: Intermediate Technology Publications, pp. 181–206.

Dunham, A. (1959). *Community Welfare Organization: Principles and Practice*. New York: Thomas Crowell.

Freire, P. (1970). *Pedagogy of the Oppressed*. New York: Herder and Herder.

Freire, P. (1973). *Education for Critical Consciousness*. New York: Seabury Press.

Fisher, R. (1990). Grassroots Organizing in the Community Center Movement, 1907–1930. In N. Betten, & M. J. Austin, (Eds.). *The Roots of Community Organizing, 1917–1939*. Philadelphia: Temple University Press, pp. 76–93.

Fisher, R. (1994). *Let the People Decide: Neighborhood Organizing in America*. New York: Twayne Publishers.

Fisher, R. & Karger, H. J. (1997). *Social Work and Community in a Private World: Getting Out in Public*. New York: Longman.

Galper, J. H. (1980). *Social Work Practice: A Radical Perspective*. Englewood Cliffs, NJ: Prentice Hall.

Gilbert, N. & Specht, H. (1977). *Planning for Social Welfare: Issues, Models and Tasks*. Englewood Cliffs, NJ: Prentice-Hall.

Gittell, R. & Thompson, J. P. (2001). Making Social Capital Work: Social Capital and Community Economic Development. In S. Saegert, J. P. Thompson & M. R. Warren, (Eds.). (2001). *Social Capital and Poor Communities*. New York: Russell Sage, pp. 115–135.

Green, G. P. & Haines, A. (2008). *Asset Building and Community Development*. Thousand Oaks, CA: Sage.

Grogan, P. & Proscio, T. (2000). *Comeback Cities: A Blueprint for Urban Neighborhood Revival*. Boulder, CO: Westview Press.

Grosser, C. (1973). *New Directions in Community Organization: From Enabling to Advocacy*. New York: Praeger.

Gutierrez, L. & Lewis, F. A. (Eds.). (1999). *Empowerment and Women of Color*. New York: Columbia University Press.

Harper, E. B. & Dunham, A. (Eds.). (1959). *Community Organizing in Action*. New York: Association Press.

Hart, J. K. (1921). *Community Organizing*. New York: Macmillan.

Hyde. C. (1986). Experience of Women Activists: Implications for Community Organizing Theory. *Journal of Sociology and Social Welfare*, 13 (3): 522–544.

Immergluck, D. (2004). *Credit to the Community: Community ReInvestment and Fair Lending Policy in the United States*. Armonk, NY: M. E. Sharpe.

Karger, H. J. (1987). *Sentinels of Order: A Study of Social Control and the Minneapolis Settlement House Movement, 1915-1950*. Lanham, MD: University Press of America.

Karger, H. J. (2005). *Shortchanged: Life and Debt in the Fringe Economy*. San Francisco, CA: Berrett-Koehler.

Kramer, R. (1999). The Rise and Decline of CO at Berkeley. In J. Rothman, (Ed.). *Reflections on Community Organizing*. Itasca: Peacock, pp. 277–292.

Kretzman, J. & McKnight, J. (1993). *Building Communities from the Inside Out: A Path Toward Finding and Mobilizing a Community's Assets*. Evanston, IL: Institute for Policy Research, Northwest and University.

Krishna, A. (2002). *Active Social Capital: Tracing the Roots of Development and Democracy*. New York: Columbia University Press.

Lane, R. P. (1939). The Field of Community Organizing. In H. W. Knight (Ed.). *Proceedings of the National Conference of Social Work*. New York: Columbia University Press, 496–511.

Laufer, A. (1978). *Social Planning at the Community Level*. Englewood Cliffs, NJ. Prentice Hall.

Lindeman, E. C. (1921). *The Community: An Introduction to the Study of Community Leadership and Organization*. New York: Association Press.

McClenehan, B. A. (1922). *Organizing the Community*. New York: Century.

Midgley, J. (2008). Microenterprise, Global Poverty and Social Development. *International Social Work*. 51 (4): 467–479.

Midgley, J. & Livermore, M. (1998). Social Capital and Local Economic Development: Implications for Community Social Work Practice. *Journal of Community Practice*. 5(1/2): 29–40.

Naparstek, A. J. & Dooey, D. (1997). Community Building. In R. Edwards et al. (Eds.). *Encyclopedia Social Work, 19th Edition, 1997 Supplement*. Washington DC: NASW Press.

O'Connor, A. (1999). Swimming Against the Tide: A Brief History of Federal Policy in Poor Communities.' In R. F. Ferguson & W. T. Dickens (Eds.). *Urban Problems and Community Development*. Washington DC: Brookings Institution Press.

Perlman, R. & Gurin, A. (1972). *Community Organization and Social Planning*. New York, Wiley.

Peters, A. H. & Fisher, P. S. (2002). *State Enterprise Zones: Have they Worked?* Kalamzaoo, MI; Upjohn Institute.

Petit, W. (1928). *Case Studies in Community Organization*. New York: Century Publishers.

Putnam, R. D. with Leonardi, R. & Nanetti, R. Y. (1993). *Making Democracy Work: Civic Traditions in Modern Italy*. Princeton: Princeton University Press.

Reza, M. H. & Ahmmed, F. (2009). Structural Social Work and the Compatibility of NGO Approaches: A Case Analysis of Bangladesh Rural Advancement Committee (BRAC) *International Journal of Social Welfare*, 18 (2): 173–182.

Rivera, F. G. & Erlich, J.L. (Eds.). (1992). *Community Organizing in a Diverse Society*. Boston, MA: Allyn and Bacon.

Rothman, J. (1968). Three Models of Community Organization Practice. In *National Conference on Social Welfare: Social Work Practice*. New York: Columbia University Press, pp 16–47.

Rothman. J. (1999). Historical Context in Community Intervention. In J. Rothman, (Ed.). *Reflections on Community Organizing*. Itasca: Peacock, pp. 277–292.

Ross, M. (1955). *Community Organization: Theory and Principles*. New York: Harper.

Rubin, H. J. & Sherraden, M. S. (2005). Community Economic and Social Development. In M. Weill (Ed.). *The Handbook of Community Practice*. Thousand Oaks, CA: Sage Publications, pp. 475–493.

Sherraden, M. (1991). *Assets and the Poor: A New American Welfare Policy*. Armonk, NY: M. E. Sharpe.

Sherraden, M. (Ed.) (2005). *Inclusion in the American Dream: Assets, Poverty and Public Policy*. New York: Oxford University Press.

Sherraden, M. S. & Ninacs, W. (Eds.) (1998). *Community Economic Development and Social Work*. New York: Haworth.

Smock, K. (2004). *Democracy in Action: Community Organizing and Social Change*. New York: Columbia University Press.

Steiner, J. F. (1925). *Community Organization: A Study of its Theory and Current Practice*. New York: Appleton-Century.

Taylor, S. H. & Roberts, R. (Eds.) (1985). *Theory and Practice of Community Social Work*. New York: Columbia University Press.

United Kingdom, Colonial Office (1954). *Social Development in the British Colonial Territories*. London: HMSO.

United Nations (1955). *Social Progress through Community Development*. New York.

Weil, M. (1996). Model Development in Community Practice: An Historical Perspective. In M. Weil (Ed.). *Community Practice: Conceptual Models*. Binghampton, NY: Haworth Press, pp. 5–68.

Weil, M. & Gamble, D. N. (1995). Community Practice Models. In R. Edwards et al. (Eds.). *Encyclopedia of Social Work.*, 19th ed. Washington, DC: NASW Press, pp. 577–593.

Wilkinson, Maposa, S. (2008). Jansenville Development Forum: Linking Community and Government in the Rural Landscape of the Eastern Cape Province, South Africa. In A. Mathie & G. Cunningham (Eds.). *From Clients to Citizens: Communities Changing the Course of their Own Development*. Rugby, Warwickshire: Intermediate Technology Publications, pp. 237–260.

Yan, M. C., Lauer, S. and Sin, R. (2009). Issues in Community Rebuilding: The Task of Settlement Houses in Two Cities. *Social Development Issues*, 31 (1): 39–54.

PART III

Conclusion

10

Limitations and Prospects of Developmental Social Work

JAMES MIDGLEY AND AMY CONLEY

This book has argued that developmental social work has positive implications for the social work profession and those it serves. In addition to describing the history, features, theories, and practice interventions, specific examples of how developmental social work can inform professional practice have been given. These have been drawn from core social work practice fields such as child welfare, aging, mental health, disability, and community practice. Although it is true that developmental social work has long been associated with community and macro-practice interventions, it has already been argued that developmental ideas can also be applied in conventional social work practice fields.

Although the book's contributors have adopted a constructive posture and shown the benefits of using a developmental approach, its limitations also need to be considered. As with other social work approaches, it is desirable that developmental social work should be subjected to critical scrutiny. The following discusses some of the limitations and challenges of the developmental approach. Some of these relate specifically to implementation issues whereas others examine the implications of the developmental approach for social work theory, practice, and other professional issues. Although these limitations are candidly discussed, they are balanced by a firm belief that developmental social work offers promising prospects for enhancing the well-being of social work's clients.

Developmental social work involves what was described in Chapter 2 of this book as a "paradigm shift," which requires that social work's institutionalized ways of operating be modified. However, unless the nature of this shift is clearly articulated, there will be uncertainty and confusion among those who are supportive of the developmental approach. Unfortunately, advocates of developmental social work have not always offered a clear and coherent explanation of what developmental practice involves. As noted in Chapter 1, many accounts of developmental social work have been infused with rhetorical and hortatory notions that provide few concrete examples of how practitioners can implement a developmental approach. Consequently, debates about the practical relevance of developmental social work have often been vague and ambiguous. This is a major limitation of developmental social work.

This issue has surfaced in recent debates about developmental social work in South Africa, where concern has been expressed about how the country's pressing problems of child neglect and maltreatment can be met through developmental interventions. Loffell (2008, p. 85) points out that the promotion of a developmental approach has created "ambiguity and uncertainty" among child protective social workers who have been urged to abandon conventional interventions for a vaguely formulated, rights-based, developmental approach. She notes that the problems of child neglect, abandonment and abuse in South Africa are of huge proportions, and although the current child protective system is far from satisfactory, it offers a modicum of protection. To dismantle the system without having a clearly defined alternative in place could be disastrous.

Loffell reports that many South African social workers are supportive of the developmental approach, and she has no quarrel with academics who have promoted developmental ideas. But she is concerned that the government has advocated developmental interventions without addressing pressing implementation challenges. Although its rhetoric paints a beguiling vision in which child welfare services will be committed to prevention and social rights, the task of meeting the needs of maltreated children is left to the nonprofit sector, which operates under extremely difficult conditions. The situation is exacerbated by contradictory governmental policy statements. Many of these statements are critical of social work's conventional, individualized approach and urge the adoption of a human rights approach based on the 1989 United Nations Convention on the Rights of the Child. However, as she points out, a rights-based approach will still be enforced through the legal system and will require individualized compliance interventions that are not very different from those used by social workers. As this example reveals, uncertainty about social work's developmental role is a major limitation of this approach. Hopefully, this book will help to clarify matters.

Another limitation of the developmental approach is continued resource constraints. This is a major challenge in many countries, including the United States, which is among the world's richest nations. It is one thing for advocates of developmental social work to extol its benefits but another to ensure that adequate personnel, funds, and other investments are available. As noted in Chapter 1, advocates of the developmental approach insist that adequate resources be allocated if those served by the profession are to utilize their strengths and respond effectively to the challenges they face. Although the social work literature has said relatively little about the need for social investments, it is not sufficient to assume that pressing social needs will be met by simply exhorting clients to utilize their strengths and draw on their assets. Nor is it sufficient to educate them about the oppressive conditions they face without offering effective alternatives. To bring about significant improvements in social conditions, tangible investments will be needed. This will require the allocation of resources by the community through the institution of the state.

Developmental programs that promote community living, prevention, and adequate services and supports are expensive. Housing, education and job training, access to transportation, employment placements, and other interventions that help people with special needs live normal lives in the community require personnel and budgetary allocations. Similarly, investments that enhance capabilities through, for example, education and employment training programs, job supports, assistance with micro-enterprise development, and matched savings accounts cost money. Although it is true that informal support networks can be utilized, they are not a substitute for adequately funded services.

Unfortunately, many examples have already been provided regarding how governments have failed to provide adequate services and supports to those with special needs. Chapter 5 revealed that despite adopting progressive legislation, services for people with disabilities in developing countries such as India and South Africa are woefully inadequate. Western countries also face serious resource constraints, which are exacerbated by perennial budget retrenchments. These cuts impede the implementation of community-based, developmental services. As the experience of deinstitutionalization in the field of mental health reveals, closing residential facilities and transferring residents into the community without providing comprehensive services that facilitate normal community living has had serious consequences in many Western countries. Another example comes from the United States, where the Head Start Program experienced a significant reduction in funding in recent years even though its contribution to child well-being is widely recognized. Despite its achievements, only a small proportion of young children from deprived communities are enrolled in the program and, with the current recession, ongoing governmental support may be tenuous. Budgetary retrenchments such as these pose a serious challenge to those who wish to implement a community-based child welfare system.

Although resource constraints impede the effective implementation of the developmental approach, a solution to this problem can be found if political leadership and electoral support is mustered. Hard decisions about priorities and balancing revenues and expenditures need to be taken. Although opinion polls in the Western countries have shown that voters are supportive of government social services spending, they are not always enthusiastic about paying additional taxes to meet these costs. It is in this regard that the developmental approach may prove to be attractive. Because social investments produce positive rates of return, politicians and voters should be educated about their wider economic benefits. Professional social work associations have a major role to play in advocating for the expansion of developmental social services. By forging coalitions with nonprofit organizations, trade unions, women's organizations, and others, they can exercise political influence to address of the resource problem.

Shortages of professional personnel also hamper the effectiveness of the developmental approach. Social workers comprise a small proportion of those employed in the human services in many countries. Even in the United States, which has the largest number of professional social workers in the world, social worker shortages remain a perennial problem. Although there has been a significant increase in the numbers of students enrolled at American schools of social work in recent years, many human service positions traditionally filled by social workers remain vacant. The problem is exacerbated by the narrowing of social work roles as other professionals increasingly assume what were historically social work's fields of expertise. For example, family therapy is now a recognized mental health profession and increasingly, family and other therapists are being employed in mental health agencies that previously relied on professional social work. Similarly, social workers are no longer major players in the field of community organization, which is today populated by political activists, sociologist, lawyers, city planners, economists, and local volunteers.

In view of these shortages, it may seem redundant to propose that social workers transcend their current professional roles and encroach on the activities of others. Instead, it may be argued that the developmental projects discussed in this book should be undertaken by those who have proper training and experience. Of course, it is a limitation of the developmental approach that relatively few social workers have expertise and experience in the field. Accordingly, some will question whether the developmental interventions discussed in this book are relevant to social work at all. Because social workers have extensive practice experience of working in child welfare, mental health, geriatric programs, corrections, and similar social services, it may be argued that they should concentrate their efforts in these fields rather than pursuing new ones. For example, in corrections, social workers have acquired valuable experience in managing therapeutic groups and counseling those with substance abuse and mental health problems. Because they do not have much knowledge of re-entry programs that require job training, small business management skills, and similar interventions, many correctional social workers will understandably be reluctant to abandon their conventional professional roles in corrections.

On the other hand, it may be argued that social work needs to expand rather than retrench its scope. In fact, it may be advantageous for the profession's future if it embraces developmental activities. This will also enhance the profession's ability to serve its clients. It should also be noted that many of the developmental activities discussed in this book are not alien to social work. Although it has been argued that a paradigm shift will be required, the shift may not be as extensive or radical as many believe.

Nevertheless, the issue of limited expertise does need to be addressed, and appropriate modifications to social work education should be made. This is particularly relevant to the developing countries where Western practice models have been widely adopted although they are largely inappropriate to the economic, social, and cultural circumstances of these countries. The issue is also relevant to the Western countries, where more needs to be done to introduce developmental ideas and practice experiences to social work educational programs. In many developing countries, social workers are involved in a number of developmental activities for which they have received little if any training. It is a reflection of their inventiveness that many engage in income-generating projects without adequate educational preparation. Their contribution could be significantly strengthened if appropriate courses in developmental social work were provided.

Another limitation is a shortage of teaching and research resources. Although this book is intended to fill a gap in the literature, more relevant teaching materials such as textbooks and manuals suited to the needs of different countries are needed. With the publication of social development textbooks in India, South Africa, and elsewhere, progress has undoubtedly been made. In addition, scholarly publications should be more accessible internationally and research findings should be more widely shared. Opportunities for faculty members in the Global South to publish in well-established journals need to be redoubled. In many low income countries, they do not have access to these journals, primarily because of their high cost. Ways of including these colleagues in international scholarly endeavors and facilitating the publication of their research is urgently needed. This is just one limitation that can be overcome through international cooperation.

Scholarly discourse on social development has intensified in recent years, revealing a number of concerns about the normative implications of this approach. One concern is the "economistic" nature of developmental interventions. Social workers, who are by inclination and professional education committed to a "helping" approach by which they show compassion to those in need and provide them with counseling and services, may be troubled by developmental social work's emphasis on economic activities. Social work, they argue, is not about compelling people to work or acquiring job skills or establishing micro-enterprises; rather, it is about alleviating suffering. Others believe that by promoting economic participation, developmental social work is compatible with neoliberalism, which is inimical to the profession's beliefs and values. Instead of promoting capitalistic forms of enterprise, developmental social workers should campaign for social structural change. A similar normative critique comes from those who believe that developmental social work is essentially conservative and fails to advocate for radical social change. Others believe that the overriding sources of injustice today are expressed through intolerance, discrimination, and racism and that it is social work's primary goal to address these injustices. Developmental social work, they believe, fails to contribute to the struggle for identity, recognition and respect and does not promote emancipatory, transformational, and social structural practice. Criticisms of this kind have been voiced on several occasions, although it should be noted that they are not always addressed exclusively at developmental social work but at social work in general.

Although it is true that developmental social work and the wider field of social development are focused on economic activities, this does not imply the advocacy or endorsement of market liberalism. As shown earlier in this book, the advocates of market liberal fundamentalism pose a serious challenge to developmental social work by retrenching statutory social services, reducing resources for social investment, imposing user fees and undermining collective responses to social need. The importance of social workers collaborating with progressive political leaders, trades unions, and others to challenge neoliberalism's effects has already been emphasized. In addition, there are clear differences between market liberalism and the interventionist developmentalism espoused by developmental social workers. This interventionism is inspired by the statist ideologies of social democracy and socialism. Although neoliberals vigorously oppose state intervention in economic and social affairs, and argue for self-reliance and individual effort, it has been shown already that developmental social work requires collective action and significant public resources. Developmental social work also rejects neoliberalism's individualist ideology and actively promotes collective action, particularly at the community level. Numerous examples of how developmental social workers collaborate with local groups and nonprofit organizations to promote social change have been provided earlier in this book.

Nor is it true that developmental social workers reject social activism. It has been shown in the previous chapters of this book that developmental social work is strongly committed to advocacy, human rights and social justice. Indeed, the social development literature is replete with references to these ideals, and numerous examples of how developmental social workers have effectively mobilized community support and advocated vigorously for social change have been given. The concept of progressive social change is fundamental to developmental social work. Similarly, the notions of human rights, peace, and social justice are integral elements of the developmental approach.

Nevertheless, some writers ignore developmental social work's position on social change or otherwise dismiss it. For example, in his comprehensive account of social work theories, Payne (1997, p. 213) argues that although the advocates of social development (and community development) "make much" of their commitment to social justice, they merely "confirm and promote the existing social order." On the other hand, he believes that Marxist, "anti-oppressive" and "empowerment" approaches effectively challenge the existing order. This is a dubious claim. Although some academic social workers have indeed made extensive use of the rhetoric of resistance and transformation, the profession's contribution to bringing about meaningful social change has been negligible and few social workers have participated in the ongoing struggles for social justice being waged in different parts of the world.

On the other hand, the implementation of the developmental perspective both in social policy and social work has produced significant results. It has fostered progressive change, alleviated poverty, promoted community participation, and brought about significant improvement in people's lives. This contention can be substantiated with reference to international macrodata, which show that there have been significant social improvements resulting from the adoption of developmental interventions. These have been accompanied by enhanced democratic participation, human rights, and social justice in many countries. This is not the case in countries where Marxist ideology has been implemented by oppressive communist governments or by dictators who use populist rhetoric and the power of the state to preserve their privileges. Indeed, populist rhetoric has seldom formed the basis for sustained social and economic development. In the form of *conscientization* and empowerment, radical populism has a major role to play in promoting social justice and change, but it has hardly resulted in the transformation of the existing social order. On the other hand, the statist social democratic tradition that informs much social development thinking has an impressive track record, not only in Europe but also in a number of developing countries as well (Sandbook et al., 2007). As was noted in Chapter 1, social democratic and Keynesian ideas have been implicit in much social development, and they have inspired effective state intervention, which has resulted in significant improvements in living standards for the large numbers of people. In addition, these improvements have been achieved through a democratic and participatory political and policy-making process.

Developmental interventions have also brought about significant social improvements at the community level in many countries. Community economic development projects are not narrowly focused on economic activities but involve local community building, peoples' participation, and popular mobilization. In many cases, they involve a high degree of activism on the part of local communities and particularly women who specifically use economic projects as a vehicle for empowerment. In India, for example, women's groups that combine activism with cooperative economic activities, such as SEWA, have proliferated in recent times. Similarly, in the United States, local people have effectively combined participatory, activist, and developmental strategies to improve their communities. This is true even of large-scale, "top-down" initiatives such as the federal government's EZ/EC program, which was discussed in Chapter 9. Although the EZ/EC program may be said to "operate within the existing social order," a recent report by the federal government's Department of Housing and Urban Development (HUD) (2009) shows how an initial investment by this program in the city of Philadelphia has been augmented by local financial and logistic support with the result that numerous nonprofit organizations providing services to needy families have benefited. Local schools have also improved and various initiatives focused on at-risk young people have been established. Although it is easy to dismiss these achievements, they have positive implications for the lives of people living in deprived communities.

On the other hand, the contribution of these critical perspectives should not be minimized or defensively rejected. In fact, they play a vital role in assessing the effectiveness of the developmental approach and remind developmental social workers of the ongoing need to campaign for human rights and social justice. There is a real danger that a narrow focus on economic projects can lead to the neglect of these wider concerns. Again, social work advocacy is needed to change negative attitudes and confront discriminatory practices. This is particularly relevant in the fields of mental health and corrections, where those who seek to live in the community often face stigma and other obstacles. Similarly, many of the people social workers serve are from minority and immigrant communities that encounter institutionalized discrimination, limited opportunities, and blatant racism. Developmental interventions are unlikely to resolve these problems unless these wider challenges are addressed. As argued in Chapter 1, the removal of barriers that inhibit economic participation is a key developmental strategy. If social workers form coalitions with other advocacy groups and campaign in a systematic way, then discrimination can be challenged. Conventional community practice skills should be vigorously used to involve local leaders, churches, the business community, and nonprofit organizations to create opportunities for vulnerable and disadvantaged clients to participate fully in the life of the community. Advocacy at the political level is equally important. By forming coalitions with political leaders, developmental social workers can campaign for progressive legislation that addresses these challenges in a systematic and authoritative way.

A critical perspective is also needed to ensure that the limitations of developmental interventions are recognized and addressed. For example, although economic participation through employment or self-employment is a useful mechanism for securing improvements in living standards, economic participation must be meaningful, remunerative, and satisfying. Exploitative low-wage employment is hardly the way to promote people's well-being. There are other limitations as well. In poor communities, social investments can enhance economic participation and improve living standards, but many local people do not, for various reasons, participate in these activities. It should also be recognized that increased economic participation among poor people with a limited education may only bring modest albeit meaningful benefits. For example, micro-enterprise does not offer a magical solution to the poverty problem, as has been implied in the literature. Although micro-enterprises do raise incomes, few participants are likely to become wealthy. Microenterprise is not suited to everyone and generally, better educated and highly motivated participants are likely to succeed. This example suggests that microenterprise initiatives should form a part of a comprehensive strategy designed to address the poverty problem (Midgley, 2008).

Similarly, employment placement for those facing challenges arising from disability, mental illness, or previous incarceration is not likely to result in a highly remunerative career trajectory. The problem of gender inequality in employment and the fact that many women served by social workers are engaged in low-wage employment must also be recognized. The problem is exacerbated because many are minorities and immigrants who face discrimination. On the other hand, employment helps meet material needs, fosters integration, and facilitates the realization of aspirations. By recognizing these limitations, developmental social workers are better placed to advocate for improved wages, regulation, and employment conditions. They can also advocate for adequate support such as affordable childcare, transportation, and other investments that facilitate meaningful work.

Unfortunately, the profession has not played an active role in campaigning for domestic workers, cleaners, office janitors, and other low-wage workers, most of whom are minorities and immigrants. By joining with the unions and other advocates, social workers can translate their social justice rhetoric into tangible action. The active involvement of professional associations will also be needed.

There is also a risk that claims about the benefits of economic participation may be exploited by those who oppose government social intervention. Often, social assistance and other supports are terminated once recipients find employment because, it is claimed, they are now self-sufficient and able to care for themselves. In the United States, politicians on the political right successfully campaigned for the abolition of the country's AFDC system on the grounds that poor women with children, who were the primary recipients of the program, were capable of working. This resulted in the mid-1990s in the so-called "welfare reform" initiative, which dramatically reduced the numbers receiving benefits without significantly reducing the poverty rate. However, many needy women—especially those with disabilities, mental illness, and other special needs—have found that their standards of living have not been sufficiently raised by engaging in low-wage employment. Another example of how successful developmental programs can be exploited by the political right comes from Tanner (2003) of the libertarian Cato Institute in Washington, which has consistently campaigned against government intervention in social welfare. Tanner cites Michael Sheraden's (1991) research into Individual Development Accounts (IDAs) to support the Institute's antistatist beliefs and to bolster the claim that the inculcation of self-reliance and individual responsibility through IDA savings programs can have a significant impact on poverty without governmental involvement. He conveniently neglects Sherraden's insistence that savings by the poor be appropriately matched, preferably from public resources. As these examples show, advocates of developmental social work need to affirm their commitment to the collectivist and egalitarian values that inform the developmental approach.

In addition to recognizing the need for ongoing support and services, it is clear that some clients will not be able to participate in economic projects and will require extensive long-term care, sometimes in residential settings. It has been claimed developmental social workers ignore those who are not able to participate in and the productive economy. Although it is true that developmental social workers seek whenever possible to foster community living and participation in economic and social activities, they are not indifferent to those who require long-term maintenance. Rather, they urge that a balance between social work's remedial, maintenance, preventive, integrative, and developmental functions be found. These different functions were described in Chapter 1, where it was noted that the profession has failed to balance them properly. Although remedial interventions have historically dominated social work, advocates of other approaches such as developmental social work risk dismissing the contribution of remedial and maintenance services. As Loffell's (2008) discussion on child welfare in South Africa reveals, a proper emphasis should be given to both conventional and developmental interventions.

As argued in this book, this can also be achieved by discharging social work's remedial functions through community-based, developmental interventions.

A final limitation is a dearth of systematic research into the effectiveness of developmental social work. Because developmental social work is committed to cost-effective practice, it may reasonably be expected that a good deal of outcome data has been collected to determine whether the interventions discussed in the major fields of practice chapters in this book have their intended impact and whether they do so at optimal cost. Unfortunately, this is not the case! As in many other fields of social work, outcome research has not being given high priority by developmental social workers, and practice decisions are seldom based on rigorous studies that differentiate between effective and noneffective interventions. Of course, some social work scholars have for many years campaigned for the systematic adoption of rigorous evidence-based and outcome research methodologies. Although they have made considerable headway, it cannot be claimed that social work practitioners today make routine use of outcome research. It is to be hoped that their continued efforts will succeed and persuade both academic and professional colleagues of the utility of systematically evaluating social work interventions.

One reason for the limited use of evidence-based and outcome research in developmental social work is that evidence-based research is often identified with clinical practice, which has little appeal in developmental circles. In addition, evidence-based research is still widely criticized for allegedly abrogating social work's humanistic and liberal ideals, undermining professional judgment and promoting managerialism. Of course, this criticism is not only voiced by developmental social workers but by many other social workers,—particularly those persuaded by critical and postmodernist ideas. Although there is indeed a risk that the rhetoric of cost-effectiveness may be used to legitimate cost-cutting and service retrenchments, it is desirable that research methodologies be judiciously used to test the efficacy of social work practice. Research of this kind has a long and venerable history. By evaluating outcomes, this research enhances social work's effectiveness with positive implications for those the profession serves.

One positive development is that outcome research is now more frequently used by colleagues in cognate disciplinary fields, and various developmental interventions have been evaluated, albeit with limited success. Their efforts should inspire developmental social workers to utilize evidence-based methodologies when testing their own interventions. They also show how outcome studies can be designed and implemented. This should facilitate the utilization of similar methodologies by social workers. Of particular value are numerous meta-outcome studies, which evaluate several individual studies of the outcomes of particular projects. This approach has the advantage of not relying on one but on several studies. Obviously, this permits a more thorough assessment of the evidence and determines whether positive or negative trends are substantiated by several studies.

Although a good deal of progress has been made by colleagues in other disciplines to test social development interventions, the limitations and challenges of this outcome research need to be recognized. One is example is an extremely thorough study of welfare to work programs for people with disabilities in the United Kingdom undertaken by Bambra, Whitehead and Hamilton (2005). Noting that the British government had over the years introduced a number of programs designed to help people with disabilities secure employment, these researchers sought to determine how effective these policies had been. They began by undertaking an exhaustive search of a large number of studies into welfare-to-work programs for people with disability in the United Kingdom and found no less than 5,000 studies of this kind. However, the vast majority of these studies were not sufficiently focused on employment activation nor on assessing outcomes, with the result that only 16 were appropriate for inclusion in the analysis. Although they concluded that welfare-to-work programs had a positive effect, shifting between 11% and 50% of clients into employment, none of the studies had controls, and therefore it was not possible to determine if the welfare-to-work programs themselves were responsible for moving clients into employment or whether this resulted from other factors. As this meta-analysis reveals, much more needs to be done to provide the research data on which outcome assessments in social development can be based.

In addition to these technical problems, outcome research is subject to different normative interpretations. As Kirp (2007) revealed in his exhaustive analysis of preschool childcare programs in the United States, methodological difficulties have been augmented by the very different ideological perspectives of supporters and opponents of these programs. Kirp points out that the Head Start program in the United States has been particularly controversial and that those who oppose the program have highlighted the findings of outcome studies that show little differences between children who were in the program and those who were not. Even carefully designed studies are subject to normative interpretations. He cites one study that found different outcomes for different ethnic groups and notes that the author was vilified for publishing results that did not fit the preconceptions of the program's supporters who were unwilling to accept these differences. The problem is exacerbated by the way outcome research has been reported by the media. News reports have tended to simplify very complex findings and to reduce them to rhetorical statements, which have been seized on by politicians on both sides of the issue.

Nevertheless, despite these challenges, outcome research plays a vital role in determining which policies and programs are effective. Despite their limitations, these and other studies of developmental interventions point the way forward to the adoption of a more coherent and systematic approach to evaluation. They show that it is possible to test the efficacy of particular interventions through utilizing rigorous evaluation methodologies. In the future, it is hoped that accounts of developmental interventions in the fields of practice discussed earlier in this book will explicitly draw on research of this kind. By collecting evidence of effectiveness, these interventions can be modified and improved so that they do indeed meet the needs of the clients they serve.

By recognizing the various limitations of developmental social work discussed in this chapter, the advocates of developmental social work should be able to respond and find viable solutions. However, it should be recognized and that no social work approach will be flawless or universally commended. Nevertheless, this book has attempted to show that the developmental approach presents positive opportunities for the social work profession and offers the prospect of more effectively meeting the needs of the people it serves. Its emphasis on progressive social change, improving material welfare, fostering client participation and community living, and above all, its advocacy of social investments that build on strengths and empower clients are consonant with the profession's values and commitments. It also supports the profession's historic commitment to promote wellbeing for all and help create just and democratic societies. Hopefully, developmental ideas and practice approaches will find their proper place in the repertoire of social work interventions, and will be more widely adopted.

REFERENCES

Bambra, C., Whitehead, M. and Hamilton, V. (2005). 'Does 'Welfare to Work Work? A Systematic Review of the Effectiveness of the UK's Welfare to Work Programmes for People with a Disability or Chronic Illness.' *Social Science and Medicine*. 60 (4): 1905–1918.

Fernald, L. C. H., Gertler, P. J. and Neufeld, L. M. (2008). 'Role of Cash in Conditional Cash Transfer Programs for Child Health, Growth and Development: An Analysis of Mexico's Opportunidades.' *Lancet* 371: 828–837.

Kirp, D. L. (2007). *The Sandbox Investment: The Preschool Movement and Kids-first Movement*. Cambridge, MA: Harvard University Press.

Loffell, J. (2008). 'Developmental Social Welfare and the Child Protection Challenge in South Africa.' *Practice: Social Work in Action*. 20 (2): 83–92.

Midgley, J. (2008). 'Microenterprise, Global Poverty and Social Development.' *International Social Work*. 51 (4): 467–479.

Payne, M. (1997). *Modern Social Work Theory*. Chicago, IL: Lyceum Books.

Sandbrook, R., Edelman, M., Heller, P. and Teichman, J. (2007). *Social Democracy in the Global Periphery*. New York: Cambridge University Press.

Sherraden, M. (1991) *Assets and The Poor: A New American Welfare Policy*. Armonk, NY: M. E. Sharpe.

Tanner, M. (2003). *The Poverty of Welfare: Helping Others in Civil Society*. Washington, DC: Cato Institute.

US Department of Housing and Urban Development [HUD] (2009). 'Local Partnership Promote Long Term Prosperity.' *Research Works*, 6 (5): 1–2.

INDEX

National Alliance to End
  Homelessness, 148
National Association for Colored
  Women, 37
National Center on Child Abuse and
  Neglect, 37
National Child Savings Accounts, 47
National Community Mental Health
  Centers Act (1963), 75
National Conference of Charities and
  Correction, 126
National Family Caregiver Support
  Program, 64–65
National Incidence Studies (NIS), 34–35
National Institute of Mental Health, 75
National Mental Health Act (1946), 75
National Mental Health Association, 76
National Runaway Switchboard, 150
National Senior Volunteer Corps, 63
neglect, 33–37, 39, 43, 92, 96, 147, 150
neighborhood building, xx, 6, 168–69,
  171–73, 180
neighborhood organizing
  approach, 3. 20
New Deal programs, 6, 115–16
  New Deal for Disabled People,
    115, 116
  New Deal for Lone Parents, 115, 116
  New Deal for the Long-Term
    Unemployed, 115
  New Deal for Young People, 115
New Door Ventures, 160
New Freedom Commission on Mental
  Health, 74
New York Society for the Prevention of
  Cruelty to Children, 36
nonrelative child care, 38, 43

older adults, value of, 58
Older Americans Act, 59, 62, 64
Omnibus Budget and Reconciliation Act
  (OBRA), 109
Oportunidades, 112, 122

Options Program, 136
outreach model, traditional, 151

paradigm shift, 193
parens patriae, 41
participatory approach, 8
pathology, 6, 14, 17
peer support, 80
pension days, 121
Perkins, Frances, 6, 108
Persons with Disabilities Act of 1995, 100
Philippines Employment Assistance
  Program, 122
physical abuse, 33
Pittsburgh Council of Associated
  Charities, 172
Poor Law model, 106, 110, 112
post-incarceration interventions, 134
poverty threshold, 78
preventive function, 4, 40
prisons/prisoners
  housing, 138
  integration, 134
  mental health, 132
  micro-enterprise, 139, 153
  microfinance, 139, 153
  re-entry, 133–34, 136–137, 140
  rehabilitation, 134
prison-to-parole programs, 141
probation and parole system, 131
productive aging, 58–59
  definition, 55
  and successful aging, 60
productivist approach, xiv, 21
productivity, xviii
Progresa, 112
Progressive social change, 198
Promotoras, 122
psychiatric approach, 5
psychotherapeutic counseling, 17,
  105, 126
psychotic disorders, 72
Purpose Prize, 63

Printed in the USA/Agawam, MA
January 16, 2013

571957.011